Decarcerating America

Decarcerating America

FROM MASS PUNISHMENT
TO PUBLIC HEALTH

Edited by Ernest Drucker

THE NEW PRESS

25 YEARS

NEW YORK
LONDON

Requests for permission to reproduce selections from this book should be mailed to:
Permissions Department, The New Press, 120 Wall Street, 31st floor,
New York, NY 10005.

Published in the United States by The New Press, New York, 2018
Distributed by Two Rivers Distribution

ISBN 978-1-62097-279-3 (e-book)

LIBRARY OF CONGRESS CATALOGING-IN-PUBLICATION DATA

Names: Drucker, Ernest M., 1940-
Title: Decarcerating America : from mass punishment to public health / edited
  by Ernest Drucker.
Description: New York : The New Press, [2018]
Identifiers: LCCN 2017042771 | ISBN 9781620972786 (hc : alk. paper)
Subjects: LCSH: Imprisonment—United States. | Prisons—Law and
  legislation—United States. | Criminal justice, Administration of—United
  States. | Punishment—United States. | Correctional law—United States. |
  Law reform—United States. | Imprisonment—Social aspects—United States.
Classification: LCC KF9730 .D43 2018 | DDC 364.60973—dc23 LC record available at
  https://lccn.loc.gov/2017042771

The New Press publishes books that promote and enrich public discussion and understanding of
the issues vital to our democracy and to a more equitable world. These books are made possible
by the enthusiasm of our readers; the support of a committed group of donors, large and small;
the collaboration of our many partners in the independent media and the not-for-profit sector;
booksellers, who often hand-sell New Press books; librarians; and above all by our authors.

www.thenewpress.com

Composition by Westchester Publishing Services
This book was set in Fairfield

Printed in the United States of America

2 4 6 8 10 9 7 5 3 1

Contents

Introduction
Decarcerating America

ERNEST DRUCKER

It used to be that most people saw drugs and crime as social diseases, and prison as the cure. But in the last few years a major shift in thinking has allowed us to understand that prisons themselves are the disease, having now taken on the epidemic proportions known as "mass incarceration." Mass incarceration is destroying hundreds of communities and millions of families across America as we lose the health and well-being of vast swaths of our society.

This was the case I made in my book *A Plague of Prisons*—that mass incarceration is a deadly and tenacious epidemic that damages the lives of individuals, families, and communities. It's a new kind of epidemic that results in a long list of chronic disabilities across the population of seventy million Americans with criminal records. The epidemic is particularly acute among the poorest minority communities, where the immediate public health effects of mass incarceration now include reduced life expectancy, higher infant mortality, and elevated rates of acute and chronic illnesses among those who have been in prison or had a family member incarcerated. The epidemic has also ravaged the vast majority of prisoners released and returned to their communities, many with deep wounds and new traumas from prison life and from being isolated through long separations from families and social supports. And yet, in order to end mass incarceration, we must greatly increase the number of people being released from prisons, exacerbating the public health problem of prisoner reentry.

The broad case against mass incarceration has been made in many other books and articles, and in the streets of Ferguson, Baltimore, and other cities where activists are striving to make black lives matter. The case has been made on the floors of legislative halls, in courtrooms, in classrooms, in state budgets. There is now a broad and growing base of support for ending mass imprisonment in America. Indeed, the emerging consensus that we simply cannot lock up so many people in prisons and jails stands to be one of the greatest victories for justice in America in our lifetimes.

To be sure, the 2016 presidential campaign brought a resurgence of "law and order" rhetoric and calls for harsher punishment. But at the same time (and, in some cases, even in the same place), a growing momentum has emerged to end this nation's globally unique overreliance on incarceration. In 2016 alone, major strides in criminal justice reform were made, including victories such as Proposition 57 in California and State Questions 780 and 781 in Oklahoma, which stand to reduce both states' prison populations dramatically. Voters elected progressive candidates as local prosecutors and sheriffs in places including Illinois, Florida, Texas, and Arizona—outcomes that would have been unthinkable even five years ago. Although federal policy is influential in setting both law and tone, criminal justice remains largely a state-based and local issue—and often a bipartisan one. So there remains reason to be hopeful, regardless of the spectacle of presidential politics.

Now it is time to ask, "What is next?" Specifically, to ask, "We've built a giant bureaucratic system that incarcerates two million people at a time—how do we get those people out of prison, stop more people from entering prison, and dismantle this system, all without doing further harm?" This is the project of decarceration and the subject of this book.

Decarceration will be a complex undertaking that demands more than one approach. The primary objective of this book will be to present one of the first comprehensive sets of solutions to this problem. Since the problem is so complex, and since there are many solutions that must be made to work in concert, the best way to begin is to draw on the specific expertise of people who have spent their lives understanding a discrete part of mass incarceration and enacting innovative and experimental solutions to dismantle it. No one person has all the answers, but each contributor to this book has a solution to offer.

The overall goal is to reduce the size of our nation's prison system. The standard for evaluating our success or failure must be whether we have deconstructed mass incarceration and replaced it with a less punitive, health-based system. Rather than treating criminal justice and prison data merely as the sum of "deviant" criminal behaviors by individuals, the contributors to this book use public health and restorative justice approaches that will allow us to set targets for reducing the number of arrests, reducing the use of long-term incarceration, and replacing the current punitive prison system with a set of proven alternatives that have a positive impact on both public safety and the people who are driven to crime. In order to dismantle the current regime of mass incarceration and help people currently held in prison, we present strategies to turn off the spigot of new commitments to prison and jail; embrace a restorative, transformative, dignity-based approach to incarceration for those we feel compelled to lock up; advocate for early release and support for successful integration back into home communities; and adopt a truth and reconciliation approach to undoing the trauma inflicted on millions of Americans during this virulently punitive era in American history.

The discipline of public health has a well-developed model of prevention that breaks interventions into primary, secondary, and tertiary strategies, each designed to address an epidemic at a different stage. I have drawn on these concepts and organized this book in three parts that mirror these three categories. We fight epidemics of infectious diseases in these three ways: by preventing people from getting sick (primary), by improving care for people once they are sick (secondary), and by healing communities and individuals who are recovering from the disease and by preventing further infections (tertiary).

As applied to mass incarceration, primary prevention means reducing the number of people entering our prisons and jails. Often called the "front door" approach, primary prevention is now the goal of growing national campaigns to reform arrest and sentencing practices, with many states already beginning to reduce new admissions to jails and prisons. Primary prevention also includes early interventions to help people avoid getting involved with the criminal justice system, and others that seek to minimize the harms associated with arrest and even short-term detention. The negative consequences of even a short stint in jail, often due to the inability to make bail, can include immediate job loss, loss of child custody, and loss of housing, so the individual stakes are high. Primary interventions work to support people during this dangerous time.

Criminologists Natasha Frost, Todd Clear, and Carlos Monteiro open Part I, on primary interventions, with "Ending Mass Incarceration." Counter to the "law and order" mind-set of many Americans, Frost, Clear, and Monteiro show that reducing rates of imprisonment in the most affected communities—by not incarcerating people for drug crimes, eliminating mandatory sentences, and reducing the length of all prison sentences, among other suggestions— can actually lead directly to improvements in community safety and reduction in crime rates.

Chapter 2 provides a case study of decarceration in New York State, which has been surprisingly effective. In "Better by Half," criminologist Judith Greene and Vincent Schiraldi, a former commissioner of the New York City Department of Probation, present the lessons of their detailed study of the New York criminal justice system over the past twenty years. They find that by employing a range of interventions, New York has successfully reduced mass incarceration, with the largest drop in prison populations nationwide over the last fifteen years. Many who are stuck in the mind-set of punishment would have predicted that such a sharp decline in incarceration in New York City would have been accompanied by an equally profound increase in crime. But Green and Schiraldi show that exactly the opposite happened. Despite the fact that the city's population grew by more than a million people between 1996 and 2014, the real number of New Yorkers incarcerated in prisons and jails declined by over thirty thousand during that time. Simultaneously,

New York City saw a 58 percent decline in the eight types of serious crime tracked in the FBI's uniform crime index, while these same index crimes declined by a more modest 42 percent nationally.

"Lessons from California on Prison and Jail Downsizing" provides a case study from a different part of the country by Michael Romano, a professor at Stanford Law School, who examines the potential of legislative reform to reduce mass incarceration. The Golden State ended three-strikes sentencing, once the national vanguard of tough-on-crime politics, in 2000 through a ballot initiative. Today, California is one of the states leading the trend in decarceration. Between 2006 and 2014, in part because of a court order, California reduced its prison population by over 20 percent—more than 37,000 fewer prisoners. In the same period the total number of prisoners in all other state prisons and the federal system combined increased by almost 30,000 (2.1 percent). In fact, the total national prison population is on the decline largely due to the scale of prison downsizing in California and New York. And yet, in a further empirical challenge to the punishment mind-set, between 2010 and 2015 the rate of violent crime per 100,000 residents in California fell by 2.1 percent and the rate of property crime fell by 0.4 percent. In total, the state's crime rate has dropped to levels not seen since 1967. The recidivism rate of prisoners released early under California reforms is five to ten times better than the average recidivism rate of other California prisoners who were not released early.

"The Role of Judges in Ending Mass Incarceration," by Justice Robert Sweet, a longtime federal judge for the Southern District of New York, and attorney James Thompson, argues that judges should be leaders in acting to reduce, and eventually eliminate, mass incarceration in our country. Judges can fight mass incarceration through measures ranging from transparency in the charging process to developing a common law of sentencing, among other strategies.

In "Public Defense and Decarceration," Robin Steinberg, Skylar Albertson, and Rachel Maremont explain the crucial role that public defenders can play for indigent populations facing criminal charges. The Bronx Defenders, which Steinberg founded and where Skylar Albertson and Rachel Maremont are staff attorneys, is one of the largest and most innovative of the more than one thousand public defender offices in the United States, representing more than twenty thousand cases per year. As the authors note, "in the American criminal justice system, an arrest is never just an arrest." Even if it leads to only a minor misdemeanor conviction or no conviction at all, an arrest can throw an individual's entire life into chaos, jeopardizing employment, housing, immigration status, access to public benefits, and family unity.[1] Steinberg and her colleagues argue for holistic public defense, an approach that provides meaningful, client-centered, and relevant legal representation that expands the scope of defense advocacy to address the many enmeshed penalties faced by those involved with the criminal justice system.[2]

In the final chapter of the primary prevention section, "Making Drug Policy Reform Work for Meaningful Decarceration," gabriel sayegh, a leader in many campaigns to reform drug policy, argues for an end to the war on drugs, which is largely responsible for the explosive growth of the U.S. prison population over the last forty years. Drug law reform is necessary but not sufficient for ending mass incarceration; to end mass incarceration we will need both to end the war on drugs and to advance other reforms of the criminal justice system, including those related to violent offenses.[3] But while the majority of people in U.S. jails and prisons are not there because of drug charges,[4] data show that ending mass incarceration is not possible without ending the war on drugs.[5]

Some argue that decriminalization of drugs is "too radical" or even impossible. But such assertions ignore the local and international debate around drug policy, where attitudes are shifting. Over the past two decades, when given the option through local initiatives, voters regularly choose to roll back the drug war for more sensible approaches—passing medical marijuana laws and legalizing recreational use,[6] enacting substantive sentencing reforms,[7] and curtailing the corrupt bail bond industry, which exposes so many poor defendants who can't make bail to long periods of brutality in our violent jails.[8] In October 2016, a major report released by Human Rights Watch and the American Civil Liberties Union concluded that decriminalization should be a primary goal of drug policy reform in the United States.

* * *

We cannot, however, prevent all new cases of incarceration. Therefore, the public health model for decarceration also calls for secondary interventions, which consist of a set of tools for making conditions in prisons and jails more humane for those incarcerated in them, as well as for reducing the size of the prison population by releasing more people from prisons. There may be certain people who must be confined in prison because of the risks they pose to others. But this is best accomplished by prison programs with rehabilitative objectives and outcomes, especially mental health services and higher education, rather than through the punitive institutions prisons have become.

The number of people who should be in prison due to the threat they pose to public safety is drastically lower than the number of people incarcerated today. Work must be done to shorten prison stays and determine which prisoners should be released immediately. Secondary interventions focus on minimizing future criminal justice involvement; the evidence tells us that we can lower recidivism while releasing more people from prisons quickly without compromising public safety. This approach also addresses both individuals and populations affected by mass incarceration, proposing an array of specific plans and programs to heal the many wounds of both the victims of crime and the victims of mass incarceration.

This section of the book opens with "Transforming Our Responses to Violence," by Danielle Sered, director of the Vera Institute's Common Justice program, which bravely seeks alternatives to punishment for violent crime. Public safety includes the protection of all citizens from the effects of criminal conduct, especially from violent crime—an essential responsibility of any society and a core dimension of delivering on the promise of justice. But substantially reducing violence requires acknowledging the limitations of prisons as a strategy to both deliver safety and ensure justice. Ending mass incarceration in America will therefore require taking on the question of violence. A pioneer in the application of restorative justice methods, Sered offers alternatives to incarceration that instead allow the people who cause harm to make amends in a way that feels meaningful to all parties involved and brings healing to the wounded person in the form of a truth and reconciliation process.

In "Minimizing the Impact of Parental Incarceration," Elizabeth Gaynes and Tanya Krupat of the Osborne Association discuss the impact of parental incarceration on children, arguing that a campaign that humanizes parents and all people involved in the justice system must be a key component of decarceration. They warn of the dangers of classifying people based only on their crime, as this ensures the continued poverty, stigmatization, and social marginalization of entire families. And they remind us that the harms associated with incarceration are extended to the health and well-being of both the incarcerated and their families; the costs of institutional support for addressing and healing trauma during and after periods of a family member's incarceration must all be factored into decarceration efforts.

In "Health and Decarceration," physicians Ross MacDonald and Homer Venters, who worked together to provide medical care at Rikers Island in New York City for many years, discuss the provision of health care in jails and prison. For decarceration to succeed, they argue, the scope of correctional health services must be expanded. In particular, we must provide support for diversion efforts before incarceration and also include medication-assisted therapy (e.g., opiate maintenance treatment with methadone or buprenorphine) during incarceration. In the case of diversion, health information for frequently incarcerated people inside jail and prisons can help formulate an alternative to detention. This includes reducing the dramatically increased risk of death immediately after release from prison—ten to twelve times the usual death rate for this population—mostly due to drug overdoses in the two weeks after release.[9]

In "Release Aging People in Prison," Mujahid Farid, director of the Release Aging People in Prison Campaign, and activist Laura Whitehorn advocate for the release of aging people from prison. In New York State, the number of people over fifty years of age confined in prisons increased by more than 84 percent between 2004 and 2014, even as the total number of people locked up fell by 23 percent during the same period. Farid and Whitehorn make the case for accelerating campaigns and initiatives that can lead to the release of greater numbers of elderly prisoners, who are routinely denied parole, compassionate release, and clemency, even though they are the population posing the lowest risk to public safety. Attention has been paid to the elderly prison population, but it has taken only the form of creating geriatric prison wards, hospices, and other ways to accommodate elders behind bars. Ending mass incarceration requires radical reforms that attack the idea of permanent, lifelong punishment and enable the release of many elders serving long sentences, including for violent crimes. Even if it were possible to release all of the nonviolent drug offenders in the next ten to fifteen years, meaningful reductions would have to include the release of people convicted of violent offenses, many of whom are now over fifty-five years of age and have served long periods in prison for offenses they committed when they were young.

Finally, tertiary interventions broaden our focus from incarcerated individuals themselves to the impact of mass incarceration upon entire communities and populations by focusing on the difficult process of reentry that a former prisoner must undergo upon his or her release from prison. The tertiary approach addresses the very large population of nearly seventy million Americans with criminal records, about 50 percent of whom cycle back through the prison system within the first three years after their release because of parole violations and new arrests; it looks at treatment programs that can reduce recidivism and help reintegrate formerly incarcerated individuals into their families and communities.

In "Health Care as a Vehicle for Decarceration," Daliah Heller, former New York City assistant commissioner of health, shows how broad health care reform is a tool for supporting successful decarceration. Heller outlines harm reduction programs that originated at the peak of the HIV and drug epidemic in the South Bronx, and shows how, if continued as it was conceived, President Obama's much-disputed Affordable Care Act could function to reduce the likelihood of reimprisonment, often for violations related to continued drug use. Heller argues for supportive services to address the social determinants of health, for universal health insurance coverage, and for targeted enrollment and retention for justice-involved individuals and their families, as well as for mental health and substance use disorder care and treatment, all as a means to reduce the number of people we feel a need to lock up.

In "Come Close In," Kathy Boudin shares the personal tale of her own twenty-three years of imprisonment and its role in developing her leadership role within the Bedford Hills Correctional Facility for Women and, subsequently, in the creation of Columbia University's groundbreaking Justice Program, focused on how former prisoners can become powerful assets in decarceration. Boudin argues eloquently for a fundamental shift in how we see former long-term prisoners who may have served sentences for violent crimes, including homicide. A long-term prison experience often creates practical and social expertise that, when combined with a passion for change, can make a huge difference in movements against mass incarceration. For years, lawyers, advocates, activists, policy makers, service providers, health workers, and others have devoted themselves to improving the lives of people impacted by incarceration. Boudin makes a compelling case for including people who were imprisoned, together with those who are supporting loved ones inside, in the national conversation.

In "Dealing with Drug Use After Prison," a group of clinicians with decades of experience in the treatment of drug use—Jeannie Little, Jenifer Talley, Scott Kellogg, Maurice Byrd, and Sheila Vakharia—present a new harm reduction model designed to effectively manage drug problems after release from prisons. People with substance use disorders also have very high rates of other mental health disorders—approximately 50 percent of respondents with a substance use disorder also meet criteria for at least one mental health disorder in their lifetimes. Individuals with co-occurring disorders also tend to have more severe and enduring symptoms, are less likely to engage in treatment, are more likely to be homeless, and are at greater risk for being victimized. The harm reduction approach is specifically intended to work with this population, instead of turning to prisons and jails as a first-line defense against drug use. Harm reduction therapy treats substance misuse as a health concern, not a legal issue. It prioritizes safety and employs strategies to keep people alive and healthy. Once people have reduced their risk-taking behaviors, these mental health experts argue, they are in a better position to stabilize their mental, emotional, and socioeconomic conditions. Only then are they likely to be ready to consider changing their relationship with drugs in the more profound ways that will allow them to avoid repeated arrest and incarceration.

In "From Prisons to Ploughshares," Eric Lotke discusses ways to develop new economies for prison towns, a critical component of decarceration. Lotke explores the role of rural prisons in local economies and how alternative uses of abandoned prisons must become a positive basis for supporting the decommissioning of prisons and jails. As Patrick Mulhern, mayor of Cresson, Pennsylvania, noted regarding the closure of Cambria State Prison near Pittsburgh in 2013, "It's going to hurt the restaurants, the hardware store, every business place here is going to be affected. Five hundred employees in one fell swoop—that's an awful lot."[10] Lotke offers numerous examples of "repurposed" prisons across the country that continue to be a source of jobs and economic vitality, making the transition away from prisons and jails less contentious. Giving prison towns more economic alternatives, Lotke argues, will strengthen the case for decarceration.

Any conclusions we can draw from this book are, of course, limited by the uncertainties we now face in the United States. The Donald Trump administration has threatened and has now begun to impose massive cuts in public health and social programs, and the U.S. attorney general, Jeff Sessions, has called for reinstatement of long mandatory sentences and a resumption of the failed war on drugs. For decarceration to proceed, both as a concept and as a practical strategy, it will have to surmount the obstacles put up by the current administration, relying on the momentum of decades of reform work at the local, state, and national levels.

Decarceration will also have to address two linked challenges: reducing the size of the prison population and minimizing the many well-documented harms of the system's punitive policies. For the many millions of people who have come through our prisons and jails, these harms continue even after release, both in terms of psychological damage and in terms of the array of collateral consequences faced by former prisoners (so memorably described by Michelle Alexander as "the new Jim Crow"). In addition to the 2.2 million individuals behind bars, at the end of 2014, an estimated 4.7 million adults were under community supervision in the U.S. Approximately 1 in 52 adults in the United States was under the control of the criminal justice system, with more than 45,000 offenders newly placed on parole that year.[11] The result was the perpetuation of a vast, state-based control apparatus, employing more than 40,000 parole officers, with thousands more in the federal system. Our bloated criminal justice system (which itself employs over 2 million people)[12] must be redesigned and reconfigured to one based on the science of public health and on the goals of social justice and human rights.

The range of topics covered in this book demonstrate the many perspectives and disciplines that will be required to address the specific issues of public health and justice needed to end mass incarceration. The current rise of interest in and support for this public health approach has produced some very useful work in several vital areas directly related to the odds of survival in prison and the possibility for productive lives for the ten to twelve million adult prisoners who have been released in the last twenty years (though about 40 percent of these are currently expected to be reincarcerated within three years after release from prison). These millions of former prisoners, including many (the majority) who do not get rearrested, now live in local communities. They have been called "invisible men" in an important new book of that title by Flores Forbes, a former leader in the Black Panther Party and now vice president for community programs at Columbia University, who himself has been freed from prison for twenty-five years. Forbes is one of a large group of black men in America who are "without constituency" and "all but invisible in society"—men who have served their time and not gone back to prison and who have the potential (largely untapped) to become an important part of efforts to decarcerate America.

In addition to including the voices of those most affected by mass incarceration in the conversation about ending it, we must pay attention to lessons from an earlier era of deinstitutionalization: that of mental hospitals in the second half of the twentieth century. It is crucial that we not repeat the experiences of the dismantling of that system—a system that at peak was of a scale on par with mass incarceration, affecting about 700 per 100,000 adults in the U.S. population. Deinstitutionalization of millions of mental hospital patients took place beginning in the 1950s and lasting through the 1970s, by which time more than 95 percent of all U.S. mental hospital patients had been discharged, and most of the large institutions that warehoused them had been shut down. That earlier process (also called "decarceration" at the time) was publicly presented as a progressive initiative to get people out of the medieval conditions of many old mental hospitals. At the time, the plan was for mental health services and care to be rendered through community-based programs. Unfortunately, those programs never materialized due to the budgetary demands of the Vietnam War and the death of President John F. Kennedy, who had driven the initiative from the start. This earlier failure of public policy affected many of the same populations we see in prisons today, where about 50 percent of inmates carry major mental health diagnoses. We must certainly insist that prison decarceration not repeat the wholesale abandonment of follow-up care that occurred after the earlier decarceration.

A special area of new services is also needed to help secure the freedom of the many elderly prisoners who have served decades behind bars. This can be accomplished only with the creation of networks of support from the local communities to which they return.

The many educational and health service programs required by former prisoners must be concentrated in "reentry communities"—those communities from which most prisoners come and to which they return after release. In New York State, for example, 80 percent of all state prisoners come from six New York City communities. Because decarceration is about both getting people out of prison and the ongoing task of "getting prison out of people," these concentrations of former prisoners, even though now freed, will require a broad range of services to heal the many wounds of brutal prisons and jails. We must offer compassionate care as former prisoners strive to build new lives after release from prison.

While decreasing the prison and jail population is a key component of decarcerating America, perhaps even more consequential is addressing the long-term trajectory of the many prisoners who have reentered society and returned to the communities from which they came. Both their families and their networks of social contacts will play a key role as this population struggles to meet their most pressing needs: home, family, education, and a job. And we must provide services in the form of health care, higher education, better employment, and psychological assistance with the many problems, including drug dependence, that they face.

The good news is that we now have many new advocacy organizations and individual leaders working in the communities of reentry. It is at the community level that these new agents of change and support can make a huge difference in the fates of those communities that account for such a large portion of former prison inmates.

Among the leading groups offering this type of support is Just Leadership USA, a group founded and led by former prisoner and public policy leader Glenn Martin. Martin has tapped into the large stream of former prisoners who have had extensive experience in the criminal justice system and who after release have advocated for the provision of life-saving services and education for the population inside prison and for community supports after release.

Just Leadership's program enables more than two hundred well-trained former prisoners to become a tangible asset in the communities they come from. During periods of parole, former prisoners continue to be accountable to the criminal justice system and little else. One focus of Just Leadership is therefore on providing support for parolees that is based on community reintegration and restorative justice models, rather than the continued punitive surveillance of the criminal justice system. One specific program of this group in New York City is the campaign to close New York City's notorious Rikers Island, an effort that has generated significant support and gained the commitment by New York City mayor Bill de Blasio to eventually close down the jail.

On the primary prevention side are restorative justice programs such as the one pioneered by Common Justice and led by Danielle Sered for the Vera Institute. These programs also create and operate vital community-based services to intervene at the time of arrest with violent youthful offenders, the group that everyone agrees is the most difficult for the criminal justice system to address. But these cases are also proving most amenable to high-impact restorative justice and reconciliation methods at the community level, with crime victims and their families recognizing the value of these programs and offering impressive levels of support. By creating a new space in the criminal justice system for meaningful contact between offender and victims, these restorative programs achieve the aims of effective reconciliation and healing at the community level.

Some of the other intervention models discussed in the book include harm-reduction approaches to drug addiction and its treatment. Two important areas to address are HIV/AIDS and drug overdoses, a set of public health issues that are newly urgent because of the increase in people injecting opiates. With the United States having seen more than 65,000 overdose deaths in 2016 alone and several outbreaks of AIDS cases in states that had not experienced them in the last decade, a new area of public health and prevention programs has arisen. These include the wide employment of lifesaving naltrexone, a narcotic antagonist medication that reverses opioid overdose and saves many lives. In this area of public health an important role has emerged for law enforcement personnel.

We now also see a growing and very progressive role for the police in decarceration. At the front end—in terms of primary interventions—there is a role for police working with early diversion programs to prevent arrest and jail time. Law Enforcement Assisted Diversion (LEAD) is a partnership between local police and mental health organizations and personnel that operates pre-booking diversion programs. These were first developed in the United States in Seattle, where the community used this approach to address low-level drug and prostitution crimes in King County. These pre-booking, community-based diversion programs are designed to divert those suspected of low-level drug and prostitution offenses away from the courts and jail and to replace prosecution with case management and other supportive services. Follow-up studies show that intervention groups are significantly less likely to have been arrested compared with the control groups.

This work has spawned a new international movement, with the Center for Law Enforcement and Public Health (CLEPH), founded in Melbourne, Australia, in 2011, working globally to identify and support examples of progressive initiatives on the part of local police in the United States and abroad. The hallmarks of the center's program are the partnership with law enforcement and its emphasis on the translation of research and knowledge into action and practice. CLEPH's vision ranges from the very local to the global. In collaboration with others around the world, the center is building capacity, interest, and activities across the whole range of investigation and influence: research, teaching, advocacy, networking (including peer support and education), and engagement with other sectors/disciplines.

At the back end—in terms of tertiary interventions—there is a role for the police in addressing the social stigma and the many restrictions imposed upon former felons as they work to reestablish community and family lives after prison. Most notable is the work of the Law Enforcement Action Partnership (LEAP) in building strong police-community ties, which are essential for police to do their job effectively and keep their communities safe. Trust in the police is dangerously low in many communities today, with people reluctant to speak with officers, witnesses unwilling to come forward, and many crimes going unreported. As LEAP puts it, "The keys to restoring this trust are allowing officers to divert appropriate individuals to intensive support programs, so police can focus on crime; improving departmental support and training for officers; and reforming policies that put officers at odds with the communities they serve."

It should come as no surprise that we need to build new lines of support for employment, health care, and affordable housing programs in the United States. These areas remain a major challenge, and not only for convicted felons. It will take a lot of imaginative and locally grounded support for such programs in order to equip communities with large reentry populations to address the needs of former prisoners—a real challenge in the face of the Trump administration's systematic stripping away of federal funds for all such programs.

The political future of the United States is now an open issue, and its intersection with mass incarceration must now become an open topic of debate and include more efforts at change. The future of mass incarceration in America will likely be decided in the next few years. I hope this book offers a road map to the mass *decarceration* this country sorely needs.

Notes

1. Robin Steinberg, "Heeding Gideon's Call in the Twenty-First Century: Holistic Defense and the New Public Defense Paradigm," *Washington and Lee Law Review* 70 (2013): 968; Sarah R. Berson, "Beyond the Sentence—Understanding Collateral Consequences," *National Institute of Justice Journal* 272 (September 2013): 25.

2. Steinberg, *supra* note 2; Smyth, *supra* note 3. The Supreme Court affirmed the responsibility of defense attorneys to address enmeshed penalties in *Padilla v. Kentucky*, 559 U.S. 356 (2010).

3. The Urban Institute analyzed the statistics relating to individuals under correction control across the United States and focused on policy changes in fifteen states to create an online tool called the Prison Population Forecaster. The Forecaster allows the user to recommend a variety of sentencing reform proposals to achieve decarceration. What becomes immediately clear to the user is that policy reforms principally relating to drug offenses will not at all be sufficient to end mass incarceration. See Ryan King et al., "The Prison Population Forecaster: State Prison Population," Urban Institute, 2015, http://webapp.urban.org/reducing-mass-incarceration.

4. Approximately one in five people is incarcerated for a drug offense. Prison Policy Initiative, "Mass Incarceration: The Whole Pie 2016," March 14, 2016 (updated with a new 2017 version), https://www.prisonpolicy.org/reports/pie2016.html.

5. Roughly half of people in federal prisons are serving time for a drug offense, and the number of people in state prisons for drug offenses today is ten times greater than it was in 1980. Sentencing Project, "Issues: Drug Policy," 2017, http://www.sentencingproject.org/issues/drug-policy.

6. See *supra*, fn. 23.

7. In 2014, voters in California made history by passing Proposition 47, which reduced the penalties for simple drug possession, petty theft, shoplifting, forgery, writing a bad check, and receipt of stolen property, resulting in dramatic reductions to the state prison population and investments in drug and mental health treatment, school programs,

and victims' services. See My Prop 47, http://myprop47.org. In 2012, California voters had approved Prop 36, which required that a "third strike" be a serious or violent felony (previously, a "third strike" could be any felony). See Aaron Sankin, "California Prop 36, Measure Reforming State's Three Strikes Law, Approved by Wide Majority of Voters," *Huffington Post*, November 7, 2012.

8. See Nick Wing, "Our Bail System Is Leaving Innocent People to Die in Jail Because They're Poor," *Huffington Post*, February 23, 2017.

9. Ingrid A. Binswanger et al., "Release from Prison—A High Risk of Death for Former Inmates," *New England Journal of Medicine* 356 (January 11, 2007): 157–65.

10. Dan Strumpf, "With Fewer to Lock Up, Prisons Shut Doors," *Wall Street Journal*, February 10, 2013.

11. Laura M. Maruschak and Thomas P. Bonczar, "Probation and Parole in the United States, 2012," Bulletin, Bureau of Justice Statistics, Department of Justice, December 2013, NCJ 243826.

12. Matthew R. Durose, Alexia D. Cooper, and Howard N. Snyder, "Recidivism of Prisoners Released in 30 States in 2005: Patterns from 2005 to 2010—Update," Special Report, Bureau of Justice Statistics, Department of Justice, April 2014, NCJ 244205.

PART I

Primary Prevention

1

Ending Mass Incarceration
Six Bold Reforms

NATASHA A. FROST, TODD R. CLEAR, AND CARLOS E. MONTEIRO

Across almost two-thirds of the states, we are witnessing policy reform to curtail further prison population growth, with dozens of states reconsidering the utility of inflexible sentencing structures and contemplating the repeal of mandatory sentences.[1] Some of the current approaches to criminal justice reform—including most of the current justice reinvestment approaches to prison population reduction—will not effectively reduce mass incarceration in the near term. Without question, in the long term these approaches might work, but they will take years, indeed decades, to manifest meaningful reductions in prison populations. Real reductions in current incarceration rates will require reform efforts far bolder than those currently being pursued. Specifically, reform to end mass incarceration will require sentencing reductions across all categories of offending that would take sentencing back to where it was in the 1980s.

What follows are critiques of the two popular approaches to decarceration—justice reinvestment initiatives as they are now implemented, and early release strategies for low-level offenders—followed by six bold reforms that we believe can rapidly reduce incarceration rates without compromising public safety.

The Problem with Justice Reinvestment Initiatives

Justice reinvestment initiatives are those reforms that seek to reduce rates of incarceration through the use of evidence-based approaches, taking the money that would have been invested in incarceration and reinvesting it locally.[2] The approach is often touted as a way to reduce our reliance on incarceration without compromising public safety.[3] In the several years since Eric Holder's Justice Department popularized the term, policy makers, researchers, and practitioners have in many respects been won over by the idea of justice reinvestment, which has become the en vogue approach to serious criminal justice reform, with dozens of states receiving federal assistance to launch justice reinvestment initiatives and additional states signing on every year.[4]

The justice reinvestment model, initially proposed by Eric Cadora and Susan Tucker, however, focused not only on reducing the country's reliance on prisons and jails but also on reallocating savings to communities most devastated by crime and incarceration.[5] Justice reinvestment initiatives launched thus far, however, have not remained true to Tucker and Cadora's original vision.[6] Instead, many of the initiatives created under the banner of justice reinvestment remain tethered to the provision of criminal justice and correctional services in the usual forms of more probation and enhanced community correctional supervision.[7]

Where justice dollars saved are reinvested, they tend to be reinvested not in communities but rather in community-based supervision schemes. Across many jurisdictions, probation has, for example, benefited from greater investments in bolstering the community-based supervision it provides.[8]

Although these approaches are well-intentioned, we are not very optimistic about getting sizable reductions from either the intensive supervision strategies or recidivism-based strategies most often associated with justice reinvestment initiatives. Intensive supervision strategies have never really been promising as alternatives to prison sentences, for two reasons. First, they are nearly always used as alternatives to regular probation rather than as alternatives to prison. This is particularly true when judges decide who gets to go into intensive supervision programs. In other words, rather than serving as alternatives to prison for those who would have otherwise been sentenced to prison, regular probation typically becomes intensive supervision probation (ISP) for a subset of offenders. The only way this can be overcome is to allow correctional administrators to take people out of prison and put them onto ISP, and then it starts to look like parole. And if administrators are in charge of the ISP decisions post-sentencing, then judges will send people to prison in the hopes that they will be selected for ISP. How could you guarantee that an ISP population would be drawn only from the truly prison-bound? You *might* get there if you allowed intensive supervision strategies as an option for cases where mandatory prison terms apply. But programmatically, how would you make the intensive supervision programs large enough to get reductions of any meaningful size in the number of people behind bars? And if you are going to go after mandatory penalties, why not just eliminate them altogether? The effect would be much larger.

The second problem with intensive supervision programs is the "intensive" part. Watching people closely while they are in the community always uncovers problems, especially with an at-risk or high-risk population such as people who have committed serious enough felonies to make them otherwise candidates for prison sentences. There is always a threat: "We will be watching you closely, and if we see anything we don't like we will send you right to prison." That means that any potential reductions in the number of prisoners through intensive supervision programs evaporate in the face of the number of parole returns that intensive supervision produces through enforcement of its rules. So we are skeptical that ISP-style strategies can get us reductions in prison populations that amount to much. We feel much the same way about in-prison treatment and rehabilitation programs intended to reduce recidivism rates.

We should invest in programs that are intended to rehabilitate offenders and prepare them for reentry *because it is the right thing to do*. That said, rehabilitating offenders and preparing them for reentry will not bring about an end to mass incarceration anytime soon. Most meta-analyses find that well-designed and well-implemented rehabilitation programs reduce recidivism rates by about 20 percent.[9] In other words, through correctional programming a recidivism rate of 40 percent might become a recidivism rate of 32 percent. This is certainly worth doing, but producing meaningful reductions in the number of people in prison over time by simply trying to affect return-to-prison rates will take a very long time. Crucially, the recidivism reduction potential of programming assumes that all programs are well run *and* that there actually is a suitable effective program for every person. It is much more likely that less than half of all programs will be well run. It is also more reasonable to assume that for a large proportion of people behind bars, there is no "known and proven effective" program that fits their problems (whatever their problems are). Correctional programming is costly and resources are scarce, so we would have to assume that for some proportion of those for whom we do have a proven and relevant program to address their problems, there will be no space available for them in that program.

So even a wildly optimistic recidivism reduction strategy would have to be working with, say, at least 25 percent of all those released from prison and reducing their return-to-prison rate from 40 percent to 32 percent. Under that sort of model, it will take a very long time to experience meaningful decreases in the size of the prison population (and that is if there are no compensatory changes in technical failure rates that would result from the intensive community supervision that would follow release from these effective correctional programs).

Why Early Release Strategies for Low-Level Offenders Are Not Enough

The rhetoric of reform always tends to be that we should start releasing low-level offenders, such as property offenders, first-time offenders, and those convicted of drug or public order crimes. But even a cursory glance at the numbers of people currently incarcerated in state and federal prisons quickly illustrates that even if we were to release all of those people en masse tomorrow, we would cut our imprisonment rate in half, but we would still have more than 700,000 people in prisons around the country. Virtually all of those would be serving very long terms for crimes of violence, facing dismal pros-

Table 1.1. State and Federal Prisoners in 2014

	TOTAL		State		Federal	
Violent	**718,900**	**47%**	704,800	53%	14,100	7%
Property	**267,200**	**18%**	255,600	19%	11,600	6%
Drug	**304,500**	**20%**	208,000	16%	96,500	50%
Public Order	**215,400**	**14%**	146,300	11%	69,100	36%
Other	**12,000**	**1%**	10,600	1%	1,400	1%
TOTAL	**1,518,000**		1,325,300		192,700	

Table constructed using data from Appendix Tables 4 and 5 in E. Ann Carson, *Prisoners in 2014* (Washington, D.C.: Bureau of Justice Statistics, 2015).

pects for release, and our imprisonment rate would once again begin to creep upward with each new admission, as it did over the past several decades.

How Do We Reduce the Prison Population Effectively?

Let's begin with the assumption that meaningful reductions in the number of prisoners would require us to get at least a million people out of the prison system. That would bring our imprisonment rate down to about 200 per 100,000—large by international standards but no longer "mass." How do we do that?

If we went back to the sentencing policies of 1980, we would very soon get 1980 prison populations, or lower. To be clear, the causes of mass incarceration as a phenomenon are complex, but the cause of prison population growth mechanically has been the sentencing policy changes that occurred mostly over the two decades between 1980 and 2000. These sentencing policy changes served to increase both the number of people going to prison and the amount of time that they would stay there.[10] Without question, undoing the sentencing policy changes that occurred through the 1980s and 1990s has to be part of the solution.

Only two functions determine prison population size—who goes into prison and how long they stay.[11] Sending fewer people to prison is surely one-half of the equation, but it is, in many ways, the easier half. Reducing length of stay is the heavy lift, and it absolutely has to be on the table. Moreover, doing it for people convicted of violent crimes also has to be on the table.

We should reduce sentences for people convicted of "violent" crimes for at least three reasons. One, most violent crime is far more mundane than most imagine—fights, drunken assaults of friends and acquaintances, hurting a loved one. The thing most people fear when they hear the term "violent"—a person hiding behind a bush and jumping out to hurt a stranger—is very, very rare. The most common version of this is armed robbery, and most armed robberies are committed by very young men, for whom the possibilities of redemption are pretty high. Why would we want to keep a twenty-year-old in prison into his forties, when the effect of prison has completely been achieved by the time he reaches his early thirties? The same can also be said, by the way, for sexual violence that is not domestic violence.

People who are released from prison after having served time for "violent" crimes have much lower recidivism rates than people released after serving time for drug or property crimes, and their recidivism rates for repeat violence are about the same as everyone else's.[12] In other words, keeping them longer has very little to do with public safety, and more to do with our need to express our outrage at their conduct by making them stay longer than, say, drug dealers or burglars. Because we have so enhanced what we do to burglars and drug dealers, we cannot do something reasonable to those facing sentences for violence. In other words, the sentences for violent crime reflect our inflated punishment scale for all crime, not just violent crime.

Expressing our collective outrage has been a driving force for increasingly punitive sentencing policy for several decades now, but it is useful to remind ourselves of the American Friends Service Committee report *Doing Justice*. When Andrew von Hirsch and colleagues laid out the just deserts framework in the early 1970s, they argued that punishments should be scaled to match crime severity and blameworthiness, with more severe crimes warranting more severe punishments, but they were scaling in terms of years, not

decades. They argued for penalties between one and five years for most offenses and emphasized that prison sentences longer than ten years should be
exceptionally rare.[13]

If, as proposed below, we were to stop incarcerating low-level property
and drug offenders altogether, *sentences of five to ten years for crimes of violence would eventually seem long again.* It is only because we have increased
the scale of all penalties so dramatically over the past four decades that incarcerating someone for ten years can seem too lenient.

For someone who has never been to prison, the difference between one
and two years does not seem very big. To someone counting the days and
minutes until they can go home, the difference between one and two years
feels immense. When the time to release is decades, it is virtually impossible to imagine that future, and so it should not be surprising that hopelessness sets in and behavior management becomes difficult. Although prisons
themselves are not a central focus of this chapter, we would be remiss if we
did not note that prisons in which prisoners have incentives to behave—
like the hope of release—are easier to manage and run.

Age matters a lot with respect to recidivism. People who have reached
their late thirties and forties are simply less of a risk to reoffend. They don't
all have to eventually get released, but we should certainly allow some to be
released. Anyone who has been inside a prison with a sizable population of
offenders serving sentences of life without parole has witnessed the futility
of continuing to keep some of these offenders behind bars, no matter how
violent their original crime. Prisoners who cannot walk or breathe without
assistance pose virtually no threat to public safety, and prisons make for
very expensive nursing homes. It is not that these offenders necessarily
deserve to be released, but more that it is not worth the cost of keeping
them.

Next to age, prior history is arguably the single most important predictor
of recidivism. However, we must always be cognizant of how punishment-
imperative-era policies have contributed to amplifying the power of this
predictor in the lives of some. The growing school-to-prison-pipeline literature

demonstrates that in some communities, starting at a very young age, school behavior is being used to identify "trouble" kids who are then increasingly surveilled and routinely disciplined.[14] As in the adult realm, most violent juvenile offending involves mundane, simple acts like an after-school street fight, rather than an elaborate plan to go on a shooting spree. The problem, however, is that school conduct problems and after-school street fights are being used by schools and juvenile justice systems to build a case for surveilling these youth and as an argument for targeting their schools and communities. With the advent of zero-tolerance policies, these kids quickly find themselves on the road to school suspension and eventual expulsion, and all signs suggest those roads lead directly or indirectly to prison.[15]

Schoolyard fights are being used in many ways as habitual offender policies are used later in the criminal career trajectory, essentially adding first, second, and third strikes for some when others are not getting any strikes at all. We have created the stereotypes of the street thug and that of the infamous superpredator, and the power of these profiles to create images that resonate should not be denied. Until we shift policies that control the labeling of some youth as dangerous, would-be criminal offenders, we will continue to provide support for the argument that the usual suspects really do deserve prison.

Six (Not-So) Radical Policies for Rapid Decarceration

Rates of incarceration have some effect on rates of crime; however, most of the leading scholars suggest that the impact is modest.[16] Analyses of the relationship between crime and incarceration have attributed between 10 and 25 percent of the crime decline to the rise in imprisonment rates.[17] It is no secret that crime has fallen precipitously over the past two decades, creating a historical moment where crime is at about the same rate it was in the 1970s (see Figure 1.1). We no longer need an incarceration rate five times higher than it was in that era.

Figure 1.1: U.S. Crime and Incarceration Rates 1930–2014

We offer six principles for effectively ending mass incarceration in the next decade.

Bold Reform #1: Don't Send People to Prison for Drug Crimes

One of the least controversial of our proposals is to stop sending people to prison for drug crimes. The supply-side criminal justice approach to drug interdiction taken in the war on drugs has not made a dent in the demand for drugs. A public health approach to drug use would refocus the efforts on addressing the problems of substance abuse and addiction that drive the demand for illegal drugs in the first place. As America confronts its latest drug crisis—the current opioid epidemic—Americans are increasingly willing to see drugs and drug addiction as a public health issue and not as a criminal justice issue. The shifting attitudes likely in part reflect the reality that opioid addiction is as prominent in middle-class suburban communities as it is in inner-city communities.[18]

Regardless of the reason for the shift, it is the case that, for the most part (and except in the federal system), drug offenders go to prison for *very* short terms anyway. Drug offenders are the quintessential offenders who cycle from communities to prisons and back again. For example, almost half of Ohio's prison admissions serve less than a year and are released.[19] This cycling of offenders into and out of prisons has its own damaging effects, which are beyond the scope of this chapter and which have been documented extensively elsewhere.[20] Needless to say, churning drug offenders into and out of prisons where treatment options are few and post-release outcomes are dismal has done little to address the underlying problem of drug addiction and demand. Nor can cycling drug offenders into and out of prisons affect rates of drug availability given the well-known phenomenon of replacement in drug markets (for every drug dealer who goes to prison, there are several at the ready to take his place).

Keeping drug offenders out of prisons and beginning to address drug use and addiction as a public health issue could mean that upward of 400,000 prisoners are dealt with through means other than incarceration. Almost 100,000 of those are the drug offenders who make up more than 50 percent of the federal prison population (see Table 1.1). It is often assumed that these are the drug kingpins of the world, but research demonstrates relatively few (less than 6 percent) of those serving time in prisons for drug offenses are actually involved in mid-level or high-level drug operations.[21] It is time that we recognize the limits of the war on drugs and begin treating drug use and abuse as a public health problem that cannot be solved by a criminal justice response. Indeed, most of the serious reform efforts to date have focused on undoing some of the policies most closely associated with the war on drugs, and while this is surely a good start, it is not *and will not* be enough. If we released all currently incarcerated drug offenders, we would still boast an incarceration rate among the highest in the world, with more than a million people in prison for offenses other than drugs.

Bold Reform #2: Eliminate Mandatory Sentences

Mandatory sentences need to be eliminated and not just for drug offenses, but for all offenses, *including violent offenses*. Two arguments are made on behalf of mandatory penalties—increasing deterrence and reducing sentence disparity.

Evidence has mounted that the sentencing stage of the justice system is not the best place to enhance deterrence. Studies show that deterrence is best achieved by swift and certain sanctions rather than severe ones. By the time a case reaches sentencing, swiftness has long been a moot issue. Certainty is related more to the likelihood of apprehension than it is the likelihood of a severe penalty. A recent review by the National Academy of Sciences concluded there is no evidence that mandatory penalties imposed at sentencing have much deterrent value, and given what we know about deterrence, it is likely that their value in producing it is near zero.[22]

It has always been a myth that mandatory sentences have reduced disparities. They have simply hampered our ability to detect disparities easily because the decisions that affect the ultimate sentence occur long before the offender shows up in court, when the prosecutor decides whether and how to charge an offense. The United States Sentencing Commission was established by the Sentencing Reform Act of 1984 under the auspices of bringing more fairness and certainty to sentencing and addressing disparities in criminal justice sentencing. Less than a decade after being established, however, the commission found that the application of mandatory minimum sentencing was tied directly to the race of the defendant, "where whites are more likely than non-whites to be sentenced below the applicable mandatory minimum."[23] Marc Mauer, a leading expert on sentencing policy, contends that mandatory sentences have produced such disparities because (1) America's drug war was waged on communities of color and policing efforts were concentrated in those communities, and (2) mandatory policies are often based on prior convictions, and defendants of color are more likely to have prior criminal justice records than their white counterparts.[24] In other words, the disparities that mandatory sentences were intended to address had little effect because decision points at earlier stages were so crucial in determining who faced the mandatory penalties to begin with.

Bold Reform #3: Bring Down the Length of All Sentences

If all currently prescribed sentence lengths were multiplied by a factor of 0.3, we would get a scale of penalties that look more like those seen in the rest of the world, and much more the way sentencing across the United States looked prior to the 1980s. Sentences beyond ten years should be rare. Sentences of life should be eliminated. There should be no such thing as life without the possibility of parole. Without question, even a short stay in prison is damaging to a person's life prospects in ways that have been extensively documented.[25] Lengthy sentences only magnify these detrimental effects.

The observation that penalties in the United States are extreme by comparison to other democracies has been made by many writers. Recently Michael Tonry pointed out that the long sentences in the United States are the cornerstone of its high rates of incarceration.[26] For example, the United States currently has more than 150,000 people serving life sentences, a kind of permanent prison population today that is close to the total number of prisoners in 1970.[27]

U.S. sentences were not always outside international norms. A rash of sentencing "reforms" in the 1980s and 1990s are the reason our sentences are so high today compared to most of the rest of the world. This means that the United States does not need a "new" sentencing regime, but rather a simple return to normative regimes of the past.

Sentencing is only part of the problem—the core issue is length of stay. It is worth noting that sentences imposed by judges have flattened in recent years, but actual time served on those sentences has significantly increased. In order to truly reduce sentences to meaningful levels, the mechanisms of release from prison, such as parole, early release, and special release, must also be activated in ways that maintain meaningful reductions in length of stay.

Bold Reform #4: Reduce or Eliminate Recidivism Enhancements

Recidivism rates are high. They always have been, and until we take sustained approaches to long-term crime prevention more seriously, they always will be. Before the 1980s, judges sentencing individual offenders standing before them typically sentenced a repeat offender to a longer term than they would have a first-time offender. It made sense to do so; there should perhaps be an enhancement of sentence for the offender who has not learned his lesson. But, at the time, offense history was just one of a myriad of considerations taken into account at sentencing. Through the 1980s and 1990s, habitual and repeat offender legislation was passed to dramatically increase the length of prison terms these offenders would serve, regardless of the circumstances of the offense or of the offender. These statutes often double or triple and sometimes quadruple the sentence that a repeat offender can expect to receive. Moreover, these enhancements are often mandatory. Statutorily prescribed sentence enhancements should be eliminated or vastly reduced. It is time that we renew our faith in the judiciary to hand out sentences that achieve the punishment's objective without compromising public safety.

Some will argue that restoring judicial discretion could result in vastly different sentences for similarly situated offenders, but it is hard to argue that this is somehow radically worse than identical sentences for very different types of offenders. More important, most of the discretion that results in disparities in criminal justice outcomes occurs long before the offender is standing before a judge—that discretion occurs in communities as police patrol the streets, and in the back rooms of district attorney offices as attorneys decide charges and bargain cases.

Bold Reform #5: Age Should Matter and All Criminal Records Should Expire

It is well established that age and prior criminal history are the two most salient predictors of recidivism. Just as it is impossible to change the past, it is impossible to stop the aging process, and we should use this pair of facts to make more intelligent sentencing decisions. Virtually all offenders eventually age out of crime, and research has consistently demonstrated that even the most active offenders age out of crime around the age of thirty-five.[28] Acknowledging this criminological fact would mean that people who are in their forties should be considered for release annually—no matter what their offense. The works of the some of the most prominent scholars in the field suggest that criminal careers do not last very long. Blumstein and colleagues, for example, using arrest data, tracked this age-crime curve for eight index offenses (murder, rape, robbery, aggravated assault, burglary, larceny theft,

33

theft, and arson) and found that the typical adult career for committing these offenses is five to ten years.[29]

We must find ways to truly expunge juvenile and adult records, because opening the prison gates and releasing large numbers of offenders will not accomplish much if we use their criminal records to send them right back in. While the call for ending mass incarceration through policy changes may seem challenging, it is relatively easy when compared with the challenge of changing how the usual suspects are perceived or treated when they encounter agents of the criminal justice system (including the police, the prosecutor, and the frequently all-white jury). Changing how we perceive individuals will have a lot to do with what story they have in their records and who has access to those stories. Crucially, the relevance of those stories becomes more attenuated with the passage of time, but the books are never closed. Criminal justice is one of the few realms where transgressions—even the most minor of transgressions—can be held against a person for life. It can no longer be argued that these records must remain accessible for decades because they continue to be relevant. Research has demonstrated that with each year that passes, a prior record becomes less determinative of future criminal conduct. After approximately seven years, a person with a prior criminal record is virtually indistinguishable from a person without one.[30]

If we are going to use age and criminal records against individuals in sentencing because research consistently shows that they are salient predictors of future criminal conduct, then we should similarly use the equally convincing research that tells us that age eventually makes continued incarceration futile and that prior criminal records eventually become meaningless.

Bold Reform #6: Stop Returning People to Prison for Technical Violations

There are many, many things that can be done to those who fail to abide by the terms of their supervision, but returning them to prison on a technical violation of the conditions of parole should not be on the table. Given their expense, prison beds should be considered a rare commodity, and those seeking to fill those beds should be required to justify the expense through cost-benefit analysis. Even the most rudimentary analysis would demonstrate that there is very little utility in returning technical violators to prison, even for short stays.[31]

Together these six principles would mean that prisons were reserved for those offenders who are truly dangerous and those prisoners would only stay for as long as they were actually dangerous. Some of those offenders might be so dangerous that they can never be safely returned to the community, but we would argue those would be very few.

If we committed to doing these six things, we would, in just a matter of years, end up with prison and jail populations that looked more like those of our European counterparts. Given the European experience, and our own (prior to the 1970s), we could do this without compromising public safety.[32] The effects of these changes would be enormous and rapid, and would soon make mass incarceration a fact of history rather than a present conundrum. A few years ago, in a report called *Unlocking America*, a team of leading correctional scholars proposed a simple reform platform similar to ours: eliminate prison for drug and public order crime, reduce length of stay to 1988 levels, and abolish imprisonment for technical violations of probation and parole.[33] They calculated the effect of these changes on correctional system populations starting in 2010, all else being equal. If we had done this in 2010, we would have 600,000 fewer people in prison today.

There is no question in our minds that the vast majority of those currently incarcerated in prisons around the country could be released with a negligible impact on public safety. For most Americans, life in the early 1970s, when there were just 200,000 prisoners, did not look vastly different from life in 2016, when there are 1.5 million (and that doesn't include the 700,000 that cycle through America's jails each year). We should not forget, though, that life for all those serving time in prisons and their families, and for the millions more who can expect to serve time in prisons during their lifetime, looks very different today than it did forty years ago. Lives are permanently altered by this experience— and not just the lives of those who are incarcerated, but the lives of children and families who are left behind and the lives of those living in communities that have been devastated by criminal justice policies that

35

have criminalized entire generations of mostly male, mostly poor, and mostly black residents.

If we could get to a prison population that was at a minimum half of what it is today in just one decade, then intensive supervision might become a realistic alternative to incarceration and all those who need correctional programs while incarcerated might be more likely to get them. Let us be clear that although we began by critiquing these approaches, we are not opposed to these as correctional strategies. On the contrary, we would be very much in support of such strategies if we work first to dramatically reduce the size of prison populations. With a much smaller base prison population, those approaches too could have meaningful and lasting effects on the number of people returning to prison—and that should ultimately be an aim.

We have made an argument with a series of proposals for immediately and dramatically reducing the number of offenders who go to prison and for drastically cutting the amount of time even the most dangerous offenders will spend there. These ideas might sound radical, even today when people are more open to decarceration arguments than they have been in decades, but most of what we have suggested would simply return U.S. sentencing systems and structures to the place they were before crime and drugs became a national obsession and increasingly harsh punishment became an imperative.

If we want to end mass incarceration, we can do so.

Notes

1. Ram Subramanian and Ruth Delaney, "Playbook for Change? States Reconsider Mandatory Sentences," *Federal Sentencing Reporter* 26, no. 3 (2014): 198–211.

2. Todd R. Clear, "A Private-Sector, Incentives-Based Model for Justice Reinvestment," *Criminology and Public Policy* 10, no. 3 (2011): 585–608; Marshall Clement, Matt Schwarzfeld, and Michael Thompson, "The National Summit on Justice Reinvestment and Public Safety: Addressing Recidivism, Crime, and Corrections Spending," Justice Center, Council of State Governments, 2011.

3. Nancy G. La Vigne, "Justice Reinvestment at the Local Level Planning and Implementation Guide," 2010.

4. Council of State Governments, "Massachusetts Names Working Group for Justice Reinvestment Initiative," news release, October 29, 2015; Nancy LaVigne et al., *Jus-

tice Reinvestment Initiative State Assessment Report (Washington, DC: Urban Institute, 2014); Nicole Porter, *The State of Sentencing 2015: Developments in Policy and Practice* (Washington, DC: Sentencing Project, 2016).

5. S. Tucker and Eric Cadora, "Justice Reinvestment: To Invest in Public Safety by Reallocating Justice Dollars to Refinance Education, Housing, Healthcare, and Jobs," Ideas for an Open Society occasional papers vol. 3, no. 3, 2003.

6. Natasha A. Frost, Carlos E. Monteiro, and Beck M. Strah, "Cost-Effective and Accountable Criminal Justice Policy," *Advancing Criminology and Criminal Justice Policy*, 2016, 441.

7. Mark A.R. Kleinman, "Justice Reinvestment in Community Supervision," *Criminology and Public Policy* 10, no. 3 (2011).

8. Frost, Monteiro, and Strah, "Cost-Effective and Accountable Criminal Justice Policy," 441.

9. Don A. Andrews, Ivan Zinger, Robert D. Hoge, James Bonta, Paul Gendreau, and Francis T. Cullen, "Does Correctional Treatment Work? A Clinically Relevant and Psychologically Informed Meta-analysis," *Criminology* 28, no. 3 (1990): 369–404; Lois M. Davis et al., *Evaluating the Effectiveness of Correctional Education: A Meta-Analysis of Programs That Provide Education to Incarcerated Adults* (Santa Monica, CA: RAND Corporation, 2013); Mark W. Lipsey and Francis T. Cullen, "The Effectiveness of Correctional Rehabilitation: A Review of Systematic Reviews," *Annual Review of Law and Social Science* 3 (2007): 297–320.

10. Todd R. Clear and Natasha A. Frost, *The Punishment Imperative: The Rise and Failure of Mass Incarceration in America* (New York: New York University Press, 2014). See also Natasha A. Frost and Todd R. Clear, "Theories of Mass Incarceration," in *The Oxford Handbook of Prisons and Imprisonment*, ed. John Wooldredge and Paula Smith (New York: Oxford University Press, 2016).

11. Todd R. Clear and James Austin, "Reducing Mass Incarceration: Implications of the Iron Law of Prison Populations," *Harvard Law and Policy Review* 3 (2009): 307; Natasha A. Frost, *The Punitive State: Crime, Punishment and Imprisonment Across the United States* (New York: LFB Scholarly Publications, 2006); Natasha A. Frost, "The Mismeasure of Punishment: Alternative Measures of Punitiveness and Their (Substantial) Consequences," *Punishment and Society* 10, no. 3 (2008): 277–300.

12. Matthew R. Durose, Alexia D. Cooper, and Howard N. Snyder. "Recidivism of Prisoners Released in 30 States in 2005: Patterns from 2005 to 2010—Update," Special Report, Bureau of Justice Statistics, Department of Justice, April 2014, NCJ 244205.

13. Andrew Von Hirsch and Committee for the Study of Incarceration, *Doing Justice: The Choice of Punishments: Report of the Committee for the Study of Incarceration* (Boston: Northeastern University Press, 1976).

14. Nancy A. Heitzg, "Criminalizing Education: Zero Tolerance Policies, Police in the Hallways, and the School to Prison Pipeline," in *From Education to Incarceration:*

Dismantling the School-to-Prison Pipeline, ed. Anthony J. Nocella, Priya Parmar, and David Stovall (New York: Peter Lang, 2014); Kelly Welch and Allison Ann Payne, "Racial Threat and Punitive School Discipline," *Social Problems* 57, no. 1 (2010): 25–48.

15. Nancy Heitzeg, "Criminalizing Education."

16. William Spelman, "The Limited Importance of Prison Expansion," in *The Crime Drop in America*, ed. Alfred Blumstein and Joel Wallman (Cambridge: Cambridge University Press, 2005).

17. Marc Mauer, "The Impact of Mandatory Minimum Penalties in Federal Sentencing," *Judicature* 94 (2010): 6.

18. Although we are encouraged by the shift, we would be remiss if we did not explicitly acknowledge the race and class dimensions of how drug use and abuse get framed. Black Americans residing in our nation's urban communities did not receive the same compassion during the crack cocaine epidemic that the mostly white Americans residing in suburban communities are experiencing as we confront the current opioid crisis. This is of no small consequence because the way in which an issue gets framed has substantial implications for how we respond to it. Drug control policies during the crack cocaine era called for a heavy-handed criminal justice approach that usually carried lengthy, often decades-long prison sentences. In 2010, President Obama signed the Fair Sentencing Act, which sought to address disparities in sentencing that for decades disproportionately subjected black and other minority offenders to the criminal justice system. Prior to the Fair Sentencing Act, federal guidelines created a series of mandatory minimum sentencing policies. Although mandatory minimums were popular and widely adopted across the states, the treatment of crack cocaine and powder cocaine in calculating minimum sentences in the federal system stood out as one of the most controversial policies to date. During this punitive era, a gram of crack cocaine was considered equivalent to 100 grams of powder cocaine, despite the fact that the two were pharmacologically identical. While the Fair Sentencing Act was a major step toward righting a wrong, reducing the sentencing disparity for crack cocaine and powder cocaine offenses from 100 to 1 to 18 to 1 is a small victory and proved largely inconsequential in terms of the overall impact on prison populations. In 2009, for example, the U.S. Sentencing Commission projected that after ten years, federal prisons would see an estimated reduction of only four thousand inmates as a result of the change.

19. E.A. Carson, "Prisoners in 2014," Bureau of Justice Statistics, Department of Justice, 2015, NCJ 248955.

20. Natasha A. Frost and Todd R. Clear, "Coercive Mobility," in *Oxford Handbook of Criminological Theory*, ed. Francis T. Cullen and Pamela Wilcox (New York: Oxford University Press, 2012); Todd R. Clear et al., *Predicting Crime Through Incarceration:*

The Impact of Rates of Prison Cycling on Rates of Crime in Communities (Washington, DC: National Institute of Justice, 2014).

21. Eric L. Sevigny and Jonathan P. Caulkins, "Kingpins or Mules: An Analysis of Drug Offenders Incarcerated in Federal and State Prisons," *Criminology and Public Policy* 3, no. 3 (2004): 401–34.

22. Daniel S. Nagin and John V. Pepper, *Deterrence and the Death Penalty* (Washington, DC: National Research Council, 2012); Daniel S. Nagin, "Deterrence in the Twenty First Century," *Crime and Justice* 42 (2013).

23. United States Sentencing Commission, "Special Report to the Congress: Mandatory Minimum Penalties in the Federal Criminal Justice System," 1991.

24. Mauer, "The Impact of Mandatory Minimum Penalties in Federal Sentencing," 6.

25. Bruce Western and Christopher Wildeman, "The Black Family and Mass Incarceration," *Annals of the American Academy of Political and Social Science* 621, no. 1 (2009); Anke Ramakers, Robert Apel, Paul Nieuwbeerta, Anja Dirkzwager, and Johan Wilsem, "Imprisonment Length and Post-Prison Employment Prospects," *Criminology* 52, no. 3 (2014): 399–427; Bruce Western and Leonard Lopoo, "Incarceration, Marriage, and Family Life," Department of Sociology, Princeton University, 2004.

26. Michael Tonry, "Remodeling American Sentencing: A Ten-Step Blueprint for Moving Past Mass Incarceration," *Criminology and Public Policy* 13, no. 4 (2014): 503–33.

27. Ashley Nellis and Ryan S. King, "No Exit: The Expanding Use of Life Sentences in America," Sentencing Project, 2009; Ashley Nellis, "Throwing Away the Key: The Expansion of Life Without Parole Sentences in the United States," *Federal Sentencing Reporter* 23, no. 1 (2010): 27–32.

28. Alex R. Piquero, David P. Farrington, and Alfred Blumstein, *Key Issues in Criminal Career Research: New Analyses of the Cambridge Study in Delinquent Development* (Cambridge: Cambridge University Press, 2007).

29. David P. Farrington, Maria M. Ttofi, Rebecca V. Crago, and Jeremy W. Coid, "Prevalence, Frequency, Onset, Desistance and Criminal Career Duration in Self-Reports Compared with Official Records," *Criminal Behaviour and Mental Health* 24, no. 4 (2014): 241–53.

30. Alfred Blumstein and Kiminori Nakamura, "Redemption in the Presence of Widespread Criminal Background Checks," *Criminology* 47, no. 2 (2009): 327–59; Megan C. Kurlychek, Robert Brame, and Shawn D. Bushway, "Scarlet Letters and Recidivism: Does an Old Criminal Record Predict Future Offending?," *Criminology and Public Policy* 5, no. 3 (2006): 483–504; Shawn D. Bushway, Paul Nieuwbeerta, and Arjan Blokland, "The Predictive Value of Criminal Background Checks: Do Age and Criminal History Affect Time to Redemption?," *Criminology* 49, no. 1 (2011): 27–60.

31. M. Michael O'Hear, "Justice Reinvestment and the State of State Sentencing Reform," *Federal Sentencing Reporter* 29, no. 1 (2016).

32. Jody Sundt, Emily J. Salisbury, and Mark G. Harmon, "Is Downsizing Prisons Dangerous?," *Criminology and Public Policy* 15, no. 2 (2016): 315–41.

33. James Austin, Todd Clear, Troy Duster, David F. Greenberg, John Irwin, Candace McCoy, Alan Mobley, Barbara Owen, and Joshua Page, *Unlocking America: Why and How to Reduce America's Prison Population* (Washington, DC: JFA Institute, 2007).

2

Better by Half
The New York City Story

JUDITH A. GREENE AND VINCENT SCHIRALDI

For much of the latter part of the twentieth century, New York was synonymous with the urban decay, crime, and mass incarceration confronting so many American cities. With the number of murders topping 2,200 in 1990, New York's jail population was bursting at the seams, peaking at nearly 22,000 inmates at Rikers Island in 1991, more than double today's population. Similarly, in 1998, the number of New York City residents in state prisons peaked at 47,315—a number that fell by more than half to 22,580 by May 2016.[1]

In the nineties, few could have imagined that in 2015, the city would experience only 350 murders—an 84 percent drop from its peak in 1990—with steep declines in other crime categories as well.[2] Writing in 2011, University of California law professor Franklin Zimring dubbed New York City's crime decline "the largest and longest sustained drop in street crime ever experienced by a big city in the developed world."[3]

Given the widely held belief among elected officials that more imprisonment was needed to control crime, a casual 1990s observer could have been forgiven for predicting that such a sharp decline in crime in New York City surely would have been accompanied by an equally profound increase in incarceration. But exactly the opposite happened.

Between 1996 and 2014, the city's combined rate of population incarcerated in prisons and jails declined by 55 percent, while the combined incarceration rate in the remainder of the United States rose by 12 percent. Despite the fact that the city's population grew by more than a million people between 1996 and 2014, the real number of New Yorkers incarcerated in prisons and jails declined by 31,120 during that time. Simultaneously, index crime—the seven types of serious crime that are tracked in the FBI's uniform crime index—in New York City declined by 58 percent, while index crime nationally declined by a more modest 42 percent.[4] By 2014, this left New York City with the lowest crime rate of the nation's twenty largest cities and the second-lowest jail incarceration rate among the largest cities, behind only Wayne County, Michigan, which includes Detroit but much of which is suburban, unlike New York City.

The past few years have marked a time of great change in U.S. prison policy, with a growing bipartisan consensus that mass incarceration should be ended (or at least curtailed). More states adopted decarceration policies addressing drug arrests, sentencing, and parole practices—leading to significant declines in state prison populations (Figure 2.1).

New York's more than 50 percent decline in jail and prison incarceration starting in the mid-1990s began at a time when incarceration rates in the rest of the United States, taken as a whole, as well as in the remainder of New York State, were still increasing. New York's decarceration experiment first flowed from a bottom-up effort to amend, repeal, and reverse the laws, policies, and practices that swept our nation into the era of mass incarceration—most particularly those involving the war on drugs. Second, the profound decline in incarceration in the nation's largest city left it one of the least incarcerated cities in America. At the same time New York was also becoming the safest city in America, giving the lie to the notion that more incarceration was needed to provide more safety.

Figure 2.1: State Prison Population Decline: Peak Year to 2014

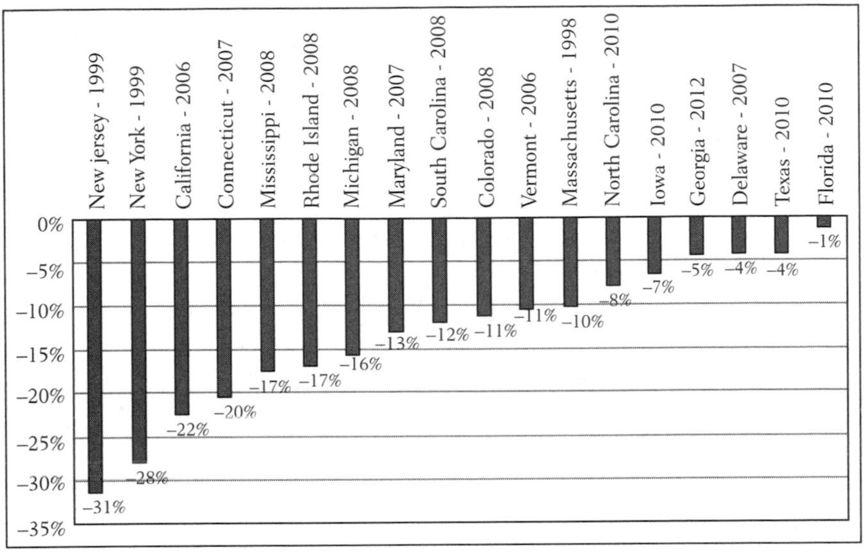

Source: Bureau of Justice Statistics

New York's State Prison Population Deescalates

One of the three most robust state experiences with decarceration has taken place in New York. During 1999, the state prison population hit an all-time high of 72,899.[5] By the end of 2015, the population had fallen by 28 percent to just 52,344 (Figure 2.2).

New York City, which drove the state's decline in prisoners, instituted a remarkable policy shift where the New York City Police Department (NYPD) was the principal factor that set the trend in motion. For decades previously, drug law enforcement in New York City had driven prison population trends, starting with enactment in 1973 of Governor Nelson Rockefeller's notorious drug law "reform" with harsh mandatory minimum sentences that became the model for the nation. Under the Rockefeller drug laws, sale of only two ounces, or possession of just four ounces, of a narcotic drug became a Class A felony, carrying a fifteen-years-to-life prison sentence. The majority of drug offense cases subject to the new law would involve much smaller

Figure 2.2: New York State Prison Population 1993–2015

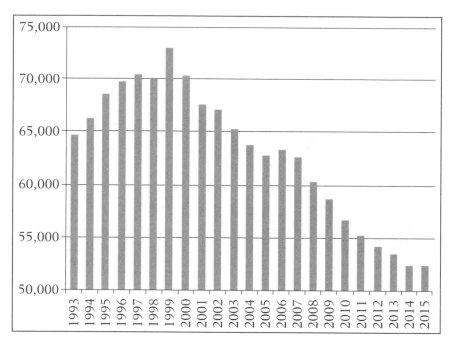

Sources: Bureau of Justice Statistics and New York State Department of Corrections and Community Supervision

weights, but the lesser-known Second Felony Offender Law, enacted along with the Rockefeller drug law, made a prison sentence mandatory for anyone convicted of any two felonies—no matter their nature—within ten years.

A national moral panic sparked in the mid-1980s by the so-called crack crisis did not exempt New York City, even though the state's drug laws were already among the toughest in the nation. In 1985 the NYPD piloted a drug enforcement dragnet called Operation Pressure Point on the Lower East Side of Manhattan, and NYPD's Tactical Narcotic Teams spread the program across the city in other neighborhoods, including East Harlem and southeast Queens.[6] The Tactical Narcotic Teams mobilized roving cadres of plainclothes and undercover narcotics officers to saturate targeted neighborhoods with intensive "buy-and-bust" operations over a three-month period before moving on to the next target neighborhood.

Intensified street drug enforcement flooded the state's prison capacity, with the number of individuals committed to prison for drug offenses rising from just 834 in 1973 to 11,225 in 1992, a remarkable thirteen-fold increase. By 1994, one-third of all New York State prison beds were holding people serving time for a drug conviction.[7] Ninety percent of them were black or Latino.

After enactment of the Rockefeller drug laws, New York legislators continued to constrict judicial discretion by toughening other sentencing laws. In 1978, longer sentences were enacted for "violent felony offenders" and "persistent violent felony offenders." Another measure increased the likelihood that young people convicted of violent crimes would receive an adult prison sentence.

Between 1988 and 1999, the state built twenty new prisons. George Pataki defeated incumbent Mario Cuomo in the 1994 gubernatorial election on a platform of "truth in sentencing" and a pledge to restore the death penalty. Legislators amended state penal laws to eliminate parole for people convicted as two-time persistent violent felony offenders, replacing discretionary release with fixed "determinate" sentences. In 1998, Pataki abolished parole for *all* people convicted as violent felons. Between 1994 and 1999, the parole rate dropped from 60 percent to 40 percent.[8]

Despite these tough-on-crime state policies, New York City's crime data showed a remarkable decrease in violent crime starting in 1991. By 2012, the city's violent crime rate had plummeted by 73 percent. Arrests for violent felonies also declined. In 1994, there were 70,880 arrests for violent felonies statewide. By 2015, that figure had fallen to 40,816. Within New York City, violent felony arrests fell by 49 percent, compared to a 22 percent decline in the rest of the state. During the same period, felony drug arrests in the city also took a dramatic tumble (Figure 2.3).

The Rockefeller drug laws were met with opposition beginning in 1973, when the governor first announced his intention to toughen sentencing laws and thereafter. In the late 1990s, students with the Prison Moratorium Project organized against the laws. In 1997, State University of New York and City University of New York students marched on the state capitol carrying banners showing dollar-for-dollar shifts in state spending from higher education to prisons. A "Drop the Rock" campaign soon spawned a broad

Figure 2.3: Felony Arrests in New York City 1994–2015

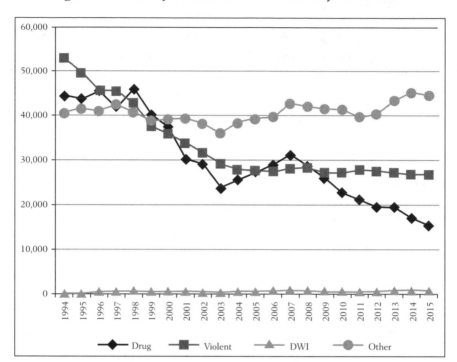

Source: New York State Division of Criminal Justice Services

coalition of organizations, including the Correctional Association of New York, the Center for Constitutional Rights, the Legal Aid Society, the United New York Black Radical Congress, the American Jewish Congress, the New York Civil Liberties Union, and the Fortune Society. Felony drug arrests in the city suddenly began a sharp decline, from 45,978 in 1998 all the way to 15,507 in 2015—a drop of 66 percent, compared to a decline of less than 20 percent in the rest of the state—even as drug use in the city remained relatively stable.[9]

NYPD enforcement priorities had shifted, with dramatic results. In just two years, the number of drug arrests fell by more than 8,000 from the high-water mark in 1998. In 1999, a well-publicized Zogby International poll of likely New York State voters had indicated that the Rockefeller drug laws were highly unpopular.[10] Twice as many voters responded that they were *more* inclined to vote for state legislators who would reduce drug sentences and give judges greater discretion than the number who said they'd be *less* inclined to do so.

New York City Wins the War

Criminologist Franklin Zimring notes that the number of officers assigned to special narcotics units grew from 1,183 in 1990 to 2,800 in 1999.[11] Yet by 2006, the narcotics force had shrunk back to 1,180. Zimring speculates that the city had simply won the drug war on its own terms, achieving the two major strategic objectives that animated the narcotic unit's expansion: driving drug markets off the streets and reducing drug-traffic-related violence.[12]

While drug related hospitalizations and drug overdose death trends remained relatively flat during this period (indicating stable prevalence of drug-using populations), police efforts were focused on affecting the nature of the city's drug markets. The almost 60 percent drop in narcotics unit strength is strong, circumstantial evidence that the reductions in open-air markets and lethal violence in drug traffic were signs of success in the department's chief priorities.[13]

Misdemeanor Drug Arrests

In 1994, New York City police commissioner Bill Bratton introduced his trademark "broken windows" policing. He ended a long-standing NYPD policy that discouraged patrol officers from arresting people for petty drug offenses, and instead he encouraged them to be aggressive with people they saw committing "quality-of-life" crimes.[14] Accordingly, misdemeanor drug arrests rose sharply from 1994 to 1996. After Commissioner Bratton retired, the sharp rise in low level arrests continued throughout the regime of his successor, Commissioner Howard Safir, peaking at 102,712 misdemeanor drug arrests in New York in the year 2000.

With a new commissioner, Bernard Kerik, misdemeanor drug arrests began a sharp decline that seemed to be an echo of the felony drug arrest decline. But in 2005 under Commissioner Ray Kelly, these arrests began to rise again to a new peak of 84,250 in 2011. By then drug reform advocates were loudly denouncing the tens of thousands of marijuana arrests that accounted for more than 40 percent of the misdemeanor drug arrests associated with the growth of "stop-and-frisk" policing practices, reaching 700,000 in its peak year.[15] The Drug Policy Alliance, in collaboration with the Marijuana Arrest Research Project, the Center for NuLeadership on Urban Solutions, and VOCAL-NY organized a campaign to stop these arrests at both the local and state levels. Commissioner Kelly responded by issuing a series of memos clarifying and liberalizing NYPD's arrest policies for marijuana, and Mayor Michael Bloomberg called for the issuance of desk appearance tickets in lieu of arrests for marijuana possession.

During the 2013 mayoral election campaign there was general agreement by the candidates to reduce marijuana arrests. From 2011 to 2015, the number of misdemeanor drug arrests plummeted by 50 percent, back to the level before Commissioner Bratton originally told the patrol troops to crack down on petty street crime.

Prosecution and Sentencing in Drug Cases

Reflecting the change in public sentiment about the issue of drugs, sentencing practices had already begun to shift across the state before the NYPD moved away from intensified drug enforcement in the early 2010s. As far back as 1990, the newly elected Kings County (Brooklyn) district attorney Charles J. Hynes decided that for many repeat felony drug offenders, their families and their communities would benefit more from treatment alternatives than from mandatory prison terms. Hynes struck a historic blow against the Second Felony Offender Law, agreeing to divert people with one or more prior felony convictions to treatment programs. Within a few years, district attorneys across the state were replicating Hynes's Drug Treatment Alternative-to-Prison (DTAP) program.

An evaluation by Columbia University's Center on Addiction and Substance Abuse found that the treatment alternative effectively diverted individuals from incarceration and reduced relapse and reoffense, even for those with significant criminal histories.[16] Participants were found to be 36 percent less likely to be reconvicted and 67 percent less likely to return to prison after two years than a matched comparison group.

The treatment program joined an already robust network of alternative-to-incarceration programs. The city's investments in these programs had been growing since the 1960s, when the Vera Institute of Justice first developed pretrial release and diversion programs that became national models, encouraging judges to send people to treatment, educational, or vocational programs instead of jail.

In the mid-1980s, New York State legislators were allocating hundreds of millions in tax dollars to expand the state's prison system, but they also began to provide substantial funding for an array of new programs designed to target defendants thought to be jail- or prison-bound with advocacy and program interventions intended to reduce the courts' reliance on incarceration. Although programs were not restricted to diverting drug cases alone, the proportion of felony drug cases that resulted in a prison sentence fell from 21 percent in 1997 to an all-time low of 11 percent in 2007.

Correctional Tools for Prison Population Management

At the state level, policy makers were working on a "right-sizing" approach to managing the prison population. They set a number of policies and programs in place to gain more control of population levels as well as to encourage those in their custody to maintain good behavior and engage in constructive activities while serving time. These included:

- *Shock incarceration,* where participants earned their GEDs. After release to parole, drug tests indicated an abstinence rate of 92 percent among Shock parolees.[17] By December 2015, 68,764 people had participated in Shock, which began at the Monterey Shock Incarceration Facility in Schuyler Country, and 73 percent of those succeeded in receiving early parole. Correctional officials

49

estimated that their early releases had saved taxpayers $1.5 billion.

- *Earned parole eligibility*, introduced in 1992 to provide people who are parole-eligible and who meet certain criteria with an "earned eligibility certificate" that enhances their chances for release at their first parole hearing. Most people who can be considered for a certificate receive one. But since 1995, when New York began to embrace truth-in-sentencing, the number of parole-eligible people in prison has declined, and many who remain parole-eligible are people sent to prison years ago with very long terms to serve. From October 2015 through March 2016, of the 3,941 people facing their initial parole hearing, 2,225 (57 percent) had been certified for early release. Of those certified, just 850 (38 percent) were granted parole. Of those denied a certificate, only 7 percent were granted parole.[18]

- *The Merit Time Program*, established in October 1997, allows people who are serving a prison term for a nonviolent, non-sex-related offense to earn a reduction of one-sixth off their minimum term, which qualifies them for early parole consideration. The reduction depends upon achievement of specific program goals— obtaining a GED or a vocational training certificate, completing an alcohol or drug abuse program, or performing four hundred hours of service on a community work crew—provided there have been no serious disciplinary infractions. Between the inception of the Merit Time Program and December 2006 (the latest year that program statistics were made available), 37,914 people had earned a merit time hearing at the parole board, of whom 64 percent were released prior to their designated parole eligibility date. On average, those granted merit time shaved about six months off their minimum sentence. A recidivism study found that the return-to-prison rate for Merit Time Program release was 31 percent, compared to 39 percent for all other releases. By 2006, Department of Corrections and Community Supervision (DOCCS) managers attributed $384 million in savings to the Merit Time Program.[19]

- *Parole release.* Until 1995, New York's penal code required that state prison sentences be "indeterminate," with judges sentencing people to a minimum typically set at one-third of the maximum. The parole board would review each case, with an initial hearing to be set in accordance with first eligibility at the minimum date. Good behavior could earn one-third off the maximum date. For example, someone sentenced to three to nine years could count on being released after serving six years at the most, unless he or she failed to earn "good time" credits. The federal Violent Crime Control and Law Enforcement Act of 1994 allocated $9.7 billion in prison expansion funding for states that gave assurances that new correctional policies (including truth-in-sentencing laws) would be implemented to provide "sufficiently severe punishment for violent offenders."[20] As a result, from 1995 forward, the number of people sentenced to indeterminate prison terms and therefore eligible for parole release steadily decreased. By 2008, the number of conditional releases (after the sentence was fully served) exceeded the number of parole releases for the first time, and by 2013, only 34 percent of releases resulted from parole board decisions.

Drug Policy Reform by Legislative Action

As described above, decades of intensifying advocacy by proponents of drug policy reform and alternatives to incarceration began to outweigh the harsh rhetoric of drug "hawks" and the "tough-on-crime" movement during the late 1990s, resulting in an unprecedented reduction in New York's state prison population. Most of that advocacy arose out of New York City, and not surprisingly, the entire decline in the state's prison population was the result of the decline in imprisoned people from New York City. Yet an entire decade would pass before legislators caught up with public sentiment and substantially revised the Rockefeller drug laws.

In the fall of 2008, key members of the New York State Assembly convened unprecedented joint hearings involving the combined leadership of six legislative committees for day-long sessions in both New York City and Rochester. National experts, public health practitioners, and local reform advocates alike voiced the need to establish a public-health-based approach to the problem of drugs. In January 2009, more than three hundred people—health professionals, law enforcement veterans, elected officials, reform advocates, drug treatment specialists, and active drug users—gathered in New York City for a conference convened jointly by the Drug Policy Alliance and the New York Academy of Medicine to spur reform.

The Speaker of the Assembly responded with a pledge that 2009 would be the year that reform of the Rockefeller drug laws would be won. On April 7, 2009, New York's governor, David Paterson, signed Article 216 of the Criminal Procedure Law.

Key elements of the reform included:

- Judicial discretion to place people convicted of drug offenses into treatment and to offer second chances when appropriate.
- Diversion from incarceration for people who commit crimes other than drug offenses because of issues stemming from substance dependence.
- Diversion eligibility for people convicted of second felony offenses.
- Opportunities to try community-based treatment without the threat of a longer sentence for failure.
- Plea deferral options, especially for noncitizen green card holders who would become deportable if they take a plea to any drug felony conviction, even if it is later withdrawn.
- Opportunities for resentencing for more than nine hundred people who were still in prison under the longer pre-2004 indeterminate terms.
- Record-sealing provisions that protect people who finish their sentences from employment discrimination based on the past offense.
- The option for a judge to dismiss a case in the interests of justice when the accused has successfully completed a treatment program.

The Impact of Drug Reform on the State Prison Population

The proportion of people admitted to serve a felony drug sentence among all new admissions in New York State prisons has been declining since 2000. While the passage of reforms was clearly a major victory for advocates in the battle against harsh drug war policies, little difference in the curve in commitments to New York State prison for drug offenses can be discerned pre- and post-passage of those reforms (Figure 2.4), perhaps because public opinion about the ineffectiveness of the laws had been shifting for decades, and judicial and prosecutorial practices had already changed accordingly.

Average sentences for people convicted of a drug felony also fell between 2000 and 2013, from twenty-seven months to nineteen months, along with a drop in the percentage of people within the overall prison population

Figure 2.4: Percentage of Drug Admissions Among All New Admissions to New York Prisons 2000–2013

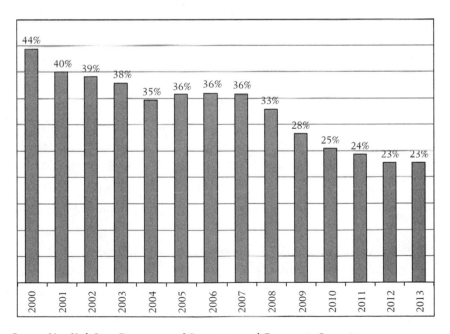

Source: New York State Department of Corrections and Community Supervision

Figure 2.5: Percentage of People with Drug Convictions in New York State Prisons 1996–2014

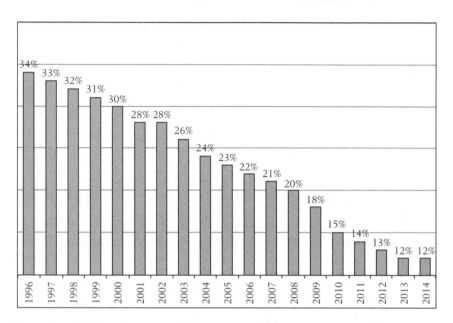

Source: New York State Department of Corrections and Community Supervision

serving time for a drug conviction. All told, in 1996 24,000 people were serving a felony drug sentences in New York's state prisons. At the end of 2014 there were fewer than 6,700—a breathtaking 72 percent decline.

The cumulative effect of refocusing NYPD drug enforcement priorities, the shifting drug sentencing trends in the city courts, the use of incentivized release programs by the DOCCS, plus several legislative reforms—including the long-fought-for 2009 Rockefeller drug law reform—had a substantial impact on New York State's prison population. Between 2000 and 2014, with 15,601 fewer people serving time on drug convictions, the overall prison population fell by 17,289. With thousands of empty prison beds, New York's correctional managers have been able to greatly reduce their prison capacity, saving money and making the prisons safer for both correctional staff and the people they guard.

During the Pataki administration, the Department of Corrections deactivated 2,700 dormitory beds. After the sweeping changes to the Rockefeller drug laws enacted in April 2009, three small minimum-security prisons were closed and annexes were shuttered at six prisons that otherwise remained in operation. The DOCCS estimate was that some $52 million was saved over the next two years.[21] By 2014, DOCCS managers had closed a total of thirteen prison facilities, and $24 million in economic development money had been allocated to assist local communities affected by prison closures.[22]

New York City's Use of Jail

As with the New York State prison population, the decline in New York City's jail population has been dramatic and driven by the shift in NYPD priorities along with substantial changes in courtroom decisions to eschew jail and local probation—which can often act as a feeder system to jail. The degree of decarceration within the city system has sparked serious discussions among policy makers and advocates about closing the notorious jail facilities on Rikers Island and relocating people incarcerated in New York City's jails to smaller, borough-based facilities—an idea with substantial media and public support that became a mayoral pledge in 2017, as the incumbent mayor, Bill De Blasio, sought reelection.[23]

The population of the New York City Department of Correction at Rikers Island has declined from a historic high of 21,688 in 1991 to 9,762 at the end of April 2016, a remarkable 55 percent decline. Jail population levels are determined by two factors: the number of people who enter the jail, and the amount of time they are confined until released. Since 1998, the average length of stay for people convicted of either felonies or misdemeanors has increased only a bit,[24] but the large decrease in admissions for both offense categories has resulted in a much lower jail population, nonetheless (Figure 2.6).[25]

Pretrial Release in New York City

Since the overwhelming majority of those in jail under the custody of the New York City Department of Correction are detained pretrial (87 percent as of May 26, 2016), what happens with the pretrial population has an important

Figure 2.6: Felony Admissions and Average
Days to Release 1998–2015

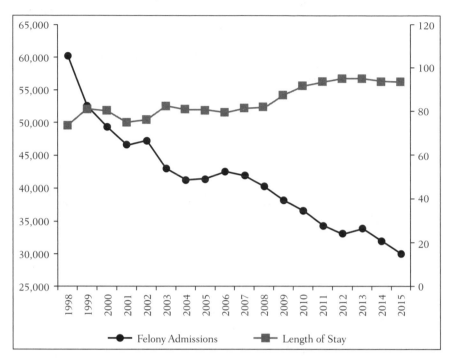

Source: New York City Department of Correction

impact on New York City's jail population. New York City detains fewer of those arrested than most other large urban jurisdictions, and over the past decade or so, releases of defendants at arraignment have increased.

Founded in 1973 as the Vera Institute's Manhattan Bail Project, New York City's Criminal Justice Agency (CJA) became the nation's pioneer in the use of a risk assessment instrument to advise courts on the likelihood that a defendant would return to court for the next court date if released on recognizance in lieu of bail at the hearing. Recent research on pretrial release shows that defendants in New York City were more likely to be released prior to case disposition (74 percent) than defendants in the seventy-five other largest urban areas nationally (58 percent). Nonfinancial release in New York

City also made up a larger portion of releases (50 percent) than was the case for the other large urban areas (25 percent).[26]

From 2004 to 2014, the percentage of people released on their own recognizance increased.[27] For those individuals recommended for release on their own recognizance by the Criminal Justice Agency, 83 percent were released in 2014, compared to 78 percent in 2004, and for people evaluated as medium risk, 72 percent were released in 2004, compared to 79 percent in 2014. But arraignment judges appear to have become more liberal in general over this period, since 50 percent of those for whom CJA did *not* recommend release were released on recognizance anyway in 2014, compared to only 38 percent in this category who were released in 2014.[28]

A substantial majority of individuals in all recommendation categories made their court appearances as required, although higher appearance rates were associated with positive recommendations. In 2014, 7 percent of defendants in both felony and non-felony cases who were recommended for release failed to appear, as did 11 percent of those evaluated as moderate risk. By comparison, 22 percent of non-felony defendants who were not recommended for release failed to appear. In addition to near-universal screening of defendants for release on their own recognizance, in 2014 CJA operated bail-expediting programs in the four largest New York City boroughs—programs that assisted defendants for whom bail was set to contact relatives and friends for help in posting bail.

The Sentenced Population

In addition to the decline in felony arrests (and particularly felony drug arrests) described above, there has been a dramatic change in dispositions—the final decisions that the court makes in criminal cases, including sentencing—of people arrested for felonies and misdemeanors in New York during this time period.

According to the New York State Division of Criminal Justice Services, prison sentences (of a year or more) declined sharply as a portion of all felony case dispositions, while shorter sentences to jail (i.e., for less than one year) rose slightly as a percentage of case dispositions. Overall, these substantial reductions in prison commitments (and small increases in the percentage of cases sent to jail) made a large contribution to reducing the city's combined incarceration rate, since people committed to jail have shorter lengths of stay than those committed to prison.[29]

Furthermore, even though jail sentences rose as a *percentage* of all felony cases disposed of, the overall *number* of jail sentences declined by 4,738 due to the 33 percent decline in felony cases handled by New York City courts between 1996 and 2014. In other words, the decline in felony arrests accounted for *all* of the decline in jail commitments for felony arrests, and then some.

A different trend appears with the misdemeanor arrests and dispositions, although the misdemeanor trend also nets out to substantially fewer jail commitments. Misdemeanor arrests rose from 181,817 in 1996 to a peak of 237,818 in 2011 before falling to 215,352 in 2014, a net increase of 18 percent or 33,535 misdemeanor arrests.

However, jail as a disposition for misdemeanor arrests declined during this period. In 1996, 25 percent of all misdemeanor cases were sentenced to jail, compared to only 20 percent in 2014. In total, despite the fact that there were 33,535 *more* misdemeanor arrests in 2014 than in 1996, 1,954 *fewer* cases in New York City ended in a jail sentence in 2014 than in 1996.

As with state prison sentences, incarceration of people for drug offenses led the way in reducing the jail population in New York City. From 1996 to 2016, the number of people incarcerated in New York City's jails for drug offenses declined by 73 percent, which made up more than half (52 percent) of the entire jail population decline during that time period.

Formal probation supervision can be another route to incarceration for some individuals insofar as failure to abide by conditions of probation can result in jail or, less frequently, prison terms. From 1996 to 2014 in New York City, probation sentences and the number of people on probation declined considerably, early discharges from probation increased, face-to-face supervision decreased, and probation violations were substantially reduced.

In 1996, 7 percent of felony cases and 0.7 percent of misdemeanor cases were sentenced to probation; in 2014, those rates were 4 percent and 0.3

percent, respectively. All told, the number of people sentenced to probation declined by two-thirds from 1996 to 2014, from 16,285 to 5,313. An analysis by the State Division of Criminal Justice Services for this chapter found that the number of people on probation in New York City declined by 33 percent between 1996 and 2015, compared to a 20 percent decline in the rest of the state.

In addition to these court-driven changes, the New York City Probation Department itself reduced the onerous nature of probation and probation violations. In 1996, the probation department reduced face-to-face supervision by initiating monthly reporting to an electronic kiosk rather than more frequent face-to-face supervision for low-risk and otherwise deserving people on probation. Further, early discharges from probation increased nearly six-fold between 2007 and 2012.[30] A state analysis showed that only 3 percent of those discharged early from probation in 2011 were reconvicted of a felony within a year of discharge.

The Probation Department's use of violations declined significantly. Just between 2009 and 2013, probation violations declined by 45 percent.[31] By 2013, only 3 percent of people on probation in New York City experienced probation violations, compared to 11 percent in the rest of New York State.[32]

Overall, in 2014, the number of felony and misdemeanor cases resulting in conditional (including a requirement such as community service) and unconditional discharges and fines exceeded the number sentenced to probation, jail, and prison *combined*. As New York was becoming a safer city, its courts were dismissing many more cases, and relying less frequently on prison, jail, and probation and more heavily on fines and conditional and unconditional discharges.

Declines in Crime and Incarceration in the Nation's Largest City

From the mid-1990s to the present day, New York City experienced a well-publicized decline in crime that Franklin Zimring has described as the "Guinness Book of World Records crime drop," exclaiming that the decline in crime in New York was "so dramatic we need a new way of keeping score."[33]

Less well publicized has been the city's dramatic and simultaneous decline in incarceration. New York City's dramatic combined reduction in incarceration and crime has left it as one of the safest and least-incarcerated cities in the United States. And while the city's incarceration rate fell by 48 percent from 1991 to 2014, the violent crime rate fell by 73 percent.

Based on data like these, it would be hard to argue that either New York City's reduction in reliance on prison or jail sentences or its low combined incarceration rate is jeopardizing the public safety of the city's residents. On the contrary, while New York's incarceration rate fell by 55 percent between 1996 and 2014, its violent crime rate fell by 54 percent—this at a time when incarceration in the rest of the country and New York State continued to rise.

In terms of sheer numbers, the contrast between New York City and the rest of the nation is even more dramatic. From 1991 to 2014, the city held 46 percent fewer people in jail and prison, while the rest of the nation increased the number of people behind bars by 34 percent. And although national data are not yet available for comparison, the combined prison and jail population decline for New York City reached 50 percent at the end of April 2016, down from its highest level at the end of 1998 (Figure 2.7).

What Does It All Mean?

Inspired by the refrain from "New York, New York," "If I can make it there, I'll make it anywhere," we believe that a number of lessons can be drawn from the New York experience.

Lesson 1: Whereas calls to reduce America's incarceration rate by 50 percent may seem outlandish to some, our findings support the notion that a 50 percent reduction in incarceration is not an unrealistic goal, at least for large American cities (and advocates can help to get us there). New York City's experience also points out that advocacy-driven decarceration efforts are more likely to seek and win audacious goals—like a 50 percent reduction in incarceration—than are technocratically driven approaches.

Lesson 2: Less can be more when it comes to incarceration and supervision. During this period of sharply declining crime and incarceration in

Figure 2.7: People in State Prisons and Local Jails Comparing New York City with the Rest of the United States 1991–2014

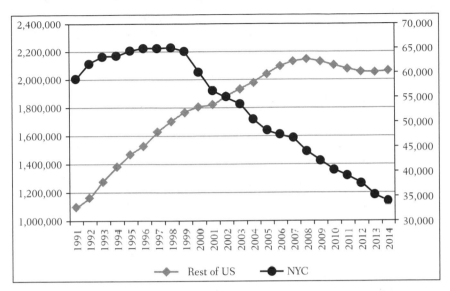

Source: Bureau of Justice Statistics

New York City, New York's judges, prosecutors, and probation officials made less use of prison, jail, and probation while increasing their use of pretrial release, dismissals, adjournments in contemplation of dismissal, conditional and unconditional discharges, and fines—all sanctions whose connection with incarceration is attenuated. Not only are 2.2 million people in prison and jail in America, but 4.7 million people—one in fifty-four adults—are on probation or parole. About one-third of prison admissions are a result of parole violations,[34] and in 2004, 330,000 people had their probation revoked for non-compliance.[35]

Research has found that supervising people who present a low risk of reoffending not only wastes resources but also can increase the likelihood of rearrest, as informal forms of social attachment and control are replaced by less effective government controls and supervision.[36] New York policy makers may have discovered that a justice system that reduces incarceration and supervision in favor of informal, less intrusive dispositions and community-based programs addresses public safety in a less dehumanizing and more effective manner.

Lesson 3: Programs may be having an impact, but they need to be evaluated. New York City has a wide array of alternatives to incarceration, funded by federal, state, local, and philanthropic dollars. Indeed, in 2015, the state and city budgets for New York City's array of alternatives to incarceration amounted to $12 million and $11 million, respectively. The city also spent an additional $18 million to fund the Criminal Justice Agency.

Lesson 4: As we reduce overall incarceration, much still needs to be done to impact the system's stark racial disparities. While Latinos declined as a portion of the DOCCS population from 31 percent in 2000 to 24 percent in 2016 and experienced smaller declines in their proportion of the city's jails, the disproportionality of African Americans stayed frozen in place throughout this unprecedented decline in incarceration in the city. African Americans, who make up 23 percent of New York City's population, made up 51 percent of the DOCCS population in 2000 and 49 percent of the DOCCS population in 2016. Likewise, between 1992 and 2016, the percentage of those incarcerated in New York City jails who were African American barely moved, declining from 56 percent to 54 percent. Much more needs to be done to address these stark disparities, in New York and nationwide, as we continue to grapple with mass incarceration.

Conclusion

New York's unprecedented reduction in reliance on incarceration has been a bottom-up, advocacy-driven, community-focused strategy, as opposed to a top-down, technocratic, elite-consensus approach. In New York, public officials and policy makers have been relentlessly pressured by vigorous demands from advocates, organizers, and activists, who have also worked tirelessly to educate the public about the need for a more humane and effective criminal justice system. And some of those same advocates traveled in and out of the corridors of power, influencing the city's system to make more parsimonious use of incarceration, which as a result became the policy goal of a succession of city and state governments.

The experiences in California and New Jersey, which embraced many of the same objectives as New York, suggest that a determined drug policy reform campaign is just one effective arrow in the decarceration quiver. These states demonstrated that the strategic use of litigation to spur a long-overdue devolution of correctional responsibilities and costs to local authorities, or just to wake up a slumbering parole board, can be highly effective. In states where ballot measures and referenda are available, they can be employed to make end runs around obstinate elected officials, provided they are accompanied by the sophisticated, adequately funded political campaigns that have succeeded in California.

New York City, New Jersey, and California have made impressive progress toward reversing mass incarceration. These three states have come to lead the nation in reducing reliance on incarceration, but each state has accomplished this distinction using different decarceration strategies over different time frames. What they all have in common is that they won large reductions that corresponded with better-than-average declines in crime, proving that the level of public safety actually being provided by mass incarceration may indeed be, as the National Research Council has concluded, "highly uncertain."[37]

As states and localities look to downsize incarceration, they may also need to bolster their community-based services, supports, and opportunities to successfully absorb people returning to communities from jail and prison, as well as to increase confidence among court officials and other system stakeholders that locking them up in the first place may be avoided. Doing so in areas of concentrated poverty, which tend to be African American and Latino neighborhoods in urban areas that disproportionately contribute residents to state prisons and local jails, may also help reduce the racial and ethnic disparities that continue to plague our criminal justice system.

We hope that people in states where there is still plenty of low-hanging fruit (e.g., people sentenced to jail or prison for low-level drug and property crimes, or violation of the requirements of community supervision) will find encouragement in these three states' accomplishments to move more boldly along this trajectory. Our view is that, judging from what has been accomplished so far in the leading states, the necessary elements for success have been bold reform agendas, organizational moxie, and powerful public engagement.

But enormous challenges remain, and we look to the three leading states to tackle yet more ambitious agendas. Our prisons have become mental health institutions by default. Sentences for people convicted of violent offenses are grossly excessive, compared to such sentences in our nation's history and in other well-developed democracies. Our zeal for mandatory sentencing enhancements, "truth in sentencing," and "three strikes" sloganeering must give way to permit greater judicial discretion in dealing with defendants as individuals. And we must foster a realization among the public that if the goal is public safety, long prison terms are far more costly and generally less effective than treatment interventions.

These problems will not lend themselves easily to technocratic top-down solutions. They will take years of bottom-up advocacy, organizing, and public engagement to effect systemic change and promote more effective and humane solutions. But we are confident that the states already in the lead will continue to struggle with these challenges.

Notes

1. The authors would like to thank the following people for providing insights and data for this article: David Aziz, director of research at the New York State Department of Corrections and Community Supervision; Reagan Daly, associate research director at the Institute for State and Local Governance at the City University of New York; Brian Leung, juvenile justice planner at the New York City Mayor's Office of Criminal Justice; Freda Solomon, senior research fellow at the New York Criminal Justice Agency; and Eric Sorenson, director of population research at the New York City Department of Correction.

2. Pervaiz Shallwant & Mark Morales, *NYC Officials Tout New Low in Crime, but Homicide, Rape, Robbery Rose*, WALL ST. J., Jan. 4, 2016.

3. Franklin Zimring, *How New York Beat Crime*, SCIENTIFIC AMERICAN, Aug. 1, 2011.

4. Both crime and incarceration have continued to decline in New York City to the present day, but 2014 is the most recent time period for which national comparisons are possible. The FBI Uniform Crime Reports index crimes in two categories: violent

crimes (aggravated assault, forcible rape, murder, and robbery) and property crimes (arson, burglary, larceny-theft, and motor vehicle theft).

5. ALLEN J. BECK, U.S. DEP'T OF JUSTICE, PRISONERS IN 1999 (2000), *available at* http://www.bjs.gov/index.cfm?ty=pbdetail&iid=928.

6. Lynn Zimmer, *Proactive Policing Against Street-Level Drug Trafficking*, 9 AM. J. POLICE 43 (1990), *available at* http://www.popcenter.org/responses/police_crackdowns/pdfs/zimmer_1990.pdf.

7. STATE OF NEW YORK, DIVISION OF CRIMINAL JUSTICE SERVICES, NEW YORK STATE FELONY DRUG ARREST, INDICTMENT, AND CONVICTION TRENDS 1973–2008 (2010), *available at* www.criminaljustice.ny.gov/pio/annualreport/baseline_trends_report.pdf.

8. Mary Beth Pfeiffer, *Parole Denials Negate Crime Drop*, POUGHKEEPSIE J., Nov. 16, 2000.

9. FRANKLIN E. ZIMRING, THE CITY THAT BECAME SAFE: NEW YORK'S LESSONS FOR URBAN CRIME AND ITS CONTROL (2011).

10. Holly Catina, *Politics of Drug Reform*, N.Y. TIMES, May 26, 1999.

11. ZIMRING, *supra* note 9.

12. *Id.* at page 116.

13. *Id.* at page 116.

14. Judith A. Greene, *Zero Tolerance: A Case Study of Police Policies and Practices in New York City*, 45 CRIME & DELINQ. 171 (1999).

15. Queens College professor Harry Levine has compiled marijuana arrest data since 1997. His analysis is available at http://qcpages.qc.cuny.edu/~hlevine.

16. NATIONAL CENTER ON ADDICTION AND SUBSTANCE ABUSE AT COLUMBIA UNIVERSITY, CROSSING THE BRIDGE: AN EVALUATION OF THE DRUG TREATMENT ALTERNATIVE-TO-PRISON (DTAP) PROGRAM (2003), *available at* http://www.centeronaddiction.org/addiction-research/reports/crossing-bridge-evaluation-drug-treatment-alternative-prison-dtap-program.

17. STATE OF NEW YORK, DEP'T OF CORRECTIONS & COMMUNITY SUPERVISION, SHOCK INCARCERATION 2007 LEGISLATIVE REPORT (2007), *available at* http://www.doccs.ny.gov/Research/Reports/2007/Shock_2007.pdf; STATE OF NEW YORK, DEP'T OF CORRECTIONS & COMMUNITY SUPERVISION, IMPACT OF 2009 DRUG LAW REFORM (2010), *available at* http://www.doccs.ny.gov/Research/Reports/2010/DrugLawReformShock.pdf.

18. STATE OF NEW YORK, DEP'T OF CORRECTIONS & COMMUNITY SUPERVISION, EARNED ELIGIBILITY PROGRAM SUMMARY SEMIANNUAL REPORT: OCTOBER, 2015–MARCH 2016 (2016), *available at* http://www.doccs.ny.gov/Research/Reports/2016/EEP_Report_Oct15-Mar16.pdf

19. STATE OF NEW YORK, DEP'T OF CORRECTIONS & COMMUNITY SUPERVISION, MERIT TIME PROGRAM SUMMARY, OCTOBER 1997–DECEMBER 2006 (2007).

20. H.R. 3355, 103rd Cong. (1993–94), http://thomas.loc.gov/cgi-bin/query/z?c103:H.R.3355.ENR.

21. State of New York, Dep't of Corrections & Community Supervision, *Fact Sheet: 2009 Prison Closures*, http://www.doccs.ny.gov/FactSheets/PrisonClosure09.html.

22. State of New York, Dep't of Corrections & Community Supervision, *Press Release: Department of Corrections Details the State's Plan to Right-Size the New York's Prison System*, Feb. 5, 2014, http://www.doccs.ny.gov/PressRel/2014/Budget_Testimony_2014-15.html.

23. Neil Barsky, *Shut Down Rikers Island*, N.Y. Times, July 17, 2015.

24. This is the time for which length-of-stay data is available.

25. These population totals include, in addition to felonies and misdemeanors, a variety of other categories (people jailed for violations or held on bench warrants, etc.). Length-of-stay data for each category were not available.

26. Mary T. Phillips, Criminal Justice Agency, A Decade of Bail Research in New York City (2012).

27. CJA's recommendation process changed in 2003, so only data from then until 2014, the most recent year available, are reported here. Mary T. Phillips, Russell F. Ferri, and Raymond P. Caliguire, Criminal Justice Agency, Annual Report 2014 (2016).

28. People interviewed by CJA staff generally fall into three recommendation categories depending on their risk score: recommended for ROR (low risk); moderate risk for ROR; not recommended for ROR (high risk). Mary T. Phillips and Raymond P. Caliguire, Criminal Justice Agency, Annual Report 2004 (2006); Phillips, Ferri, and Caliguire, 2016.

29. The combined incarceration rate is the rate at which people are in the custody of the city's jail complex, combined with the rate at which people are serving sentences imposed by city judges in the custody of the state DOCCS.

30. New York City, Department of Probation, Do More Good: A Progress Report from the NYC Department of Probation (2014).

31. *Id.*

32. State of New York, Office of Probation and Correctional Alternatives, State Probation Plan Data Summary (2013).

33. Joe Domanick, *The New York "Miracle,"* The Crime Report, Oct. 16, 2011.

34. P.M. Guerino et al., U.S. Dep't of Justice, Prisoners in 2010 (2011), *available at* http://www.bjs.gov/content/pub/pdf/p10.pdf.

35. Pew Center on the States, When Offenders Break the Rules: Smart Responses to Parole and Probation Violations 3 (Nov. 2007), *available at* http://www.pewtrusts.org/~/media/legacy/uploadedfiles/pcs_assets/2007/when20offenders20break20the20rulespdf.pdf.

36. Harvard Kennedy School Program in Criminal Justice, Executive Session on Community Corrections, Consensus Paper (forthcoming).

37. Comm. on Causes and Consequences of High Rates of Incarceration, Nat'l Research Council of the Nat'l Academies, The Growth of Incarceration in the United States: Exploring Causes and Consequences (2014).

3

Lessons from California

MICHAEL ROMANO

Once California was the national vanguard of tough-on-crime politics; today it is one of the states leading the trend in the opposite direction. Over the past decade, and during the past five years in particular, no other state has grappled as vigorously with its prison policies or enacted and implemented more reforms to reduce its prison and jail populations than the Golden State. In fact, to the extent that the total *national* prison population is on the decline, it is largely attributable to prison downsizing in California. This is par-tially due to California being among the most populous states in the country and partially due to the scale of reform enacted there. Between 2007 and 2015, California reduced its prison population by more than 44,000 prison-ers (over 20 percent). Over the same period of time, the combined popula-tion of all other state prisons and the federal system decreased by about 30,000 prisoners (less than 2 percent).[1]

Much of California's prison downsizing came at the behest of the United States Supreme Court in response to reprehensible conditions within the state prison system. In 2011 the Court ruled in *Brown v. Plata* that California's prisons were unconstitutionally overcrowded and ordered the state to limit the number of inmates in its prison system to approximately 113,000 inmates (or 137.5 percent of the prison system's design capacity).[2] At the time, that meant a reduction of approximately 35,000 inmates. The state legislature responded with the enactment of the Public Safety Realignment Act (AB 109), providing that most new nonviolent offenders be incarcerated in county jails rather than the state's prisons, thus greatly reducing the strain on the state prison system.

The following year, California voters overwhelmingly enacted a ballot measure (Proposition 36) to reform the harshest aspects of the state's infamous three-strikes law—which at the time was the most punitive noncapital sentencing law in the country and accounted for over a quarter of all prisoners in California. Two years later, in 2014, California voters approved another ballot measure (Proposition 47) reducing sentences for drug possession, shoplifting, and several other low-level street crimes.[3] The popular movement for sentencing reform in California is so strong that Governor Jerry Brown, who did not publicly support earlier reform measures, sponsored his own successful statewide ballot measure in 2016 to keep the state's prison population in check, the Public Safety Rehabilitation Act of 2016 (Proposition 57), which increases early parole and in-prison credit-earning opportunities.[4]

To the extent that California's sentencing reforms can be evaluated in terms of the crime rate since the enactment of these policy changes, the results are encouraging. Both violent and property crime rates have decreased since 2010, the year before *Plata* and the first sentencing reform was enacted. Between 2010 and 2015, the rate of violent crime per 100,000 residents in California fell by 2.1 percent and the rate of property crime fell by 0.4 percent.[5] In total, the state's crime rate has dropped to levels not seen since 1967.

For obvious reasons, special attention has been paid to the recidivism rates of prisoners released early under California's sentencing reforms. These results are encouraging as well, with those recidivism rates five to ten times better than the average recidivism rate of other Californian prisoners who were not released early.[6] There are several reasons for the success rate of prisoners released early under California's reforms, including the fact that the reforms targeted older nonviolent prisoners with low likelihood of future recidivism, a public safety screen by courts that could veto the release of dangerous prisoners, and increased reentry support services targeting this group of released inmates.[7]

While important work remains to be done in California—state prisons remain overcrowded, too many people who pose no risk to public safety remain imprisoned, the mentally ill still bear a disproportionate burden of harsh sentencing policies, and recent state data project an increase in the population of mentally ill prisoners over the next few years—the trend is undeniably positive. This chapter describes some of the key reasons California has been successful in downsizing its prisons, presenting the results as a model for other jurisdictions to follow and as encouragement to policy makers in California to continue its unfinished business.

California's prison reforms did not come easy. Almost all of California's prison downsizing reforms came in the face of fierce political opposition from state lawmakers, most of whom identify as progressive Democrats, including Governor Jerry Brown.

Most of these officials came to office in the wake of the Willie Horton advertisements in the 1988 presidential election and Bill Clinton's 1994 crime bill. It's hard to overstate the legacy of Horton on criminal justice policy, especially among Democrats. In June 1986, while serving a sentence of life without parole for murder in Massachusetts, Horton was permitted to spend a weekend in the community as part of a furlough program designed to rehabilitate inmates. He didn't report back to prison, as instructed. Instead, he traveled to Maryland and, among other things, raped a woman and assaulted her boyfriend. The story came to prominence two years later when Massachusetts governor Michael Dukakis ran for president against George H.W. Bush, whose campaign publicized the Horton case relentlessly. Negative publicity about Horton is widely considered the single most important factor undermining Dukakis's substantial lead over Bush at the time. The effect was amplified in California, where two years earlier three justices of the state supreme court, including the chief justice, were ousted by voters due to their opposition to the death penalty. State voters then enacted the California's three-strikes law (Proposition 184) in 1994, followed by a cascade of subsequent voter initiatives restricting parole and increasing punishments for firearm offenses, juvenile offenders, gang members, and sex offenders. Predictably, California's prison population swelled to over twice the system's designed capacity.

The first step toward prison downsizing in California came in the form of class action lawsuits alleging that the state's prisons had become so crowded that mentally and physically ill inmates were being deprived of basic psychiatric and medical care.[8] In 2011, after more than a decade of litigation in lower courts, the U.S. Supreme Court agreed that California's prison crowding conditions were so bad that they violated basic human dignity and the Eighth Amendment's prohibition of cruel and unusual punishments. In *Plata*, the Court affirmed a lower court ruling that the only legitimate remedy was reducing the number of prisoners, and it ordered the state to reduce its inmate population dramatically. A special three-judge panel was empowered to monitor the prison population reduction and enforce a long-term "durable" solution to California's prison overcrowding crisis.

Grudgingly, the California legislature complied with *Plata*, enacting legislation "realigning" the state's justice system by imprisoning people convicted of nonviolent crimes in county jails rather than state prisons. The move was partially a political sleight of hand. Officials insisted that no prisoners were being released early—but in reality most of the state's jails themselves were already overcrowded and under their own court-ordered population caps, so policy makers must have known that the jails would be forced to release inmates early when they received the influx of new inmates who were no longer sentenced to state prison. (Indeed, in 2014, the state jails reported releasing more than fifty thousand inmates early due to overcrowding.) In any event, the state prison population dropped precipitously as a result of the *Plata* ruling and subsequent realignment legislation—from more than 200,000 inmates when the *Plata* case was filed to 129,000 by January 2017.[9]

The second major reform in California ameliorated the state's three-strikes law. Because that law was enacted by ballot measure, amendments or reforms to the legislation also had to be enacted by popular vote (or by a politically unobtainable two-thirds vote of the legislature). The Three Strikes Reform Act of 2012 (Proposition 36) impacted fewer total prisoners com-

Figure 3.1: Three-Strikes Sentences for Violent and Nonviolent Crimes

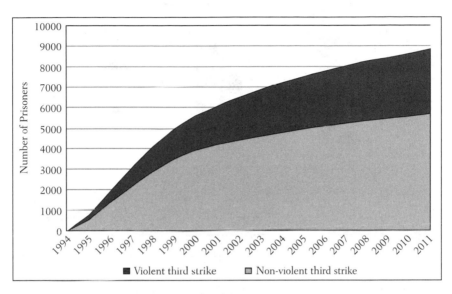

pared to *Plata* and realignment, but it had far-reaching political impact considering the infamy of California's three-strikes law and the approach to releasing prisoners under Proposition 36.[10] Prior to the reform campaign in 2012, California's three-strikes law was the harshest and most widely used noncapital sentencing scheme in the United States. More than ten thousand prisoners had been sentenced to life under the law since its enactment in 1994, most of whom were convicted of a nonviolent third-strike offense. Prisoners were sentenced to life for crimes as minor as shoplifting a pair of tube socks, simple possession of $5 worth of cocaine, or attempting to steal a dollar in loose change from a parked car.[11] In addition, and not unpredictably, a disproportionate number of the inmates sentenced to life under California's three-strikes law for minor crimes were mentally ill.[12]

It's also no surprise that California's three-strikes law exacerbated the disproportionate impact of sentencing laws on people of color, especially African Americans.

Figure 3.2: Race and Three-Strikes Sentencing

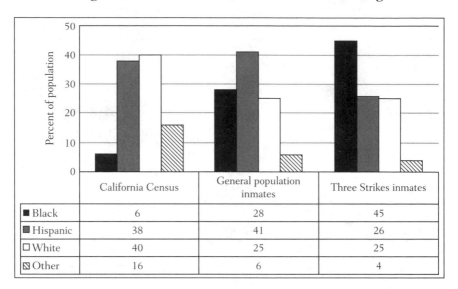

	California Census	General population inmates	Three Strikes inmates
■ Black	6	28	45
■ Hispanic	38	41	26
□ White	40	25	25
⊠ Other	16	6	4

Proposition 36 eliminated life sentences for nonserious, nonviolent crimes and was enacted by 70 percent of the California electorate.[13] The success of California's three-strikes reform contributed to the national conversation about prison downsizing and was one of the first specific pieces of criminal justice reform legislation that was endorsed by conservative leaders, including conservative activist Grover Norquist, and law enforcement officials, including Bill Bratton, commissioner of the New York City Police Department and former Police Chief in Los Angeles.[14]

Perhaps the most groundbreaking aspect of Proposition 36 is that it was one of the first prison downsizing laws to permit the release of prisoners who were behind bars at the time of its enactment. Typically, legislation that reduces criminal sentences (including California's realignment measure) operate prospectively from the date the reform was enacted—changing the law for future cases only, rather than also reaching back to adjust sentences for prisoners who committed their crimes prior to enactment of the reform legislation. As a result of Proposition 36, more than 2,200 prisoners sentenced to life for minor crimes have been released from custody and returned to their communities. As discussed in more detail below, the recidivism rate of those released under the reform has been many times better than that of the average inmate released from prison in California.

The success of Proposition 36 begat California's third, and perhaps most far-reaching, prison downsizing reform: Proposition 47, the Safe Neighborhoods and Schools Act of 2014. The measure was so titled because it created a mechanism to redirect the financial savings associated with the reform (from reduced prison and jail costs) into a state fund to support K-12 education, mental health treatment, and services to support crime victims. It targeted an idiosyncrasy in California sentencing law that permits prosecutors to elevate even the most minor crimes (e.g., shoplifting and simple possession of a fraction of a gram of drugs) from misdemeanors to felonies. Under Proposition 47, six of the most common so-called "wobbler" crimes were designated as mandatory misdemeanors. This impacted tens of thousands of cases in California and resulted in the early release of more than thirteen thousand inmates in state prisons and jails, causing the state's prison population finally to fall below the population threshold ordered by the Supreme Court in *Plata*. As with those prisoners released under Proposition 36, the state prisoners freed early under Proposition 47 have performed remarkably well as a group, with a recidivism rate far better than anyone could have anticipated or hoped for.[15]

As of spring 2017, Californians are waiting for a third successful sentencing reform ballot measure to go into effect: Proposition 57, the Public Safety Rehabilitation Act of 2016, which was enacted by voters in November 2016. Proposition 57 provides an opportunity for early parole to some nonviolent offenders and permits the state Department of Corrections to reset rules that reduce prison sentences for good behavior and participation in prison programming. Remarkably, Proposition 57 was authored and sponsored by Governor Jerry Brown and his administration. Although Governor Brown is a Democrat and widely considered one of the county's most progressive leaders, he vociferously fought the overcrowding-reduction order in *Plata* and refused to endorse Propositions 36 or 47. It's also remarkable that a sitting governor would sidestep the legislature, both houses of which are controlled by fellow Democrats, and take an issue directly to voters. It seems he did so because California voters appear more supportive of prison reform than their elected representatives are.

Proposition 57 gives prison officials flexibility to adjust the sentences of current inmates and provide some control over the state's overall prison population. Undoubtedly, the governor hopes the measure will satisfy the three-judge panel overseeing the California's prison system that the state finally has a durable solution to the state's prison crowding crisis and bring to a close the class action litigation that spurred the state's prison downsizing movement in the first place.

In some ways, the success of prisoners released under the California reforms over the past five years may be the most important—and hardest-to-explain—lesson to be drawn from California's reforms. Seemingly, the odds would be especially great against the prisoners released from three-strikes sentences under Proposition 36: they were being released from indeterminate life sentences, and inmates serving life sentences in California were generally barred from prison programming and reentry services.[16] Further, by their very status as three-strikes inmates they were proven recidivists. And as the Supreme Court noted in *Ewing v. California*, the justification of the three-strikes scheme was the incapacitation of inevitable recidivists: "the class of offenders who pose the greatest threat to public safety: career criminals."[17]

Therefore, it comes as some surprise that the recidivism rate of those inmates sentenced under the three-strikes law and released under the reforms enacted in 2012 is many times better than that of the average inmate leaving prison in California. According to the California Department of Corrections, the recidivism rate of prisoners released under Proposition 36 is 9 percent over the three years following enactment of the reform. The recidivism rate of all other prisoners released in California over the same period of time is 53 percent.[18] Even the fiercest opponents of Proposition 36, including prosecutors, have publicly acknowledged that the reform is "working well."[19]

The recidivism rate of prisoners released under Proposition 47—California's 2014 follow-up to three-strikes reform, which retroactively reduced the sentences of even more prisoners—is also very encouraging. Although there has been less time to evaluate the recidivism rate of prisoners released under

Figure 3.3: Recidivism Rates of Prisoners Released Under Propositions 36 and 47

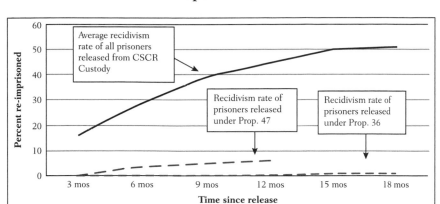

Proposition 47, one year after its enactment the recidivism rate of more than four thousand state prisoners released under the reform was less than 10 percent.[20] (By comparison, the one-year recidivism rate of all other California state prisoners was 42 percent.)

There are some theories about why prisoners released under California's sentencing reforms are doing so well. First, released three-strikes inmates are generally older than the typical parolee, and one would rightly anticipate that their recidivism rate would be lower. However, prisoners released under Proposition 36 outperform other prisoner cohorts by such a large degree that something else must be at work to explain the dramatically low recidivism rates.

Second, neither Proposition 36 nor Proposition 47 resulted in the automatic release of prisoners. In order to win a reduced sentence under either reform, each prisoner had to appear before a trial court judge, who had discretion to deny resentencing if the prisoner continued to pose an "unreasonable risk of danger to public safety."[21] At first blush, this public safety screen might explain a lot of the recidivism data. On closer review, however, the judges' review and discretion to deny resentencing had little impact: more than 95 percent of inmates eligible for shorter sentences under Propositions 36 and 47 received them.

Third, the California legislature allocated special funds to support reentry of prisoners released under Proposition 36.[22] In addition, Proposition 47

Figure 3.4: Recidivism Rates of Different Categories of California Prisoners

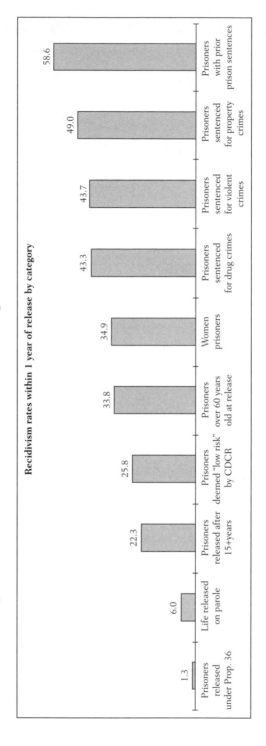

Recidivism rates within 1 year of release by category

Prisoners with prior prison sentences	58.6
Prisoners sentenced for property crimes	49.0
Prisoners sentenced for violent crimes	43.7
Prisoners sentenced for drug crimes	43.3
Women prisoners	34.9
Prisoners over 60 years old at release	33.8
Prisoners deemed "low risk" by CDCR	25.8
Prisoners released after 15+years	22.3
Life released on parole	6.0
Prisoners released under Prop. 36	1.3

provided for state parole supervision of inmates released under its resentencing procedure, rather than oversight by underfunded and understaffed county probation officers.[23] These services undoubtedly helped, but it is unclear how many prisoners availed themselves of these reentry support services. Because the services offered to those released under Proposition 36 were largely voluntary, it is difficult to measure the effect of the intervention for those who self-selected to receive services.[24]

Fourth, some research suggests that the Proposition 36 release process itself may contribute to improved outcomes. The theory is that lack of recidivism, or desistance from crime, involves a cognitive transformation in an offender's identity from prisoner to law-abiding citizen—and, further, that a ceremonial event marking the transition can help facilitate a lasting new identity.[25] Every prisoner released under Proposition 36 won the approval of the court that originally sentenced him or her to life behind bars—approval in the form of an order finding that the prisoner is no longer a threat to public safety.[26] In addition, the law itself was passed with the overwhelming support of California voters, which may further add to a public acknowledgment that inmates released under its auspices are no longer threats to public safety.

It is undeniable that something significant is at work here. Individually, none of the most obvious explanations and hypotheses for the low recidivism rates among prisoners released under reforms enacted in California can adequately explain the phenomenon. Multiple factors are clearly at play—some of which, undoubtedly, are yet to be identified. This chapter will be a success if it inspires others to further unpack the data and develop a more comprehensive explanation, which would be valuable to prison reduction policies and reentry programs throughout the country.

Other states should also look closely at their sentencing rules, especially those imposing long sentences for nonviolent recidivists. Where we once assumed that so-called career criminals were hopeless recidivists, which the Supreme Court in *Ewing* reasoned justified life sentences even for petty crimes, the success of reforms in California should undermine those assumptions.

It may be easy to see California's prison downsizing experience as sui generis and perhaps unhelpful. After all, most other states don't have the initiative process—and even those that do don't have such active ballot measure politics. It is also unlikely that the Supreme Court will intervene in other state prison systems as it did in *Plata*. And *Plata* itself is fairly limited to specifics of California's prison crowding and sentencing policy dynamic, so the case has little precedential value for other jurisdictions.

That said, the success of multiple sentencing-reduction ballot measures in California does reflect popular support for these reforms that is broader and stronger than most people expected. Prior to the three-strikes reform campaign in 2012, prominent pollsters doubted that the public had interest in reducing prison sentences.[27] In fact, the public seems much more supportive of criminal justice reform proposals than elected officials are. California is certainly a solidly Democratic state, but its voters led the country with harsh sentencing policies in the 1990s, and California's recent experience should give lawmakers and policy officials in other states pause before they assume that their constituents remain solidly tough-on-crime.

Indeed, the politics should follow the data. The data from California show that a state can dramatically reduce its prison population and maintain a decreasing crime rate over the same period of time. As discussed above, California reduced its prison population by more than 20 percent between 2010 and 2015. Over that same period, statewide crime rates went down.[28] In addition, the prisoners released early under California's prison reform measures—even the supposedly hopeless recidivists sentenced under three-strikes laws—have a recidivism rate lower than the average inmate released from state custody.[29] California's data are consistent with the experience on the federal level. Between 2008 and 2011, more than fifteen thousand federal inmates received sentence reductions under retroactive application of sentencing guidelines for crack cocaine offenses. Follow-up studies by the U.S. Sentencing Commission showed that the guideline reforms had no negative impact on public safety. In fact, prisoners released early had a slightly lower recidivism rate than similar inmates who did not benefit from the guideline reforms.[30]

Perhaps the most important common element among the reforms discussed in this chapter is that their implementation intimately involved the court system. Most obviously, *Plata* and the ensuing realignment legislation were brought about by years of litigation and federal court oversight. Propositions 36 and 47 were passed by popular vote, but both measures required that eligible prisoners return to court in order to be resentenced and released. Under both reforms, a judge had discretion to refuse resentencing if the prisoner posed a continuing unreasonable danger to public safety.[31] Federal crack guideline reforms include a similar public safety screen, providing that judges review cases prior to ordering sentence reductions and directing them to deny resentencing applications if necessary to protect the public from further crimes.[32]

This is a new role for many judges. Today, trial court judges are mostly empowered to impose sentences immediately upon conviction, which provides an excellent vantage point to assign retribution. However, it is far from ideal for evaluating benefit to public safety or an inmate's recidivism risk. Parole boards have historically played this role, but, whether hampered by legislation, regulations, or politics, they have proven an inadequate check on the wave of mass incarceration. States would be wise to vest more authority in judges to evaluate sentences at the back end. As with California Propositions 36 and 47 and federal crack guideline procedures, courts can hear evidence from both sides and help reach an impartial and just result. Judges have also proven effective at accurately gauging recidivism risk, based on the data from California and the U.S. Sentencing Commission.

California's prison downsizing experience should inspire reformers and policy makers across the country to reexamine assumptions about criminal justice. Tough-on-crime politics no longer holds the sway it once did. Law enforcement through long prison terms and incapacitation does not enhance public safety. And government institutions, particularly courts, can and should play a larger role in encouraging and evaluating prisoner rehabilitation and facilitating positive transitions from custody to communities.

Notes

1. *See* U.S. Bureau of Justice Statistics, "Total Correctional Population," *available at ojp.usdoj.gov*; Cal. Dept. of Corrections and Rehabilitation, "Monthly Population

Reports," *available at cdcr.ca.gov*; Joan Petersilia and Francis Cullen, *Liberal but Not Stupid: Meeting the Promise of Downsizing Prisons*, 2 Stan. J. Crim. L. & Pol. at 18 (2015).

2. *Brown v. Plata*, 131 S.Ct. 1910 (2011).

3. For purposes of full disclosure, please note that I was intimately involved with the enactment of Propositions 36 and 47, including co-authoring both ballot measures and helping direct both campaigns in conjunction with and on behalf of the NAACP Legal Defense and Educational Fund and Californians for Safety and Justice, among others.

4. *Text available at safetyandrehabilitation.com.*

5. Cal. Dept. of Justice, "Crime in California (2015)," *available at oag.ca.gov.*

6. This chapter relies on the definition of recidivism used by California state officials—*i.e.,* state prisoners convicted of new crimes and returned to state prison. *See generally* Cal. Department of Corrections and Rehabilitation, "2014 Outcome Evaluation Report," (July 2015); *see also* Stanford Law School Three Strikes Project, "Proposition 36 Progress Report: Over 1,500 Inmates Released with Record Low Recidivism Rates" (2014); Stanford Law School Three Strikes Project, "Proposition 47 Progress Report: Year One Implementation" (2015).

7. *See* Erik Eckholm, "Out of Prison, and Staying Out, After 3rd Strike in California," *New York Times*, Feb. 26, 2015.

8. For an excellent analysis and history of California's prison crowding litigation, *see* Jonathan Simon, *Mass Incarceration on Trial: A Remarkable Court Decision and the Future of Prisons in America*, The New Press (2013).

9. *See* Cal. Dept. of Corrections, "Monthly Report of Population" (Jan. 2017), *available at www.cdcr.ca.gov.*

10. For a more detailed account of the Three Strikes campaign, *see* David Mills and Michael Romano, *The Passage and Implementation of the Three Strikes Reform Act of 2012 (Proposition 36)*, 25 Fed. Sent. Rpr. 4 (Apr. 2013).

11. *See, e.g.,* Matt Taibbi, "Cruel and Unusual Punishment: The Shame of Three Strikes Laws," *Rolling Stone*, March 27, 2013.

12. *See* Steinberg, Mills, Romano, "When Did Prisons Become Acceptable Mental Health Care Facilities?," Stanford Law School (2014).

13. Just prior to the election, the state legislature declined to pass a similar measure, and only three elected officials endorsed the ballot measure campaign. *See* Tracey Kaplan, "Proposition 36: Voters Overwhelmingly Ease Three Strikes Law," *San Jose Mercury News*, Nov. 6, 2012.

14. See, e.g., *New York Times*, "California's Prison Experiment," Nov. 13, 2015.

15. *See* Stanford Law School Justice Advocacy Project, "Proposition 47 Progress Report: Year One Implementation" (Oct. 2015).

16. Indeed, access to in-prison reentry preparation programming has been measured as the single best intervention to recidivism reduction in California. *See* Cal. Department of Corrections and Rehabilitation, "2014 Outcome Evaluation Report" (July 2015), at 42.

17. *Ewing v. California*, 538 U.S. 11, 24 (2003).

18. Cal. Department of Corrections and Rehabilitation, "2014 Outcome Evaluation Report" (July 2015), at 11.

19. Dan Morain, "Three-Strikes Changes Appear to Be Working," *Sacramento Bee*, April 13, 2014 (quoting San Bernardino district attorney Mike Ramos).

20. Stanford Law School Justice Advocacy Project, "Proposition 47 Progress Report: Year One Implementation" (Oct. 2015).

21. *See* Cal. Penal Code §§ 1170.126 (Proposition 36); 1170.18 (Proposition 48).

22. *See* Stanford Law School Three Strikes Project, "Proposition 36 Progress Report: Over 1,500 Prisoners Released, Historically Low Recidivism Rate" (April 2014); Eckholm, *New York Times*, Feb. 26, 2015.

23. *See* Cal. Penal Code § 1170.18(d).

24. *See also* Petersilia and Cullen, 2 Stan. J. Crim. L. & Pol. at 22 ("We also must recognize that the number of proven programs, especially for a reentry programs, is in short supply").

25. *See, e.g.*, Giordano, Cernkovich, & Rudolph, "Gender, Crime, and Desistance: Toward a Theory of Cognitive Transformation," *American Journal of Sociology, 107*(4), 990–1064 (2002); Paternoster & Bushway, "Desistance and the 'Feared Self': Toward an Identity Theory of Criminal Desistance," *The Journal of Criminal Law and Criminology*, 1103–56 (2009); Maruna, Immarigeon, & LeBel, "Ex Offender Reintegration: Theory and Practice," *After Crime and Punishment: Pathways to Offender Reintegration*, 3-2 (2004).

26. *See* Cal. Penal Code § 1170.126.

27. *See* Mills and Romano, *The Passage and Implementation of the Three Strikes Reform Act of 2012 (Proposition 36)*, 25 Fed. Sent. Rpr. 4.

28. Cal. Dept. of Corrections and Rehabilitation, "Office of Research Population Reports," http://www.cdcr.ca.gov/Reports_Research/Offender_Information_Services_Branch/Population_Reports.html; Cal. Dept. of Justice, "Crime Data," https://oag.ca.gov/crime.

29. Stanford Law School Three Strikes Project and NAACP Legal Defense and Education Fund, "Proposition 36 Progress Report: Over 1,500 Prisoners Released; Historically Low Recidivism Rate," April 2014.

30. U.S.S.C. Retroactivity Data Reports for Amendments 706, 750, and 782; U.S.S.C. Recidivism 2007 Crack Cocaine Amendment Report.

31. *See* Cal. Penal Code §§ 1170.126 (Proposition 36) and 1170.18 (Proposition 47).

32. *See* 18 U.S.C. § 3582(c)(2) (providing that courts must consider factors provided in § 3553(a), including danger to public safety, prior to reducing a prisoner's sentence).

4

The Role of Judges

JUDGE ROBERT SWEET AND JAMES THOMPSON

Judges are at the center of the criminal justice system and should be leaders in acting to reduce, and eventually eliminate, mass incarceration in our country. The judge does not define the acts that constitute crime, nor the punishment to be meted out for those acts—legislators do that. It is the judge, however, who must assure the public, the prosecution, and the defense that the process is fair and true to all legislative and constitutional constraints. It is the judge who must face the defendant and determine the sentence. It is the judge who will determine whether or not the defendant will lose his or her liberty and, if so, for how long. Even within the necessary limits to his or her role, the judge can and should act to minimize the blight of mass incarceration in America. The appropriate judicial goals in this effort are transparency with respect to the charging process, flexibility and transparency in the sentencing process, continued opposition to mandatory minimum sentences, development of diversion alternatives to trial, enhanced reentry programs, and the development of a common law of sentencing. As a central actor in criminal justice, a judge can, to a significant degree, become an agent for change.

The principal responsibility for the high level of incarceration afflicting our society belongs to drug laws and their enforcement. The statistics establish that responsibility. The Bureau of Prisons estimates that approximately half of all federal prisoners are incarcerated for drug offenses—more than the number incarcerated for all violent crimes, extortion and fraud, weapons and explosives offenses, sex crimes, immigration violations, and participation in organized crime combined. The available data indicate that this percentage results from the harsher sentences imposed on drug offenders relative to those convicted of other crimes. While drug offenders make up about half of the federal prison population, they make up only 32 percent of those convicted in federal court—a function of their longer sentences—even though these rates are down from 35 percent in 2004 and 41 percent in 1996. The problem is less pronounced but remains significant in many state prisons, despite sharp drops in the proportion convicted of drug offenses.[1]

For some, ourselves included, the criminalizing of some mind-altering substances was a national policy blunder from the outset, transforming the addictions from a health problem to a crime, forgetting the lessons of Prohibition and its enforcement. The drug war has not significantly altered drug use, but it has created a billion-dollar untaxed and illicit industry, and has sapped public resources dramatically. As of fiscal year 2016, the White House's National Drug Control Budget estimates that the federal government spends $27.6 billion on anti-drug efforts, but the full annual cost of the drug war is a multiple of that amount, once state expenditures and related costs such as law enforcement and correctional personnel are included—the Drug Policy Alliance puts the annual cost of the drug war at over $51 billion.

But we are in a period of change. The fact that twenty-nine states now permit some form of medical marijuana marks the recognition of the drug's therapeutic value, and the current trend toward legalization of marijuana (in eight states) is a sign that the laboratory of state legislation is beginning to revise what has been the all-too-accepted wisdom of criminalization of mind-altering substances.

The Charging Process

Under our system, transported from England in the early days of what was to become the United States, the executive is responsible for enforcing the law. This system places one of the key determinants of the ultimate sentence in the hands of prosecutors, who have the discretion to determine what offense to charge. The check on this power comes in the form of the grand jury, which reviews the potential charges for probable cause and is the tool by which the charging document, the indictment, is forged. There is no judicial involvement in determining who is charged for what or the applicable sentencing regimen. However, once the indictment is filed and the action is under way, the judge is responsible for seeing that all the constitutional and legislative requirements are met.

While indictments are standardized and rarely challenged, the process from charging to trial is carefully monitored. In 97 percent of cases, that process produces pleas of guilty from defendants—a sign that some vital processes of justice are missing. This result has obvious benefits for the courts in terms of time, money, and certitude. The factors producing this result in any given case are many, but foremost among them are the strength of the government's case, the use of informants and cooperating witnesses, and the plea bargaining process.[2]

The ability of the government prosecutor to offer a plea bargain is a powerful incentive for a defendant to plead guilty, and it is not uncommon for those facing the heaviest charges, sometimes because of leadership roles and participation in drug sales, to provide evidence against their former co-conspirators. In other instances the government may have the option of augmenting the charges by adding a "prior felony information," a document alerting the court to a defendant's earlier conviction on another charge, the filing of which substantially increases the penalties the bargaining defendant faces. This process deserves closer judicial scrutiny.

The Honorable Jed S. Rakoff recently wrote an article in the *New York Review of Books* entitled "Why Innocent People Plead Guilty." In it, Judge Rakoff described the way prosecutors can use the federal sentencing regime, with its mandatory minimum provisions, "to bludgeon defendants into effectively coerced plea bargains." Particularly with defendants whose prior convictions empower prosecutors to file (or not file) a prior felony information, or in drug cases, where prosecutors may choose the nature and quantities of the narcotics a defendant is charged with trafficking, defendants are often faced with a choice between accepting a plea bargain acknowledging a relatively small amount of drugs or going to trial on charges involving a large amount, which may carry a mandatory minimum sentence of a decade or more. This intense pressure, combined with the frequent gap in resources and knowledge between federal prosecutors, who have the assistance of the law enforcement officials who investigated the case, and the time- and cash-strapped defense lawyers who represent those charged with drug offenses, can lead defendants to accept guilt even when they may have had meritorious arguments against conviction. Judge Rakoff characterizes such a system as one where "it is the prosecutor, not the judge, who effectively exercises the sentencing power, albeit cloaked as a charging decision."

In *United States v. Kupa*, the Honorable John Gleeson of the U.S. District Court for the Eastern District of New York, described this practice and its effect on a particular defendant. Kupa, a Staten Island–born child of Albanian immigrants, had two prior convictions for selling marijuana before the drug arrest that brought him into Judge Gleeson's court. Federal prosecutors offered Kupa a plea bargain that would have resulted in a sentence as low as seven years and ten months in prison, but Kupa refused to admit guilt. The government then filed a prior felony information, advising the court of the two marijuana convictions. Those two prior drug convictions triggered a provision under mandatory sentencing rules that would have required a sentence of life in prison without the possibility of parole—but only if Kupa went to trial. Five weeks later, Kupa finally pled guilty to a deal providing for a sentence of 140–175 months in prison—thirteen and a half years or more—telling Gleeson that he was doing so in order to avoid spending life in prison. "I want to plead guilty, Your Honor, before things get worse," he said. Judge Gleeson sentenced Kupa to 132 months in prison, but wrote an opinion castigating the

Department of Justice for using its prior felony information power to coerce plea bargains. Gleeson concluded, "If DOJ cannot exercise its power to invoke recidivist enhancements in drug trafficking cases less destructively and less brutally, it doesn't deserve to have the power at all."

While plea bargains are essentially negotiated contracts between the parties, a negotiation from which judges are appropriately excluded, the acceptance of that plea is a judicial responsibility. In the light of Judge Gleeson's powerful reasoning, judges should probe more deeply into the bargaining process to ensure that it was not improperly coercive. These inquiries can play an important role in drawing attention to unfair practices, though the circumstances of *Kupa* show the limits of a judge's ability to alter the outcome: Judge Gleeson could have ruled that Kupa's guilty plea was coerced and thrown it out, but that would have left the defendant facing trial, and potentially a life sentence.

The Sentencing Process

The judge has the responsibility of determining and pronouncing a sentence. The judge must resolve the conflicting views of acts involved and justify the decision to the defendant (and frequently his or her family), to the victims of the crime, and to the public. The methodology and rules of this wrenching and difficult process have drastically changed over time.

In the 1970s, when one of us, Justice Robert Sweet, became a judge, the only legislative constraint was the range of penalties prescribed by Congress. There was no reporting on sentencing or information available about norms, except on a case-by-case basis. To establish consistency in sentencing even for an individual judge was a daunting task, and a comparative court-wide analysis was not possible. The judge had virtually untrammeled discretion. Appellate review was infrequent and limited to whether the sentence imposed was permissible under the law passed by Congress that criminalized the offense. The Supreme Court's jurisprudence on the issue recognized that the trial-level judge who supervised the progress of the criminal case generally had a superior understanding of the crime, the offender, and the interests involved, and so the sentence imposed was "met with virtually unconditional deference on appeal," in the words of Justice Harry Blackmun.

In practice, however, this meant that sentences could vary based on the priorities and prejudices of the judge overseeing a given case. This situation was criticized by those who sought stricter enforcement for white collar crime, for instance, and those who felt that minorities were disproportionately punished. After several years of urging, with the support of both the Reagan administration and liberals including Senator Ted Kennedy, Congress passed the Sentencing Reform Act of 1984, which created the United States Sentencing Commission and empowered it to create guidelines that would "recommend to the sentencing judge an appropriate kind and range of sentence for a given category of offense committed by a given category of offender," according to the Senate Judiciary Committee. The new guidelines system would require the judge to consider the history and characteristics of the offender, the nature and circumstances of the offense, and the purposes of sentencing before issuing a sentence within a prescribed range, which would be generated by mechanistic calculations. Judges across the country were required to go through the same steps in determining a sentence, and those steps were recorded for appellate review. (Congress did, however, provide that judges could impose sentences outside the guidelines in extraordinary cases.) Critics concluded that the guidelines impermissibly restricted the judge's authority—in 1988 *United States v. Alafriz*, the author declared them unconstitutional because they deprived defendants of their right to be sentenced as individuals and because the regime gave appointed commissioners authority over sentencing, a function reserved for the judicial branch. However, the guidelines were upheld as constitutional by the Supreme Court in *Mistretta v. United States* (though Justice Antonin Scalia agreed with the separation of powers analysis in his dissent).

As time went on, certain glaring inequities were recognized in the law of sentencing, particularly the disparity between the treatment of crack and powder cocaine. The two drugs share the same active ingredient and psychotropic effects, but the Anti–Drug Abuse Act of 1986, enacted during a period of public panic about drug abuse in general and crack cocaine in particular, required courts to treat each gram of crack cocaine—the inexpensive form primarily used in African American communities—as equivalent to 100 grams of powder cocaine, the form primarily used by white Americans, for sentencing purposes where severity of sentences was determined by the weight of the drugs involved. The effects of this disparity were particularly destructive when combined with the Anti-Drug Abuse Act's mandatory minimum provisions, which required a five-year sentence for any defendant distributing 5 grams of crack cocaine (as opposed to 500 grams of powder cocaine), and a ten-year sentence for defendants convicted of distributing 50 grams of crack cocaine (as opposed to 5 kilograms of powder cocaine). As the Supreme Court noted in *Kimbrough v. United States* (discussed in further detail below), since cocaine tends to be imported into the country in powder form before being chemically converted into crack for distribution to individual users, the disparity resulted at times in street-level sellers of crack cocaine being punished more severely than the international traffickers who were responsible for the wholesale importation and distribution of the same drugs. Because the Anti-Drug Abuse Act was passed through Congress on an emergency basis, bypassing much of the normal legislative process, there is "no authoritative legislative history," in the words of the Sentencing Commission, that would explain what empirical rationale, if any, Congress used in adopting the 100-to-1 disparity.

Although the Sentencing Commission sent reports to Congress criticizing the unfairness of the cocaine sentencing regime, Congress took no action in response. The first hint of change came thanks to the action of a federal judge. In April 2005 (shortly after the Supreme Court's seminal *Booker* decision, discussed further below), the Honorable Raymond A. Jackson of the Eastern District of Virginia refused to sentence a crack dealer named Derrick Kimbrough to the nineteen years required by the sentencing guidelines, reasoning that since Kimbrough would have received only a seven-and-a-half-year sentence for distributing the equivalent amount of powder cocaine, the case exemplified "the disproportionate and unjust effect that the crack cocaine guidelines have in sentencing." The *Kimbrough* case made its way to the Supreme Court, where a 6–3 opinion written by Justice Ruth Bader Ginsburg upheld Judge Jackson's departure, concluding that judges were empowered to deviate from the guidelines based solely on the recognition that the crack/powder disparity was unjust. Some amount of legislative relief finally arrived with the Fair Sentencing Act of 2010, which reduced the crack/powder cocaine disparity to 18-to-1, major progress from the regime that had existed before, but still far from the equivalent treatment that is warranted.

Judge Jackson was not the only member of the federal bench who strained against the rigidity of the sentencing guidelines and the inequities codified within them. Although the Sentencing Reform Act had made the guidelines effectively mandatory, judges were still authorized to issue non-guideline sentences for two reasons: either a motion from the government regarding the "substantial assistance" provided by a defendant who gave evidence to investigators, or a finding that there existed aggravating or mitigating circumstances that were not adequately taken into consideration by the Sentencing Commission. Although this latter category was intended to be used only in exceptional cases, federal judges began using it more frequently to correct guidelines outcomes that they perceived as unjust. Between 1991 and 2001, downward departures for reasons other than substantial assistance increased from 5.8 percent of sentences to 18.1 percent. The judiciary took a dimmer and dimmer view of the guidelines over this period; in a 1996 survey by the Federal Judicial Center, 73 percent of district judges and 69 percent of circuit judges felt that the mandatory guideline regime was unnecessary.

Congress reacted to these acts of judicial independence by enacting the Feeney Amendment to the PROTECT Act of 2003, which was ostensibly geared toward defending children from sex offenders, requiring the Sentencing Commission to review every downward departure (thus reducing the number of areas where judges could argue that the Sentencing Commission had not considered key mitigating factors) and changing the standard for appellate review of fact-based sentencing decisions from one that deferred to the trial judge to one that allowed appellate judges to re-decide the issues from scratch. The amendment drew widespread condemnation from legal scholars and the federal bench. Chief Justice William Rehnquist referred to it as "an unwarranted and ill-considered effort to intimidate individual judges in the performance of their duties."

The landscape of sentencing law changed fundamentally with the Supreme Court's 2005 decision in *United States v. Booker*. *Booker* essentially involved two half-opinions, each supported by a 5–4 majority of justices, that altered the Court's previous divisions. In the first half of *Booker*, written by Justice John Paul Stevens with the support of Justices Scalia, David Souter, Clarence Thomas, and Ginsburg, the Court concluded that provisions of the guidelines that enhanced sentences based on findings of fact by a judge violated the Sixth Amendment right to trial by jury. In the second half, written by Justice Stephen Breyer with the support of Chief Justice Rehnquist and Justices Sandra Day O'Connor, Anthony Kennedy, and Ginsburg, the Court determined that the Sixth Amendment problem would be solved by striking down the statutory language that had made the guidelines mandatory.[3]

The practical consequence of *Booker* rendering the guidelines advisory is that judges have largely returned to their previous ability to tailor sentences according to the circumstances of individual defendants. The guidelines remain important, however: each judge still conducts the mechanical guidelines analysis for every sentence, and the result plays an important anchoring function. Because the guidelines tell the judge and the parties what sanction a normal defendant would receive in the given circumstances, judges remain likely to impose a sentence within the guidelines range unless there is a reason not to do so.

During all of this period, and up to the present day, the factors a judge must consider in imposing a sentence have been codified in a statute—Title 18, Section 3553(a) of the United States Code. The section requires judges to consider the nature of the offense, the characteristics of the defendant, the four fundamental purposes of criminal law (retribution, deterrence, public protection, and rehabilitation), the kinds of sentences available, compliance with the guidelines and Sentencing Commission policy statements, the status of co-defendants, and restitution to victims.

The § 3553(a) factors are certainly broad enough to permit judges to consider the many problems of mass incarceration. The statute provides for the consideration of the nature and circumstances of both the offense and the defendant, as well as the need for the sentence imposed "to reflect the seriousness of the offense" and "to afford adequate deterrence to criminal conduct." While these factors alone are sufficient to permit consideration of many of the negative impacts of drug criminalization and mass incarceration, Congress might well add to § 3553(a) a provision requiring the consideration of the comparative costs to taxpayers of incarceration or community supervision. Currently, the factors do not account for the financial burden that incarceration imposes on taxpayers, which the Administrative Office for the U.S. Courts estimates at $30,621 per inmate per year. Such a revision might well appeal to those concerned about both mass incarceration and those who are sensitive to the economics of the government.

One arbitrary imposition on the judge's sentencing discretion remains: the mandatory minimum sentences resulting from Congressional legislation. The damaging effect of mandatory minimums could be seen in the *Kimbrough* case where, despite a Supreme Court decision in his favor, Kimbrough was still sentenced to the statutory minimum of fifteen years for crack cocaine, twice what he would have received had he pled guilty to distributing the equivalent amount of powder cocaine. These mandatory minimums can be set aside by the prosecution, who can grant a letter outlining the cooperation of the defendant in assisting the prosecution. The provisions are primarily applicable to drug crimes, though other offenses are covered.

Mandatory minimums and three-strike provisions are responsible to a substantial degree for the mass incarceration problem. Some amelioration of these provisions is presently under consideration in Congress at this writing, with no assured resolution. According to a report by the Sentencing Commission to Congress, as of 2010, 58.1 percent of federal prisoners were convicted of offenses carrying a mandatory minimum penalty, and 39.4 percent failed to qualify for any of the exceptions and were sentenced subject to the minimum. The data also show a significant racial disparity in the way mandatory minimums are applied, with black and Hispanic defendants subject to minimum penalties at a higher rate than non-Hispanic white defendants.

Although progress has been made in curbing the most grievous aspects of the current sentencing regime, reforms should be adopted by courts and judges that would lead to the development of a common law of sentencing. By making the outcome and reasoning of every sentencing decision available to other sentencing judges, both individually and as part of aggregated sets of data, the decisions of federal judges across the country could come to play the anchoring role currently occupied by the guidelines. Such a system could well replace the guidelines' current advisory form with judicial decisions, reflecting the reasoned judgment of a large sample of federal cases rather than the outcome of a set of mechanistic calculations.

Former district court judge Nancy Gertner has addressed this subject in an article in the *Harvard Law and Policy Review* entitled "Supporting Advisory Guidelines." Judge Gertner noted that while the guidelines were no longer mandatory, there was little background information available to judges seeking an alternative framework for sentencing. She suggested that every sentencing decision, whether in the form of a full opinion, a hearing transcript, or a standardized form, should be made searchable and available to other sentencing judges and to the public. Meanwhile, the Sentencing Commission should educate jurists not only on how to comply with the guidelines but also on alternative sentencing structures backed by social science research on best practices. Twenty years ago, during the mandatory guidelines era, one of us, Judge Sweet, recommended in the *Fordham Law Review* that all federal judges issue written sentencing opinions in each criminal case, which could then be digitized by the sentencing commission to produce a database showing statistical norms for each combination of offense and offender.

Even without a national system, there remain small-scale changes that can help lead to a common law of sentencing. Openness and clarity are served by judges filing sentencing opinions outlining the considerations underlying the sentence in each case.[4] If sentencing opinions were produced and made broadly available, norms could be devised within districts and circuits, and a significant departure from those norms could constitute a challenge on appeal to the judge's discretion. Currently, there is virtually no appellate

93

review of sentencing except for an illegal sentence or improper guidelines calculation.

Another option would be to make public the "statement of reasons" that is submitted to the Sentencing Commission in every case. In this brief, four-page form, the judge certifies whether there is a mandatory minimum sentence (or whether the defendant is somehow exempt), the results of the guidelines calculations, whether the judge is sentencing the defendant within the guidelines, and, if the judge chooses to sentence the defendant outside the guidelines range, what basis he or she gives for departing. Although the document is submitted to the Sentencing Commission and the aggregate data from these statements are the basis for much of the annual statistical report that the commission generates, the documents themselves are unfortunately not part of the public record.

The rule of secrecy that keeps these important documents sealed is a judge-made one, enacted by the Judicial Conference of the United States in 2001, meaning that judicial action could also make the statement of reasons public.[5] In fact, the District of Massachusetts has voted to make available all statements of reasons for sentences imposed in that state (outside of extraordinary cases), which has allowed for public scrutiny and statistical analysis of judicial reasoning. If this policy were enacted nationwide, norms presumably could be created from the aggregated data, effectively creating guidelines devised by those primarily responsible, the judges. Those norms and departures from them could form the basis for appellate review.

Any such reform will require careful legislation and cooperation and leadership from the Sentencing Commission. With judge-driven norms and consideration of themes set forth above, it is a safe assumption that the incarceration rate would be reduced.

Alternative Sentencing and Reentry

While judges can make a difference within the sentencing system, another approach is to attempt to craft judicially sponsored alternatives to incarceration. These efforts have been gaining momentum in recent years, and tend to take two forms: alternative sentencing programs that attempt to intervene in individual cases before a sentence is imposed, and programs that assist convicts in the reentry process upon their release from prison or jail, with the aim of reducing recidivism. Although small in scale, these programs represent an important judicial innovation that, if widely adopted, could play an important role in reducing mass incarceration.

The most promising of these programs, at least in terms of potential impact on incarceration rates, are those that take place prior to sentencing. These endeavors, which require cooperation from the relevant U.S. attorney's office given the predominant role of the prosecution in the charging process, select defendants for whom incarceration may not be an appropriate sanction and who might receive some form of lower sentence conditioned on completion of a program of rehabilitation, often involving attempts to wean the defendants off of drugs.

One such program is the Pretrial Opportunity Program (POP), which takes place in the Eastern District of New York. Led by District Judges John Gleeson and Joanna Seybert, along with Magistrate Judges Steven Gold and Gary Brown, the Pretrial Opportunity Program is a "drug court," based on the idea that many of the behaviors defendants are arrested for are grounded in drug or alcohol abuse, and that society's interests are better served by combating those addictions than by punishing behavior over which the defendants may not have full control. When a defendant enters the program, all proceedings in his or her case are adjourned for a year or more. The defendant is required to remain drug-free, to get a GED if he or she does not already have a high school diploma or its equivalent, and to seek and obtain employment. Upon defendant's completing the program, defense counsel and prosecutors evaluate the defendant's progress and negotiate an outcome, which can include felony charges being reduced to misdemeanors or being dropped altogether. Even when charges are not reduced, participation in the program is considered by the sentencing judge in determining whether incarceration is required, and how long the appropriate term would be. Although the program in the Eastern District of New York is fairly recent, initial results look promising, and the Western District has begun a similar pilot program geared toward youthful offenders, under the leadership of Judge Ronnie Abrams.

Similar programs have shown potential in districts across the country, each taking slightly different approaches. The Central District of California (based around Los Angeles) has a two-tiered program called CASA. In one tier, defendants accused of minor crimes who complete the program have their charges dropped; the second tier, consisting of defendants charged with more serious crimes that appear to be motivated primarily by addiction, rewards successful participants with a sentence of probation rather than prison. In the Central District of Illinois's PADI program, defendants who successfully complete their rehabilitation objectives receive a motion from prosecutors to lower their sentence based on "substantial assistance"—an act normally reserved only for defendants who cooperate with the government in key cases, and one that has the legal effect of authorizing a sentence below an offense's mandatory minimum. Similarly, the DREAM program in the Western District of Washington takes defendants whose crimes were motivated by substance abuse issues and puts them through an intense, one- to two-year program involving rehabilitation, drug testing, and frequent meetings with the sentencing judge. Successful participants have their charges dismissed. Other programs have met with success in South Carolina, Connecticut, and New Hampshire.

Federal judges have also created programs that work post-sentence, helping to lower the number of people incarcerated by reducing recidivism. These reentry programs provide defendants who have served their prison terms with supervision, counseling, educational and vocational services, and at times a reduction in the length of a defendant's period of supervised release. The Southern District of New York developed such a reentry program in 2010, Supervision Opportunity to Accelerate Re-Entry (SOAR), under the leadership of the late Honorable Harold Baer Jr. Those selected for the program were those who had a significant risk of recidivism but were not hardened criminals. Both prosecutors and defense lawyers were involved in selecting participants for whom services could make a difference, and successful completion of the year-long program resulted in a reduction in the term of supervised release. The Probation Department's active participation in the program was critical, as were the biweekly meetings with the reentry court's judges. Regrettably, the program fell victim to budgetary constraints in 2013. A similar system in the Eastern District, called STAR Courts, is estimated to have saved more than $2 million in prison terms avoided and supervised release terms shortened.

These innovations stand as examples of how judges can be leaders in helping to reduce mass incarceration. They also show that judges cannot do it alone; each of these programs involves a host of other actors, from federal prosecutors to the defense bar to the probation department. Neither thorough review of plea bargains, judicial pushback against the excesses of the sentencing guidelines system, nor alternative sentencing programs represents a true solution to mass incarceration. That will come only with congressional action to eliminate the criminalization of drugs, or to reduce or eliminate mandatory minimums, particularly those applicable to nonviolent drug offenses. The efforts of hundreds of diligent and principled jurists have led to lasting change in the past, particularly the demise of the mandatory guidelines system and the amelioration of the crack/powder cocaine disparity. The steps judges can take, though limited in scope, can be part of a necessary and fundamental change, as the justice system and the public recognize the damaging effect of mass incarceration on society.

Notes

1. These numbers likely understate the problem, since they do not include prisoners convicted of personal and property crimes connected to drug addiction or participation in the drug trade.

2. Although outside the scope of this chapter, the government's use of confidential informants involves its own set of dubious practices and connections to mass incarceration. As Loyola law professor Alexandra Natapoff writes in her 2009 book *Snitching: Criminal Informants and the Erosion of American Justice,* by trading lenience for testimony the government has the ability to put extraordinary pressure on defendants prior to trial and prisoners after conviction. When used unethically, this pressure can result in false testimony and improper convictions. The use of such informants is particularly prevalent in drug cases.

3. The *Booker* court also overturned the portion of the Feeney Amendment that provided for de novo appellate review of sentencing decisions. Instead, appellate courts would review sentencing decisions for "unreasonableness."

4. One of this chapter's co-authors, Judge Sweet, notes: "It has been my practice to write a full sentencing opinion for each and every criminal conviction, whether the defendant agreed to a plea bargain or was found guilty at trial. The sentencing opinion is published (or circulated to the parties if it contains confidential information) a few days prior to the sentencing hearing at which the ultimate decision is made. I believe that having these determinations written out and made available is beneficial both for the public, which has an interest in knowing what sentences are being handed down and why, and for the participants in the case. The government and the defendant have the opportunity to look into my reasoning, correct any errors in my calculations of the guidelines range, and highlight any issues that I should consider further. Co-defendants, meanwhile, have the opportunity to see how I am approaching the case and estimate what sanction they may receive, given their level of culpability in the offense."

5. The Reporters Committee for Freedom of the Press, along with several other newspapers and media organizations, recently challenged the legal grounds for keeping statements of reasons sealed as part of their efforts to obtain documents regarding the recent prosecution of former general and CIA director David Petraeus. The Honorable David C. Kessler of the Western District of North Carolina granted the motion to unseal the statement of reasons, redacting only General Petraeus's social security number.

5

Public Defense and Decarceration
Advocacy on the Front Lines

ROBIN STEINBERG, SKYLAR ALBERTSON, AND RACHEL MAREMONT

Renée is a fifty-four-year-old woman who lives alone and suffers from heart disease and bipolar disorder, as well as a bad leg.[1] She was arrested after being accused of slashing a neighbor in the face with a kitchen knife. According to Renée, her neighbors were drinking and had tried to take her clothes off, and she protected herself in the only way she knew how. Renée was charged with second-degree assault, and was released and allowed to return to her home while awaiting her next court date a month later. A week after her arrest, however, Renée received a letter in the mail that the New York City Housing Authority, notified automatically of her arrest, had started eviction proceedings against her. Disabled and mentally ill, Renée was now facing eviction from the home where she had lived for the past twenty-six years, without being convicted of a crime.

In the American criminal justice system, an arrest is never just an arrest. Even if it leads to only a minor misdemeanor conviction or no conviction at all, an arrest can throw an individual's entire life into chaos, jeopardizing employment, housing, immigration status, access to public benefits, and family unity.[2] These enmeshed penalties of criminal justice involvement—frequently referred to as "collateral consequences"[3]—often begin prior to any conviction, last long beyond the resolution of cases in the criminal and family court systems, and continue to present significant obstacles to reentry after incarceration. As the first advocates to meet with clients at the start of criminal and family court proceedings, public defenders are uniquely positioned to help clients fight the accusations against them as well as addressing these systemically enmeshed penalties before, during, and after the resolution of their cases.

Beginning in the 1980s and continuing throughout the 1990s—the peak period of growth in prison populations—policymakers across the United States added a host of far-reaching penalties to both state and federal laws, such as exclusion of felons from public housing and denial of financial aid for higher education.[4] Today, the American Bar Association's "National Inventory of the Collateral Consequences of Conviction" lists more than 45,000 enmeshed penalties in state and federal statutes.[5] With nearly seven million Americans incarcerated or under state supervision[6] and tens of millions of names in criminal record databases,[7] the impact of enmeshed penalties continues to spread throughout communities—predominantly low-income communities of color—at an alarming pace. The burden of collateral penalties weighs particularly hard on people who are reentering society following incarceration, as they aren't able to access resources such as housing, employment, or public benefits that could help them achieve stability.[8]

In this context, it is not enough for public defenders to merely advocate for clients within the narrow confines of criminal cases. Public defenders who seek to provide meaningful, client-centered, and relevant legal representation must expand the scope of their advocacy to address these enmeshed penalties.[9]

From a public health perspective, public defenders are the only ones able to powerfully disrupt mass incarceration on a client-by-client level, not just to avoid imprisonment (a primary intervention) but also, if a client has been incarcerated, to ameliorate the harm of prison upon release (a tertiary intervention). As advocates who meet with clients at the start of criminal proceedings and who are responsible for zealously representing clients' stated interests, public defenders have the opportunity to address the full range of collateral penalties before they become crises. By advocating for clients in this manner, public defenders can carry out primary interventions that not only seek to minimize or avoid incarceration but also mitigate many of the lesser-known penalties that might soon destabilize clients' lives. Concurrently, public defenders are able to engage in primary intervention by participating in community organizing projects and strategic policy reform designed to reduce inflow into the criminal justice system. By serving more generally as clients' "legal homes," public defenders can also become sources of tertiary intervention by helping clients who have already been incarcerated to better address the long-term consequences of criminal justice involvement. Holistic defense is a best practice model for public defenders to implement in pursuit of this broader vision of justice.

Holistic Defense

The Bronx Defenders has been pioneering its innovative model of holistic defense since its founding in 1997, when eight advocates united around a new vision of public defense. While members of the fledgling organization did not yet know the precise form that their new practice would take, they shared a core commitment to expanding the traditional role of public defenders by looking beyond clients' criminal cases and the existing systems to address clients' needs in the courts and beyond.[10]

The founding group of advocates listened to clients, their families, and the community, and what they found is that people often cared more about the broader civil, social, and economic consequences of their criminal cases than about the cases themselves. When clients' children, jobs, benefits, housing, and immigration status were at stake, liberty interests were not always paramount.

As The Bronx Defenders' staff learned more about clients' needs over time, the group's advocacy expanded to encompass a set of core practice areas. What began with one social worker on the initial team of legal advocates developed into a full Social Work Practice consisting of eighteen full-time social workers specializing in criminal defense, family defense, immigration, adolescent defense, and mental health support services. Similarly, the Civil Action Practice, which started with a single attorney funded through an external fellowship, grew to include twenty-six attorneys and eleven non-attorney civil advocates who provide support to clients on vital noncriminal matters such as employment, housing, public benefits, property retrieval, and immigration. Meanwhile, after staff at The Bronx Defenders watched the Administration for Children's Services drag countless clients and their children before Bronx Family Court, threatening removal of clients' children from their custody for issues related to their criminal cases, the office launched its Family Defense Practice, whose thirty-three attorneys, nine social workers, and seven parent advocates evolved to serve as the first institutional provider of parent defense representation in Bronx Family Court.

The common architecture that connects these practice areas are the four pillars of holistic defense. In sharp contrast to practice models that silo advocates into separate divisions, these four pillars embody a commitment to fully integrating services across multiple disciplines. This approach results in better case and life outcomes for our clients, higher levels of client satisfaction, and more long-term stability for clients and their families. The first pillar is the recognition that clients have a wide range of legal and social support needs that, if left unresolved, will continue to push them back into the criminal justice system. These needs include assistance with family custody issues, substance abuse, mental health issues, homelessness, lawful immigration status, and employment.

The second pillar is the importance of communication between advocates specializing in different practice areas. Dynamic and interdisciplinary communication enables advocates to strategize more effectively among themselves and with clients about how to tackle cases, address enmeshed penalties, and best connect clients to services that match their needs.

The third pillar is the interdisciplinary training that staff members at holistic defender offices must undergo in order to provide clients with the best representation possible. Advocates with interdisciplinary training are able to anticipate and identify the enmeshed penalties that their clients may face, making timely and informed referrals possible.

The fourth and final pillar of holistic defense is an emphasis on the necessity of community ties. A robust understanding of and connection to the community is holistic defenders' primary means of identifying the full array of enmeshed penalties that their clients face, building trust with clients and their families, and identifying the larger, systemic forces at play.

Holistic defense and its four pillars operate most effectively through an interdisciplinary, team-based approach. At The Bronx Defenders, although advocates are organized by practice area for the purposes of supervision and professional development, they are functionally and physically organized into teams that include advocates from every practice area. They sit together, work together, and even socialize and eat together—and as a result, they are primed to promptly collaborate on their clients' cases when multidisciplinary challenges arise. Thanks to the office's team-based structure, staff members are then able to put the four pillars into practice by continually strategizing across practice areas and referring clients to additional services—both in-house and beyond—as needed.

Teams range in size from sixteen to twenty-four advocates, with each team comprising several criminal defense and family defense attorneys, an administrator responsible for managing the team's referrals and court filings, and at least one of each of the following: civil generalist attorneys, immigration attorneys, social workers, investigators, parent advocates, and civil legal advocates. Team members participate in community engagement initiatives, where a director of policy and external affairs, a director of community organizing, and an impact litigation team help focus and direct their efforts.

While some clients—often those whose cases are resolved quickly in court—make use of only the Criminal Defense or Family Defense practices, many not only benefit from several different practice areas but also return long after the formal conclusion of their cases to take advantage of this broad array of services. The interdisciplinary structure of the office avoids the complex and confusing processes that might otherwise result from referrals to services not handled by clients' criminal or family defense attorneys. When referrals to outside organizations are necessary, advocates help their clients to navigate these transitions, often by accompanying clients to their first meetings.

Of course, while the core practice areas at The Bronx Defenders (Criminal, Family, Civil, and Immigration Defense; Social Work; Impact Litigation; and Policy and Community Organizing) cover many of the legal issues that clients face, substantial challenges exist beyond these areas. For this reason, the office also operates fifteen to twenty special projects that organize subsets of staff around narrower but no less devastating issues affecting clients. As these projects—which often begin as independent efforts by Bronx Defenders staff who identify a pressing client need—grow, they are often subsumed into preexisting practice areas, thereby continuously expanding the scope of our core areas of representation. Examples of such projects include the Adolescent Defense Project, now a subset of our Criminal Defense Practice, which provides specialized advocacy to the office's sixteen- and seventeen-year-old clients, and Healthy Mothers Healthy Babies, now a joint Family Defense Practice–Social Work Practice program, which proactively connects pregnant Bronx Defenders clients who may be at risk of losing custody of their future newborns with a variety of support services. Other special projects such as the Client Emergency Fund, which provides small-scale donations of cash or goods to clients in moments of crisis, continue to exist independently of one practice area and are instead organized by an interdisciplinary team of volunteers from across the organization.

Keeping with the fourth pillar of holistic defense, which commits the office to robust community engagement, many of these special projects involve community outreach and systemic reform. The Bronx Defenders Organizing Project, under the umbrella of the Community Organizing Practice, trains current and former clients as community activists and conducts outreach with the local Bronx community through youth justice summits, Know Your Rights sessions, and trainings on how to deescalate conflicts with the police. Special organizing projects such as the Fundamental Fairness Project have shed light to the public on the ways in which delays in case processing in the court system have rendered going through the court system the de facto punishment in the Bronx criminal courts—pressuring clients to plead guilty in order to avoid the countless court appearances that stretch out over months and years. Projects such as the Robert P. Patterson, Jr. Mentoring Program, which provides adult mentors to at-risk youth in the South Bronx, seek to provide young people with opportunities, skills, and resources that build positive community and minimize the risk of criminal justice involvement.

By making community organizing and policy advocacy integral components of holistic defense, The Bronx Defenders has been able to break down the traditional division between direct service provision and policy advocacy. Advocates work with individual clients to solve their legal problems and address the collateral consequences stemming from them. Armed with the knowledge of clients' real-life experiences, advocates are well placed to take on long-term, systemic policy change efforts. This radically shifts the community perception of public defenders away from narrowly focused criminal lawyers to problem solvers and advocates for necessary and long-overdue change.

This model of holistic defense is replicable and has spread to public defender offices across the United States. In 2010, The Bronx Defenders established the Center for Holistic Defense with funding from the Department of Justice's Bureau of Justice Assistance. Each year, the Center selects between three and six organizations as technical assistance partners, for a total of twenty-four offices to date.[11] These efforts are supplemented by more informal technical assistance such as speaking engagements and site visits. While the precise contours of holistic defense vary in different offices and jurisdictions, each organization that adopts the model follows the four pillars as a guide to implementing truly interdisciplinary advocacy. Today, organizations as distinct as the Arch City Defenders in St. Louis, Missouri, the East Bay Community Law Center in Berkeley, California, the Community Law Offices in Birmingham, Alabama, and the Tribal Defender of the Confederated Salish and Kootenai Tribes in Pablo, Montana, have incorporated some or all aspects of holistic defense into their practices.

In January 2017, The Bronx Defenders launched Still She Rises, Tulsa: A Project of the Bronx Defenders, the first replication of its holistic model outside of New York City. Having worked in Tulsa, Oklahoma, for years through the Center for Holistic Defense, staff at The Bronx Defenders became aware of the growing crisis of female incarceration in Oklahoma and across the country. Women and girls are the fastest-growing population in prisons and jails across the United States, and Oklahoma leads this trend by incarcerating 142 out of every 100,000 women, a rate more than double the national average.[12] While many of the same circumstances—poverty, drug addiction, marginalization, and mental illness—drive men and women into the criminal justice system, it became clear to The Bronx Defenders that representing women and families would present unique challenges and opportunities.

With the support of local foundations and private donors, Still She Rises opened its doors in North Tulsa, Oklahoma, as the first public defender office dedicated exclusively to representing mothers and female caregivers in the criminal justice system. As at The Bronx Defenders, each client at Still She Rises has access to an interdisciplinary team of attorneys and advocates who provide defense, representation, and support in a variety of legal and non-legal arenas, always tailored to the client's stated wishes. Staying true to the four pillars of holistic defense, which call upon advocates to adapt the holistic model to the specific jurisdiction and community served, Still She Rises has also expanded into new areas of advocacy tailored to the particular needs of women in North Tulsa. In the first few months of serving clients, attorneys and advocates came to understand that the myriad appointments, costs, and services that clients are mandated to complete post-conviction are overwhelming and onerous, particularly for those who are indigent and do not have regular access to transportation or childcare. As a result, many women were being reincarcerated for failure to comply with these conditions. Thus, the office's Post-Disposition Advocacy Team was born. By tracking clients' follow-up court dates, services and treatment program appointments, and payment schedules, as well as by serving as a liaison between clients, attorneys, the court, and service providers, post-conviction advocates assist clients in navigating the diffuse and obscure processes that follow criminal justice involvement.

In addition to providing high-quality advocacy and shedding light on the growing number of incarcerated women across the country, Still She Rises serves as a pilot program to test the holistic model—developed and refined over nearly two decades—in a new jurisdiction and with a particular client focus.

Holistic Defense and Primary Intervention

When Renée was facing criminal assault charges as well as the enmeshed penalty of eviction from her apartment, her interdisciplinary team advocated zealously on her behalf. A social worker reconnected Renée with mental health services to help her manage her bipolar disorder. A civil attorney defended her in housing court, convincing the New York City Housing Authority to delay the eviction proceedings in order to get Renée the services she needed and allow her time to resolve her criminal case. Renée's criminal attorney then incorporated her mental health treatment and her high risk of homelessness into her defense in order to advocate on her behalf in criminal court. Renée was eventually able to resolve her criminal case in a way that did not trigger automatic eviction, allowing her to stay out of jail and in her home.

Holistic defense is the best and most direct vehicle in the criminal justice system for keeping people out of prison. Effectively advocating for clients' liberty against the power of the government is a primary intervention against mass incarceration. Public defenders reduce inflow into prisons and jails every day by challenging the evidence presented against criminal defendants and advocating for individualized assessments, treatment programs, or other alternatives to incarceration.

As with many diseases, mass incarceration stems from a myriad of complex and often interconnected causes. Holistic defense both enhances public defenders' core function of zealously defending clients against criminal charges and empowers advocates to partner with clients to address the underlying causes and consequences of court involvement. A holistic defender model is driven by client decision-making, so clients guide not only case decisions but also prioritize which life outcomes are most pressing and relevant. Attorneys at holistic public defender offices are then able to help their clients reach their stated goals by leveraging the comprehensive, extended resources and perspectives provided by interdisciplinary teams.

In keeping with the fourth pillar of holistic defense, advocates at The Bronx Defenders listened to clients' experiences and learned that even short-term incarceration can produce lasting instability in people's lives. Being in jail for just a few days can jeopardize people's ability to maintain employment, family relationships, housing, and legal status, among other consequences. Many of The Bronx Defenders' clients were spending days, weeks, or months incarcerated because they were too poor to afford bail—sometimes in amounts as low as $500. Too often, clients would plead guilty in order to be released from jail, leading to adverse consequences in all areas of their lives.

In addition to bail, the extreme delays now endemic to the Bronx criminal court system also pressure clients to accept plea bargains, rather than return to court for months and even years. Court delays of up to five years for felonies have pushed the Bronx courts to what judges call "crisis levels."[13] For misdemeanors in the Bronx, it seems that the right to a trial has been all but lost. Through its "No Day in Court" study, the Bronx Defenders' Fundamental Fairness Project followed fifty-four "fighter clients"—clients who were determined to take misdemeanor marijuana possession cases to trial and challenge the evidence that government claimed to have against them. The study proved that trials are unreasonably difficult to come by for individuals charged with low-level offenses. Not a single fighter client was able to take his or her case to trial. In each case, prosecutors delayed until the client gave up and accepted a plea, a judge dismissed the case, or the prosecutors themselves dropped the charge.[14] This phenomenon is particularly troubling considering that a mere 8 percent of all cases arraigned in the Bronx in 2013 involved the most serious charges, while misdemeanors and violations were the top charges for over 70 percent of cases.[15]

Bronx Criminal Court, like the American criminal justice system in general, operates almost exclusively through dispositions other than trial verdicts. In 2013, there were more than 74,000 arrests, 95,000 summonses, and 88,000 criminal court dispositions in the Bronx, and yet only 170 criminal cases that resulted in trial verdicts. This is partially because of the excessive delays in the Bronx court system.[16] Nationwide, an estimated 90 to 95 percent of state and federal court cases are resolved through a plea bargain.[17] When clients must wait months and years to have their day in court, they are much more likely to take a plea bargain, leaving them with a devastating criminal record and likely facing severe enmeshed penalties. The damage is particularly severe for clients who were incarcerated while awaiting trial.

In response to clients' urgent need to fight their criminal cases from outside of jail, The Bronx Defenders created the Bronx Freedom Fund, New York's first-ever charitable bail fund housed in a holistic defender office. The Bronx Freedom Fund posts up to $2,000 bail for Bronx Defenders clients who are facing misdemeanor charges, allowing clients to return home to their jobs, families, and communities while awaiting trial.

The success of the Freedom Fund is clear. In its first two years of operation, it secured the freedom of more than three hundred clients, with 97 percent of them returning to all of their scheduled court dates. Each time a client returns to all of his or her court appearances, the money posted returns to the fund and is available for use in other clients' cases. Since people are much more likely to obtain favorable dispositions when they are able to fight their cases from outside jail, the Bronx Freedom Fund also plays a critical role in helping clients avoid longer terms of incarceration. Without help from the Freedom Fund, more than nine in ten defendants who cannot make bail will plead guilty and likely be saddled with a criminal record, severely impacting their ability to access housing, employment, and other services.[18] Among clients who were bailed out by the Freedom Fund, however, more than half had their cases dismissed and only one in eight clients received a misdemeanor conviction.[19]

Overwhelming data from the Bronx Freedom Fund and other charitable bail funds demonstrate that the vast majority of people return to court without paying bail or being forced to undergo treatment or services. In the summer of 2015, New York Mayor Bill de Blasio's office announced a plan to largely eliminate cash bail for people charged with low-level or nonviolent crimes. This was a long-overdue step, and one that has the potential to help break the causal connection between poverty and incarceration that the Freedom Fund was founded to alleviate. However, unlike the Freedom Fund, which merely reminds people of their court dates with calls and text message check-ins, the city's proposed alternative to bail and similar proposals created since then would likely extend the reach of the criminal justice system by forcing people to undergo services such as mental health treatment, anger management classes, or drug treatment, even though they have not been convicted of a crime, and even when such interventions do nothing to alleviate the underlying issue driving the client into the system. While this policy has the potential to reduce the total numbers of incarcerated people, it also threatens to broaden the reach of the criminal justice system, particularly over poor communities of color.[20]

For most of The Bronx Defenders' clients, holistic defense begins at arraignments and family court intake, where attorneys ask clients a series of questions.[21] These questions, which were carefully crafted to help Bronx Defenders advocates identify potential enmeshed penalties, are continually updated to reflect clients' needs as well as changes in statutory law and the political climate to best protect clients from onerous consequences. When our attorneys meet with their clients for the first time, their familiarity with the basics of their colleagues' areas of expertise enables them to use their clients' responses to recognize when to refer issues to their team members. Thanks to the structure of the office, these referrals are prompt, and referring attorneys can follow up with their colleagues as easily as leaning over the walls of their cubicles. Rather than simply processing clients through the system (as many understaffed public defenders do), advocates at holistic defender offices get to know their clients, strategize according to their strengths and vulnerabilities, and leverage that knowledge into better outcomes both inside and outside of court—humanizing clients in the eyes of judges and prosecutors.

The application of holistic defense in criminal court results in a higher percentage of non-incarceratory dispositions and, equally importantly, legal strategies that seek to mitigate the enmeshed penalties of court involvement. In 2014, The Bronx Defenders represented clients in nearly thirty thousand criminal cases.[22] According to all available data, 91.8 percent of Bronx Defenders clients received non-incarceratory dispositions.

Of course, much of holistic defense occurs beyond the doors of criminal court. In 2013 and 2014, Bronx Defenders criminal defense attorneys referred roughly 4,000 clients to civil legal services, 900 clients to family court representation, 3,500 clients to immigration advocacy, and 1,100 clients to social work support. These referrals do not include the countless instances of more informal collaboration across practice areas that occur every day at The Bronx Defenders.

As the first institutional provider of defense representation for parents accused of abuse or neglect in Bronx Family Court, The Bronx Defenders Family Defense also assisted nearly 1,000 clients in family court proceedings in 2014. Additionally, The Bronx Defenders represented approximately 197 people facing deportation in Immigration Court in 2014 through the New York Family Immigrant Unity Project (NYIFUP). Clients who come to The Bronx Defenders via family court and immigration court are eligible for all of the same interdisciplinary resources as clients who come to the office through arraignments in criminal court.

The office's Civil Action Practice assists clients with a variety of matters including public benefits, housing, employment, education, and health. In addition to the office's twenty-six civil generalist attorneys, The Bronx Defenders employs eleven civil legal advocates, who are trained to assist clients with matters that don't require licensed attorneys, such as reclaiming property taken by the police during an arrest and accessing public benefits. Civil legal advocates enable the office to offer clients a broad array of civil legal services despite the limited funding options for providing civil legal aid to people with criminal or family court involvement.

In 2014, the Civil Action Practice handled 9,000 legal matters, benefiting more than 15,500 people. The practice's major achievements for that same period include preventing the evictions of more than 300 clients and their families, resulting in over $11 million in shelter cost savings; securing access to stable, affordable housing for 48 families; preserving jobs or employment licenses for the breadwinners of 258 families; and connecting clients with cash and noncash benefits valued at over $2.5 million.

Meanwhile, Bronx Defenders immigration advocates provided advocacy to clients whose criminal court involvement might impact their immigration status and also advocated on behalf of individuals facing deportation in immigration court. In 2014, Bronx Defenders immigration attorneys and legal advocates prevented the deportation of 357 clients and obtained lawful immigration status for 29 clients. In addition to advising clients about the immigration consequences of their criminal or family court proceedings, The Bronx Defenders has, since 2014, represented detained immigrant clients facing deportation through the New York Immigrant Family Unity Project, the first universal representation program in the country for immigration court proceedings.

Since President Trump's inauguration, immigration-related concerns have become of paramount importance to criminal-court-involved clients. One of several executive orders issued in early 2017 by the Trump administration prioritizes the removal of seven categories of immigrants, including those who have been convicted of a crime, those who have been charged with a crime but not yet convicted, and those who have "committed acts that constitute a criminal offense"—broad descriptions that encompass nearly all of The Bronx Defenders' clients. As of spring 2017, New York City remains a sanctuary city, meaning that the New York City Police Department and the Department of Corrections will not automatically detain noncitizens for Immigration and Customs Enforcement. Between 2003 and 2015, Immigration and Customs Enforcement officials were stationed at Rikers Island, the largest of the city jails, to monitor and detain non-citizen inmates. Depending upon the Trump administration's promise to withhold federal funding from sanctuary cities, it is possible that New York's status as a sanctuary city could change, resulting in the arrest and detention of many more noncitizen residents and Bronx Defenders clients.

Bronx Defenders social workers frequently assist young clients with mental health needs or developmental disabilities, struggling with substance abuse and addiction, or facing serious charges (homicide, arson, and serious sex offenses trigger mandatory social work referrals). In contrast to clinical social workers, whose primary allegiance might be to the courts or to an outside agency, social workers at The Bronx Defenders are embedded in legal teams. This means that they are bound by attorney-client privilege and their primary goal is to advance clients' interests as part of holistic legal strategies. Social workers perform assessments, engage in crisis interventions, secure placements for clients in treatment programs, testify in court, and compose prepleading and sentencing reports. Social workers are on call for arraignments and are thus able to promptly assist with interviewing clients and advocating for their release. Statistics from The Bronx Defenders' Arraignment Checklist indicate that in 2014, more than six hundred clients were immediately referred for social work support following their first meetings with their criminal defense attorneys, while many more become involved with social workers as their cases progress, crises arise, referrals to community-based treatment or services are needed, or mitigation reports become essential.

Finally, The Bronx Defenders pursues systemic reforms that more broadly seek to restrict gateways to incarceration. The office maintains a robust Impact Litigation Practice, which has co-counseled cases such as *Ligon v. New York*, a major class action that established the unconstitutionality of the New York City Police Department's Operation Clean Halls program, whereby officers would stop, frisk, and often arrest people inside or near apartment buildings. The Bronx Defenders Organizing Project was active in the campaign against stop-and-frisk and continues to advocate for systemic change in the New York City criminal justice system. Additionally, as previously mentioned, Bronx Defenders staff members regularly conduct Know Your Rights workshops for members of the community so that individuals are empowered to safely and respectfully assert their legal rights when interacting with the police. In 2014 alone, Bronx Defenders organizers and advocates reached more than nine hundred people through twenty-eight workshops. These organizing projects have the potential to be a very powerful tool in combating mass incarceration through primary intervention—when community members are knowledgeable about their legal rights, they are less likely to be swept up into the criminal justice system to begin with, and they become active participants in the political process that so often tries to silence their voices.

Holistic Defense and Tertiary Intervention

Joel is a Bronx resident who came into Community Intake seeking help obtaining food stamps for himself and his children. The Human Resources Administration had denied his application for food stamps because his children's mother was collecting benefits on their behalf, even though the children lived with him. With help from The Bronx Defenders' Community Intake team, Joel successfully obtained food stamps and was able to get five months of retroactive benefits. While awaiting the outcome of his appeal, Joel was able to use The Bronx Defenders' food pantry and community-wide Thanksgiving meal to provide for his kids. The Bronx Defenders had previously represented Joel in two criminal cases, so Joel knew that he could again seek help from the advocates there.

By providing clients with seamless access to a variety of services, The Bronx Defenders creates a legal home: a single destination that people can visit when they require assistance with legal matters or related issues. Bronx Defenders clients know that they can return to the office long after the formal conclusion of their cases to receive quality support and advocacy.

People who have come into contact with the criminal justice system—particularly people who have experienced incarceration—often have limited resources available to navigate the obstacles they face and little knowledge of which organizations might be able to help them. To make matters worse, many enmeshed penalties affect the issues most critical for people to achieve stable lives: housing, public assistance, employment, and family unity.

For formerly incarcerated people who are on parole, and therefore still under the control of the criminal justice system, having access to community and social services is particularly crucial. People released to parole are generally subjected to a number of onerous conditions, including but not limited to having frequent meetings with a parole officer, finding stable employment and housing, submitting to drug testing, and avoiding police contact.[23] Unsurprisingly, given the enmeshed penalties that accompany criminal justice involvement, many people are unable to meet the conditions of their parole and are therefore reincarcerated for parole violations. In

2009, 35 percent of prison admissions were for technical parole violations such as failure to report to a parole officer, rather than as the result of a new criminal conviction.[24] When public defender offices can function as clients' legal homes, they are able to provide needed advice and support long after the formal conclusion of their cases, in addition to providing social services and facilitating tertiary interventions for people struggling with the chronic effects of incarceration and court involvement.

At The Bronx Defenders, much of the office's status as a legal home comes about informally through clients' ongoing relationships with their teams of advocates. However, staff members also take deliberate steps to make the office a place where clients feel comfortable returning in the future. The Bronx Defenders' Organizing Project serves not only as a vehicle for pursuing systemic change but also as a setting for discussions about experiences with the criminal justice system. Meanwhile, social workers and parent advocates organize initiatives such as Focus on Fathers, a discussion and support group for fathers involved with the court system, and Healthy Mothers Healthy Babies, a program that, as previously mentioned, connects pregnant clients with resources that help them give birth to healthy children and maintain unity of their families. Each year, The Bronx Defenders also hosts a community block party, a Thanksgiving meal, and a Celebration of Families for clients and community members, which provide opportunities for Bronx residents to get to know The Bronx Defenders and access resources as needed. Additionally, the physical space of the community reception area—with comfortable couches, bright and cheerful decorations, a client library, and toys for small children—sends a clear and inviting message to visitors.[25] Clients and community members are welcome to visit The Bronx Defenders' office on weekdays between 9:00 a.m. and 6:00 p.m., with or without appointments. Outside of those hours, Bronx Defenders attorneys staff a twenty-four-hour legal emergency hotline.

In 2015, more than three thousand people arrived at the doors of the Bronx Defenders' community reception space seeking assistance. Approximately 21 percent of visitors met with Bronx Defenders advocates beyond the Community Intake Team, roughly 19 percent received referrals to outside organizations, and over half received brief advice, general legal information, or one-time services. Two-thirds of visitors who met with members of the intake team sought assistance related to civil penalties, which often present significant obstacles to reentry following incarceration.

Many of the one-time services provided by the Community Intake Team are simple but effective measures that ease the burden of enmeshed penalties. For example, members of the Community Intake Team are able to review criminal records for errors and help people submit corrections so that erroneous or sealed information does not become an obstacle to obtaining employment and housing. Intake advocates are also able to screen clients to determine whether they are eligible for public benefits (including food stamps, Supplemental Security Income, and unemployment) and can help clients obtain certificates of good conduct or rehabilitation, documents that are necessary for obtaining employment in certain professions following periods of incarceration. Bronx Defenders staff members also host legal clinics in the community reception area on matters such as tax preparation or how to file a notice of claim, which preserves an individual's right to sue government officials and agencies for damages. Drawing upon its experience providing these types of services and counseling people with past court involvement, The Bronx Defenders created ReentryNet.net, an online clearinghouse for information related to enmeshed penalties and reentry following incarceration, and publishes a guide for attorneys and advocates on the civil legal collateral consequences of arrests and convictions.

Approximately 27 percent of people who met with the Community Intake Team in 2014 had previously been represented by The Bronx Defenders in separate matters and returned to the office for help with new issues. This figure demonstrates not only that former Bronx Defenders clients feel that the office is their legal home and are comfortable returning for help, but also that thousands of community members in the South Bronx with no prior interactions with The Bronx Defenders feel the same way about the office. Both insights establish that when public defenders broaden the scope of their advocacy and serve as legal homes, they are able to reach vulnerable populations that might not otherwise receive assistance.

Conclusion

Public defenders play a crucial role in reducing mass incarceration through their zealous representation of individual clients. By advocating thoroughly and effectively on behalf of clients whose liberty may be at stake, public defenders help clients minimize or avoid incarceration, thus reducing inflow into the prison or jail system.

But holistic defenders are even better equipped to combat the complex causes and consequences of criminal justice involvement because they are able to look beyond the narrow confines of a criminal case. Practicing holistic, interdisciplinary advocacy compels defenders to consider not only the enmeshed penalties that accompany criminal justice involvement, but also the larger systemic issues driving entire communities—particularly poor communities of color into the justice system. Armed with a broader understanding of these forces, as well as robust community support, holistic defenders can be the most effective advocates for individual clients while simultaneously pursuing systemic changes at the policy level.

As we consider a more hopeful future—one in which mass incarceration is no longer a defining feature of the American criminal justice system—we must seek to better support public defense by fully funding state and local defender systems and by encouraging defenders to adopt the holistic model. We now have clear evidence that holistic advocacy enhances public defenders' work and can play a critical role in facilitating effective primary and tertiary interventions against the systemic injustices of mass incarceration.

Notes

1. The names Renée and Joel used in this chapter's examples are pseudonyms.

2. Robin Steinberg, "Heeding Gideon's Call in the Twenty-First Century: Holistic Defense and the New Public Defense Paradigm," *Washington and Lee Law Review* 70 (2013): 968; Sarah R. Berson, "Beyond the Sentence Understanding Collateral Consequences," *National Institute of Justice Journal* 272 (September 2013): 25.

3. While the labels "enmeshed penalties" and "collateral consequences" are interchangeable, we use the former term in this chapter to emphasize how closely these punishments are intertwined with criminal sanctions. McGregor Smyth, "'Collateral'

No More: The Practical Imperative for Holistic Defense in a Post-Padilla World . . . Or, How to Achieve Consistently Better Results for Clients," St. Louis University Public Law Review 31 (2011): 147–48.

4. Jeremy Travis, "Invisible Punishment: An Instrument of Social Exclusion," in Invisible Punishment: The Collateral Consequences of Mass Imprisonment, ed. Marc Mauer and Meda Chesney-Lind (New York: The New Press, 2002), 17–25.

5. American Bar Association, "National Inventory of the Collateral Consequences of Conviction," http://www.abacollateralconsequences.org (last visited April 14, 2015).

6. Lauren E. Glaze and Danielle Kaeble, "Correctional Populations in the United States, 2013," Bureau of Justice Statistics, Department of Justice, 2014.

7. Gary Fields and John R. Emshwiller, "As Arrest Records Rise, Americans Find Consequences Can Last a Lifetime," Wall Street Journal, August 18, 2014.

8. Michael Pinard and Anthony C. Thompson, "Offender Reentry and the Collateral Consequences of Criminal Convictions: An Introduction," NYU Review of Law and Social Change 30 (2006); Gwen Rubinstein and Debbie Mukamal, "Welfare and Housing—Denial of Benefits to Drug Offenders," in Invisible Punishment: The Collateral Consequences of Mass Imprisonment, ed. Marc Mauer and Meda Chesney-Lind (New York: The New Press, 2002), 40–46.

9. Steinberg, "Heeding Gideon's Call"; Smyth, "'Collateral' No More." The Supreme Court affirmed the responsibility of defense attorneys to address enmeshed penalties in Padilla v. Kentucky, 559 U.S. 356 (2010).

10. For a more in-depth history of the Bronx Defenders and holistic defense, see Steinberg, "Heeding Gideon's Call."

11. Bronx Defenders, "The Center for Holistic Defense Training and Technical Sites," December 18, 2015, http://www.bronxdefenders.org/the-center-for-holistic-defense-technical-and-training-sites.

12. Sentencing Project, "Fact Sheet: Incarcerated Women and Girls," April 26, 2017, http://www.sentencingproject.org/wp-content/uploads/2016/02/Incarcerated-Women-and-Girls.pdf.

13. William Glaberson, "Justice Denied," New York Times, April 30, 2013.

14. Bronx Defenders, "No Day in Court," 2013, http://www.bronxdefenders.org/wp-content/uploads/2013/05/No-Day-in-Court-A-Report-by-The-Bronx-Defenders-May-2013.pdf.

15. New York City Criminal Justice Agency, "Annual Report 2013," available via the New York City Criminal Justice Agency online publications library at: http://www.nycja.org/library.php.

16. Office of the Chief Clerk of New York City Criminal Court, "Criminal Court of the City of New York: Annual Report 2013," available at http://www.courts.state.ny.us/COURTS/nyc/criminal/2013%20Annual%20Report%20FINAL%2072214.pdf; New

York State Division of Criminal Justice Services, "Adult Arrests: 2005–2014 (Bronx)," available at http://www.criminaljustice.ny.gov/crimnet/ojsa/arrests/Bronx.pdf.

17. Lindsay Devers, Bureau of Justice Assistance, "Plea and Charge Bargaining: Research Summary," 2011, available at https://www.bja.gov/Publications/PleaBargaining ResearchSummary.pdf.

18. The Bronx Freedom Fund, Second Annual Report, 2015, 2–4, available at http://static1.squarespace.com/static/54e106e1e4b05fac69f108cf/t/5681561eb204d52319 b86854/1451316766890/2015+Annual+Report.pdf.

19. Ibid., 4.

20. Robin Steinberg and David Feige, "The Problem with NYC's Bail Reform," Marshall Project, July 9, 2015, available at https://www.themarshallproject.org/2015/07/09/the -problem-with-nyc-s-bail-reform#.pcTOR7hLE (last visited January 30, 2016).

21. Bronx Defenders, Arraignment Checklist, http://www.bronxdefenders.org/pro grams/checklist-project.

22. While a small number of the office's Criminal Defense Practice clients come to the Bronx Defenders through community intake, the vast majority of clients are assigned to their attorneys at arraignment. The office is contracted by the City of New York to staff arraignments in the Bronx Criminal Court on certain days of the week and represents every individual arraigned during its shifts who cannot afford to pay for an attorney and for whom the office has no conflict of interest.

23. Christine S. Scott-Hayward, "The Failure of Parole: Rethinking the Role of the State in Reentry," *New Mexico Law Review* 41 (2011): 421.

24. Ibid., 437.

25. Winnie Hu, "In South Bronx, Legal Aid and a Shoulder to Lean On," *New York Times*, February 27, 2013.

6

Making Drug Policy Reform Work for Meaningful Decarceration

GABRIEL SAYEGH

The U.S. war on drugs and the brutal system of mass incarceration are inextricably linked.[1] The movements working to end the war on drugs and mass incarceration have for decades also been linked. Yet the recent successes of both these movements, along with a changing political landscape, are raising fundamental questions about the ongoing viability of this linkage. For one, ending the war on drugs alone will not end mass incarceration. While the politics are complex, the data are clear: the majority of people in U.S. jails and prisons are *not* incarcerated or otherwise detained as a result of drug charges.[2] Yet the data also show that ending mass incarceration is not possible *without* ending the war on drugs.[3] In other words, ending the war on drugs is necessary but not sufficient for ending mass incarceration. To end mass incarceration, we will need both to end the war on drugs and to advance other reforms, including those related to violent offenses.[4]

This means that participants in both the movement to end the war on drugs and the movement to end mass incarceration have an investment in finding enough common ground to ensure that there is a pathway forward where reform efforts in both movements are mutually reinforcing and can work for meaningful decarceration.

Finding Common Ground

For the last twenty-five years, finding common ground between these two movements has been relatively natural because the connections between the war on drugs and mass incarceration are, in many ways, self-evident. The drug war preceded the advent of mass incarceration and has long been understood as a major driver of mass incarceration (despite not being the sole cause). When the war on drugs was launched in 1971 by President Richard M. Nixon, there were approximately 350,000 people in prisons and jails in the United States.[5] At that time, the incarceration rate in the United States was similar to that of other industrialized Western democracies. Today, there are 2.3 million people in prisons and jails in the United States—which means that a country with 5 percent of the world's population holds nearly 25 percent of all the people in cages on the planet. Roughly 480,000 people—more than the population of Atlanta, Georgia—are incarcerated in jails and prisons for drug offenses alone.[6] The United States, through a range of policies including the war on drugs, criminalizes and locks up a huge proportion of its population, predominantly poor people and people of color, with disastrous results for public safety, public health, and human rights.[7]

More and more people are chronicling the connections between the war on drugs and mass incarceration, generating greater awareness among the general public of the problems at hand. Some of the most potent contributions in this area include books such as Michelle Alexander's *The New Jim Crow*, Carl Hart's *High Price*, Johann Hari's *Chasing the Stream*, and Todd Clear's *The Punishment Imperative*; films including Ava Duvernay's *13th* and Eugene Jarecki's *The House I Live In*; numerous reports issued by a wide array of organizations and institutions with diverse political perspectives, such as *Growth of Incarceration in the United States: Exploring Causes and Consequences* from the National Academy of Sciences, *How Many Americans Are Unnecessarily Incarcerated?* from the Brennan Center for Justice, and *Four Decades and Counting: The Continued Failure of the War on Drugs* from the Cato Institute; and countless articles and stories in a variety of print and digital media.[8]

Without question, the movements to end the war on drugs and end mass incarceration have made tremendous progress over the last twenty-five years. Made up of a diverse array of stakeholders—including formerly incarcerated people, active and former drug users, people in recovery, organizers, advocates, researchers, and more—these movements have won policy and electoral victories small and large and have succeeded in disrupting the political consensus underlying the war on drugs and mass incarceration. Even a cursory review generates an impressive list of major victories, as reform measures are now regularly advancing in state legislatures and at the ballot box in every region of the country. New York State rolled back the Rockefeller drug laws.[9] California completely overhauled its sentencing system to reduce its incarceration rate by tens of thousands through Proposition 47.[10] States from Alabama to Colorado to Michigan have enacted a range of reforms that reduce sentences, expand alternatives, and promote reentry. Cities across the country, driven by local advocacy, are taking up reforms with their police departments, and a growing number of police departments are increasingly working with community leaders to establish diversion programs to keep people out of jail.[11] More innovative public health interventions to reduce accidental overdose fatalities are being considered in cities of all sizes.[12] There have even been some important, albeit limited, reforms in Congress in recent years as political leaders on the left, on the right, and in the center have been forced by these movements to admit that the war on drugs has failed and that the nation's criminalization binge has gone too far.[13]

These movements are now larger, better funded, and more successful than ever, and they are still growing. They are arguably now mainstream. This is perhaps most evident in relation to cannabis (marijuana) policy.[14] The drug war is particularly focused on cannabis—nearly half of all drug arrests in the United States every year are for cannabis, and some states still harshly punish people for mere possession. For instance, in Louisiana, possession of even two joints can lead to years in prison.[15] Yet the drug policy reform movement has made miraculous progress over the last twenty years in its effort to fix the nation's cannabis laws; today a majority of states in every region of the country have enacted some type of reform to their cannabis laws. Twenty-nine states plus Washington, D.C., have enacted medical marijuana laws, where only medical patients with certain qualifying conditions can, with a physician's recommendation, purchase cannabis from approved vendors, or sometimes even grow their own.[16] Twenty states and Washington, D.C., have decriminalized possession of small amounts of cannabis, where criminal penalties for possession of relatively small amounts are reduced or eliminated (but the production and sale of the drug remain illegal).[17] And eight states have enacted full legalization, where cannabis production, sale, and use by adults is legal, taxed and regulated by the government, while Washington, D.C., now permits adults to grow, consume, and share cannabis but does not allow for commercial production or sales.[18] More than sixty million Americans now live in states where cannabis is legal for recreational use by adults—it is taxed, and regulated, like alcohol.

Tellingly, most of these cannabis reform victories have come thorough voter initiatives. Of the eight states with full legalization, all were enacted through voter initiatives. It's not surprising that voters, when given the option, enact reform—polling data show that 60 percent of Americans support legalizing cannabis, up from 12 percent in 1969.[19]

This mainstreaming creates its own challenges for defining a path to finally ending the war on drugs and mass incarceration. Tremendous growth in both movements means there are more and more people involved and an increasing number of new organizations. This naturally leads to more movement conflicts and debates over leadership and goals. Groups compete for limited resources from donors and foundations, fight for the spotlight, and fracture over disagreements about strategies and tactics. As both movements expand, there is a growing debate and divide between organizations about how to proceed, and about what "winning" means. The very success of these movements has brought them to a crossroads.

Finding a way forward has been made all the more complicated in the wake of the 2016 presidential election. While President Barack Obama talked openly of mass incarceration and called for an end to the war on drugs,[20] Donald J. Trump asserted himself as the "law and order" candidate, won the presidency, and appointed an attorney general, Jeff Sessions, who not just is hostile to reform but has a record of supporting mass incarceration.[21] Sessions, upon becoming attorney general, swiftly called for expanding the war on drugs.[22] The retrograde drug policy and criminal justice positions of the Trump administration, coupled with the profound political realignment still underway in the wake of the election, create even more challenges for social movements and policy reformers to find common ground to advance efforts to end the drug war and mass incarceration, let alone for these different movements to work together in complementary ways.

Here, I propose five guidelines to aid advocates in both movements. For drug policy reformers, these guidelines can help in developing and advancing drug policy reforms that will serve the interest of meaningful decarceration. For those working to end mass incarceration, these guidelines may prove useful in finding ways to make drug policy reform work for criminal justice reform more broadly.

Advancing Decriminalization

Decriminalization must form the basis for a sensible, health-based drug policy. This means decriminalizing possession and use of all drugs. It also means being careful not to advance or promote efforts that rely on explicit or implicit criminalization.

The drug war plays a unique role in criminalizing people, for mere possession and use of certain psychoactive substances. Consider that in 2013, 38 percent of Americans (more than 120 million people) had tried cannabis at least once.[23] That same year, nearly 1.5 million people were arrested in the United States on drug offenses, the vast majority for simple possession—and almost half those arrests were for cannabis alone.[24] In 2017, 45 percent of Americans (over 140 million people) said they had tried cannabis at least once, and 12 percent of Americans (nearly 40 million people) said they were currently using it.[25]

But the drug war has gone much farther than just expanding criminalization and feeding mass incarceration. In *A Plague of Prisons*, epidemiologist Ernest Drucker makes a public health analysis of mass incarceration. He writes:

Incarceration—punishment by imprisonment—is based on a set of laws established by any state or nation to assure public safety by the separation and isolation of criminals from society. By contrast, mass incarceration results from policies that support the large-scale use of imprisonment on a sustained basis for political or social purposes that have little to do with law enforcement.[26]

Since its formal launch in 1971, the drug war has further stigmatized and marginalized people for having the health problem of addiction. The drug war has exacerbated and institutionalized racial disparities.[27] It has militarized the police and significantly expanded police powers while under-mining constitutional rights.[28] It has limited access to proven public health interventions such as syringe exchange programs and proven drug treat-ment modalities such as opioid agonist treatment (methadone, buprenor-phine), consequently contributing to the spread of bloodborne illness, increased prevalence of infectious disease, and untimely, preventable deaths.[29]

The war on drugs is rooted in *punitive prohibition*, wherein criminalization takes center stage.[30] Criminalization turns otherwise law-abiding citizens who use illicit drugs into criminals; and for those people who develop a problem in their use of illicit drugs, criminalization makes those problems (addiction, overdose, etc.) into a criminal context that diminishes their chance to get help. There is some debate in the scientific community about whether drug addiction is a disease or a disorder,[31] but there is no debate that drug addiction is a health issue. And herein lies the rub. If addiction is a health issue, why do we criminalize people for experiencing the health problem of addiction? As journalist and writer Maia Szalavitz writes:

To argue that "addiction is a disease" while criminalizing possession of the drug involved in the addiction is, then, to make an impossible case. You are saying "I think your addiction is shameful and users of the drugs you take should be caged," while also claiming "You have an illness that should be treated like any other disease." Neither cancer patients, nor people with diabetes nor those with depression are put into this double bind: no actual disease is seen this way.[32]

The implications of such an approach are seen in the current opioid overdose crisis. More than half a million people have died in the United States of drug overdoses since 2000. Most opioid overdose deaths are preventable—if emergency intervention is applied in time, death can often be avoided. And many (but not all) people who die of a fatal overdose are using drugs with other people when they overdose[33]—which means, in theory, that people could call for help if the person they're with overdoses.

But most people are afraid of calling 911 because they fear that if they call emergency services, they're more likely to get a ride in the back of cop car than the back of an ambulance.[34] And they're right. In a country that has so vigorously prosecuted the war on drugs and created the thing we now call "mass incarceration," such a fear is logical. Because our policies are rooted in the criminalization approach, we've succeeded in scaring people away from calling for help when they need it, dramatically increasing the likelihood of preventable deaths.

Some may be quick to argue that decriminalization is "too radical" or, in the era of Trump and Sessions, impossible. But such assertions ignore history and the current local, national, and international debate around drug policy. While the drug war dominated the political landscape in the 1980s and early 1990s, by the late 1990s attitudes began to shift. Over the past two decades, when given the option through initiatives, voters regularly choose to roll back the drug war in favor of more sensible approaches—passing medical cannabis laws and legalizing cannabis, enacting substantive sentencing reforms,[35] curtailing the corrupt bail bond industry (which exposes so many poor defendants who can't make bail to long periods of brutality in our violent jails),[36] and more. In October 2016, a major report released by Human Rights Watch and the ACLU concluded that decriminalization should be a primary goal of drug policy reform in the United States.[37]

And it's not just in the United States that the political alignments and opinions related to drug control are changing. The debate at the global level is surpassing that in the United States, as the call to decriminalize possession and personal use of all drugs is no longer taboo or even controversial among knowledgeable actors. In 2011, the Global Commission on Drug Policy, building on the work of the Latin American Commission, issued its first report, recommending an end to "the criminalization, marginalization and stigmatization of people who use drugs but who do no harm to others."[38] The commission draws its members from the elite around the world—former heads of state, business leaders, and political leaders, including George Shultz, former secretary of state under Ronald Reagan; Kofi Annan, former secretary-general of the United Nations; Richard Branson, head of Virgin; and Paul Volcker, former head of the U.S. Federal Reserve, among many others.[39] Subsequent reports published by the commission have not only echoed this call for decriminalization but expanded on it.[40]

In 2015, then UN secretary-general Ban Ki-moon said, "We must consider alternatives to criminalization and incarceration of people who use drugs and focus criminal justice efforts on those involved in supply. We should increase the focus on public health, prevention, treatment, and care, as well as on economic, social, and cultural strategies."[41] Perhaps even more telling, in October 2015 a paper calling for decriminalization was leaked from the UN Office of Drugs and Crime. The paper's unnamed authors wrote that "decriminalising drug use and possession for personal consumption is consistent with international drug control conventions and may be *required to meet obligations under international human rights law*."[42]

In Europe, Portugal, the Czech Republic, and Estonia have all decriminalized personal possession for all drugs.[43] In 2013, Uruguay became the first country to legalize cannabis, and in 2017 it will begin selling it in drugstores.[44] Canada is on track to legalize cannabis nationally within the next year.[45] In early 2016, at the urging of Latin American political leaders, whose countries are suffering the violence of horrific drug wars, the UN General Assembly held a special session on drugs.[46] It was the first time in twenty years the UN had taken up the question of drug control policy, with many political leaders calling openly for an end to the drug war.[47]

In March 2016, the prestigious medical journal *Lancet*, in collaboration with one of the top medical schools in the world, Johns Hopkins University, convened a commission of dozens of the world's leading health scholars and scientists to study drug control policy and make recommendations.[48] The commission concluded that it was time to decriminalize drugs, writing: "Countries such as Portugal and the Czech Republic decriminalised minor drug offences years ago, with significant financial savings, less incarceration, significant public health benefits, and no significant increase in drug use."[49] These developments demonstrate that there is a growing national and international challenge to the drug war consensus, creating a new, broad foundation upon which to make more strident, bold, honest political demands regarding drug policy.

For drug policy reform to serve decarceration, it must seek to reduce criminalization at every opportunity, beginning with decriminalization—eliminating criminal sanctions associated with drug possession and use *of all drugs*.[50]

The criminal legal system is not designed or equipped to respond effectively to problem drug use or addiction and should not have the responsibility to respond to it. It should not be the avenue through which people get the medical attention they need if they have a drug problem. And, absent harm to others, the criminal legal system should not be responsible for determining what substances consenting adults choose to put into their own bodies.

For advocates working to end mass incarceration, it is imperative to avoid the trap of using criminalization as a tool to solve real or perceived drug problems. This is particularly evident when reformers call for "treatment instead of incarceration" and promote drug courts as the model to meet this important demand. Drug courts expand the scope of criminalization, reinforce false notions that drug use equals addiction, and have questionable outcomes. A 2017 report by Physicians for Human Rights put it this way: "People with substance use disorders who get treatment through the criminal justice system are still treated as criminals, and the symptoms of their illness punished as if the illness itself were a crime."[51] The best way to address a health issue is in a healthcare setting, not in a court or jail. Drug courts, therefore, are not the solution.

For drug policy advocates, it is important to consider what decriminalization means beyond the question of drugs. The drug policy reform movement has won significant success by promoting a narrative of the "nonviolent offender," distinguishing drug offenses—most of which are nonviolent—from other offenses including, and especially, violent offenses. The public and lawmakers are more sympathetic to a person detained on a drug possession charge than one detained on, say, assault. But as this distinction continues to be made by the drug policy reform movement, it increasingly puts that effort at odds with the movement to end mass incarceration, because to win, we must not allow violence to become an all-encompassing justification for incarceration, nor can we allow for the continued use of language like "offender" which serves to dehumanize and "other" people.[52]

Nowhere is this dynamic more vivid than in efforts to reform cannabis laws, most of which have used this distinction to assure the public and lawmakers that a particular reform measure wouldn't benefit "those people"—people with violent offenses on their records—but would benefit only those who committed nonviolent offenses. Not only do we need health-based approaches to drug policy, but in order to meaningfully decarcerate— to substantially reduce jail and prison populations overall—we need to develop new ways to address violence. We must actually respond to the needs of those harmed by crime (victims), meaningfully hold accountable those who commit violence, protect public safety, and find ways to accomplish these goals that do not require locking people in cages and dehumanizing them for interminable amounts of time.[53] To meaningfully contribute to decarceration, decriminalization must form the basis for how drug policy reform initiatives *and communications strategies* are developed and deployed.

Using Facts, Not Propaganda

Basic knowledge about drugs is important for advocates working on drug policy and criminal justice reform; understanding differences between drugs and being aware of the relative harm versus benefit of drugs will aid reformers in all movements. Most urgently, however, reformers must understand that people take drugs for a variety of reasons, including for pleasure; that the vast majority of people who take drugs don't have a problem; and that most who do experience a problem find a way to course-correct without formal treatment.

Compulsive, problematic drug use (addiction) is the exception and not the norm for most individuals' use of drugs. Most adults who use psychoactive substances do so without it leading to serious problems in their lives, and they successfully carry out their responsibilities, from jobs to kids to community roles.[54] This is true for familiar substances, such as tobacco, alcohol, caffeine, and cannabis, and it is also true for less familiar substances, such as cocaine, MDMA, opiates, and what are now called novel psychoactive substances.[55]

The potential for abuse of drugs, or harm caused by drug use, is real. But over the course of the drug war there has been deliberate, sustained misrepresentation of the scientific evidence about drugs to serve a political purpose of executing a drug war. Media too often report on fiction as fact, and policy makers are quick to use those accounts to formulate policies that serve a political purpose.

Promoting propaganda about drugs and drug use for political purposes is quite old, and nearly all of us have experience with it. In the 1980s, Nancy Reagan's Just Say No campaign was launched, ostensibly to teach young people about the harms of drugs, but really it was the centerpiece of the Reagan administration's effort to normalize their expanded drug war and recruit citizens to serve in it. I was in elementary school when the Just Say No program was launched; my school, like many around the country, adopted the program. Police officers came to our school to tell us that if we tried drugs, especially cannabis, even once, we'd become addicted, and that people who used drugs were bad people who should be reported to the police. Many kids in my school had parents who were participants in the countercultural drug scenes of the 1960s and early 1970s and regularly used cannabis (and sometimes other drugs). We were being asked to turn in our parents to the authorities.

When I tried cannabis myself in my early teens, I did not immediately crave heroin or other drugs, as I had been told I would. The authorities, in their zeal to keep kids off drugs, succeeded only in lying to my generation and undermining the relationship between kids and adults. Once I realized they were lying about drugs, I never again trusted what school authorities told me about much of anything else.

The misinformation and lies about drugs permeate science as well. Today this is seen frequently with regard to methamphetamine, which is practically the same, chemically speaking, as the pharmaceutical drug, Adderall.[56] Yet that hasn't stopped some scientists in the United States from concluding that methamphetamine use will "ruin your brain," frequently showing electronic images that compare the brains of people who have used methamphetamine with the brains of those who haven't. The differences are then presented as abnormalities that "prove" methamphetamine use irreparably harms the brain.[57]

One scientist decided to test this claim. Dr. Carl Hart, chair of the psychology department at Columbia University and the author of the acclaimed book *High Price*, reviewed the studies that had been conducted of methamphetamine use in humans and found that for people who used methamphetamine,

> cognitive functioning overwhelmingly falls within the normal range when compared against normative data. In spite of these observations, there seems to be a propensity to interpret any cognitive and/or brain difference(s) as a clinically significant abnormality. The implications of this situation are multiple, with consequences for scientific research, substance-abuse treatment, and public policy.[58]

Drug war propaganda, left unchecked, finds its way into healthcare as well, particularly drug treatment. For instance, there is increasing evidence that cannabis can play a very useful role in reducing harms from other drug use, like opioids, yet many treatment and healthcare providers still won't recommend cannabis because it is, well, cannabis.[59] This is a kind of modern "reefer madness" that spurs otherwise smart people to cling to propaganda because the evidence contradicts their worldview.

Because mass incarceration cannot be ended without ending the war on drugs, it is imperative that reform advocates in both movements develop the ability to identify misinformation about drugs and combat it.[60] Drug scares are routine in America—and in nearly every drug scare of the last 150 years, misinformation, propaganda, and outright lies have been used by authorities to target select populations for criminalization, most often communities of color. When these lies are repeated by advocates or assumed to be true, it inhibits our ability to advance reforms that roll back criminalization. To use a phrase coined by Dr. Marsha Rosenbaum, a scientist and longtime drug policy advocate, when it comes to drugs, it's time we "just say know."[61]

Promoting Harm Reduction

Many advocates working in drug policy reform have long known of and practiced harm reduction; indeed, the drug policy reform movement over the last thirty years has been profoundly shaped by it. Even so, not everyone in the drug policy reform movement understands what harm reduction is, and it is relatively new (if not entirely new) to many people working in the movement to end mass incarceration. As a conceptual and practical framework, harm reduction may be among the few approaches that can immediately strengthen both movements and foster more effective collaboration between them.

While there are various definitions of harm reduction, the Harm Reduction Coalition defines it this way: "Harm reduction is a set of practical strategies and ideas aimed at reducing negative consequences associated with drug use. Harm Reduction is also a movement for social justice built on a belief in, and respect for, the rights of people who use drugs."[62]

Harm reduction has its roots in public health and can be applied beyond the scope of drug use itself. For instance, consider seat belts. Auto accidents are a leading cause of death in the United States; driving in cars can be quite dangerous, even deadly. To reduce the potential for injury or harm of this dangerous activity, we wear seat belts. That's a form of harm reduction.

Harm reduction is critical in these reform spaces because it accepts that human beings throughout the world have always used psychoactive substances (drugs) and are going to continue to use them, regardless of moral or legal consequences. Most do so without legal or health problems. There are, relative to the number of people who use drugs, a much smaller number of people whose drug use turns to addiction. By acknowledging the reality that, despite best efforts to discourage or prohibit drug use, many people are going to use anyway, and some will use in ways that may harm themselves, we can craft interventions that reduce drug-related harm, save lives, and improve health and safety.

Take syringe exchange programs, which have been operating legally in many states in the United States for thirty years and much longer underground. Developed by people who inject drugs to reduce transmission of blood-borne diseases, these programs allow people to obtain clean needles to inject drugs while providing proper, safe disposal of used needles. Syringe exchange programs are responsible for dramatic reductions in the transmission of HIV/AIDS among people who inject drugs. In New York City, for example, over the last twenty years there's been an 80 percent drop in the number of HIV transmissions associated with injection drug use as a result of providing access to clean needles.[63] These programs also become a pathway for people to connect with broader services and health care. While syringe exchange is still controversial in some parts of the United States, advocates in every region of the country are convening unusual alliances of health providers, people who use drugs, and local police leaders to launch and expand syringe exchange programs. Notably, syringe exchange programs are already standard practice integrated into healthcare systems in countries throughout the world, on nearly every continent.[64]

Another harm reduction intervention proven to improve health and save lives is supervised consumption facilities—places where people can consume their drugs in a medically supervised location instead of in an alleyway, a park, the bathroom of a McDonald's or local coffee shop, or the street in between parked cars. They cannot purchase drugs there—they can only bring their own drugs to consume. Such facilities operate in nearly one hundred cities around the world, including Vancouver, Copenhagen, Berlin, Paris, London, and Sydney. The only such facility in North America operates in Vancouver, Canada; Toronto plans to open an interim site by the end of 2017. In the United States, both Seattle, Washington, and Ithaca, New York, are moving toward opening their own facilities.[65] There are no recorded deaths in any of these facilities, but there are thousands of recorded instances of people getting help and often starting on their own paths to recovery.

For those who may recoil at the idea of creating a supervised consumption facility where people would consume their drugs under medical supervision, consider that variations of such places already exist, just for substances that are already culturally accepted. People buy and consume alcohol in bars, without any medical supervision. In major airports across the country, such as Atlanta and Salt Lake City, travelers can find "smoking lounges," promoted by the airports as an amenity for travelers.[66] In these lounges, smoked tobacco—by far a greater killer than heroin—can be consumed.[67] Even though these rooms lack medical supervision and generally provide no resources to help users quit (should they wish to do so), they are a form of harm reduction. By congregating smokers in these dedicated smoking rooms, exposure of others to secondhand smoke is reduced, and airport personnel don't have to deal with travelers who are frustrated by having to exit security to smoke.

Harm reduction interventions have dramatically improved treatment options for people struggling with addiction, especially heroin addiction. The most successful interventions for heroin addiction are maintenance therapies—methadone and burprenorphine.[68] Americans may be surprised to learn that many countries, including Britain, Germany, Australia, and Denmark, allow doctors to prescribe heroin to people when methadone and buprenorphine have proven ineffective maintenance therapies.[69] These interventions have proven to be incredibly effective in treating people with serious heroin addictions.[70]

As the opioid crisis in the United States continues to expand, and the response by some law enforcement leaders and Attorney General Jeff Sessions is so hyper-focused on criminalization, it is imperative for reformers to look for interventions that are not rooted in criminalization. Interventions like syringe exchanges, supervised consumptions facilities, heroin maintenance, and other harm reduction approaches may prove enormously valuable in addressing the crisis.

Finally, harm reduction can help advocates shape more effective public health communication strategies to address drug crises. Many politicians and law enforcement agents tell people that heroin is dangerous, and frequently say that even one-time use of heroin could lead to death. What if authorities took a harm-reduction-oriented approach? With heroin, for example, rather than rely solely on a message discouraging people from using it, what if authorities were to discourage use while acknowledging that some people will use it anyway? If we acknowledged this fact in policy and practice, it might lead to public health intervention messages like this:

> Don't do heroin. But if you do, make sure you're as safe as possible. Don't use alone. Have the overdose reversal drug naloxone on hand. Call 911 in an emergency. Don't mix your heroin with other drugs—especially alcohol and benzos; the combination with depressants increases the likelihood you may overdose and die. And if you want treatment, call 555-555-5555 and you'll be connected to help.

Harm reduction, as a practice and philosophy, has been shaped by people who use drugs—those who have been marginalized, stigmatized, criminalized—and has been remarkably successful in improving public health and safety. The wisdom, experience, and insight found in the networks of people who use drugs and harm reduction service providers who work with them have strengthened the foundation of the drug policy reform movement for years and can be engaged and utilized by advocates working toward decarceration. Reform efforts in both movements should, wherever possible, be oriented around harm reduction.

Strengthening the Safety Net

To realize a health based approach, we must strengthen the social safety net in the United States and improve access to that safety net—particularly access to health care.

The drug war is a systemic response to a perceived problem (or manufactured one, depending on your perspective). In his 2011 book *Drugs, Crime and Public Health*, Dr. Alex Stevens, a professor of criminology at the University of Kent, sought to understand the differences among Western industrialized nations in health outcomes related to illicit drug use. Why, he asked, did the United States have remarkably different outcomes from other industrialized Western nations, with higher rates of overdose death, drug addiction, and incarceration? While the Netherlands and Portugal have comparatively more liberal drug policies than the United States, Sweden's drug policies are similar to the punitive approach in the United States. But even with this approach, Sweden demonstrated outcomes much more like those of the Netherlands and Portugal. What was happening to account for these differences?

The evidence, Stevens concluded, "indicates that the provision of social support is more important in affecting the levels of problematic drug use than is the stringency of drug policy . . . The levels of drug use and drug problems do not depend on the level of prohibition. They are more closely associated with the level of social equality and support."[71]

Stevens is making a transformative point. To reduce the harms associated both with problematic drug use and with our enforcement of drug laws, we must not focus exclusively on drug policy but rather need to take account of the social inequalities that shape people's lives. Sweden's outcomes look more like those of the Netherlands because both countries have, in comparison to the United States, strong social safety nets and far less economic inequality. The drug war in the United States has expanded simultaneously with a constant and steady erosion of the social safety net. And the United States has some of the highest rates of economic inequality among developed countries.[72]

To end the drug war and mass incarceration, we need a social safety net prepared and resourced to respond both to addiction and to the real harms and issues that give rise to problematic drug use and the *development* of addiction. Services must be available regardless of geography, race, class status, gender, or any other factor, and all people must be able to access those services. Stevens noted:

> Long-term solutions to drug problems require change to be effected outside the realm of drug policy. If governments do have the drug problems they deserve it is not because they have neglected to enforce their drug laws, but because they have failed to protect their citizens from the malign effects of inequality.[73]

In 2014, shortly after the implementation of the Affordable Care Act, which expanded health care access to millions of Americans, I co-authored a paper about how advocates could leverage the health care reform to end the drug war and mass incarceration. We wrote:

> At a conceptual level, the [Affordable Care Act] represents an opportunity to recast substance use disorders and drug use as a matter for public health rather than criminal justice. Second, the dramatic expansion of healthcare coverage, enabling participation in community-based care and treatment, is likely to substantially improve the quality of life for millions of people, and particularly for low-income populations and communities of color, by expanding the social safety net through access to healthcare. In turn, this expansion may serve to reduce both criminal justice system involvement and the social exclusion so familiar under the structures that have developed through the far-reaching War on Drugs.[74]

Since its passage, there has been an effort underway to repeal or destroy the Affordable Care Act (ACA). For those working to end the war on drugs and mass incarceration, this would be disastrous. Consider that close to half of the incarcerated population in U.S. jails and prisons are eligible for Medicaid coverage under the state expansion option provided by the ACA.[75] Among people who cycle in and out of U.S. jails, untreated mental illness and addiction are disproportionately high, and unstable housing or homelessness are common.[76] With Medicaid expansion, states can provide care coordination (case management) services to recipients with chronic health conditions, including mental illness and substance use disorders, as well as diabetes, hypertension, and asthma. Case management helps justice-involved individuals address their housing, legal, transportation, and other social needs, ensuring they have the capacity and stability to focus on their health issues, and reducing their risk of re-arrest as a consequence.

Repealing the ACA and other attempts to roll back or erode the safety net should be resisted by the movements seeking to end the war on drugs and mass incarceration, because the safety net is essential for the systemic change we are seeking. Expanding access to healthcare—a core feature of any real safety net—relieves law enforcement, jails, and prisons of the de facto health and social service role they have been filling in the wake of a widespread opioid epidemic, a national housing crisis, and a historically underfunded community health system. What is needed is universal health care. Without constructing and bolstering a strong social safety net for people and strengthening the foundations of a just society—including, and especially, by ensuring health care for all people—the dominant system in place, that of criminalization, will remain as the primary catchall and social control mechanism for those who are poor, marginalized, or addicted.

Centering Racial Justice and Racial Equity

Given the origins of drug control in the United States, a new drug policy must make racial justice and racial equity a core objective. Writes Joanne Csete, a member of the Johns Hopkins–Lancet Commission on Drug Policy and Health, "[U.S. drug] policies have their roots in a racist and reactionary calculation."[77]

For drug policy reform and criminal justice reform alike to serve the goal of decarceration, it is imperative to address the ways in which racial discrimination and racial bias have been baked into existing drug policies, institutions, and systems for hundreds of years. From slavery to Jim Crow to redlining to the drug war and mass incarceration, the historical legacy of white supremacy, racial discrimination, and racialized violence profoundly shapes our criminal legal system and drug policies today.

The use of criminalization as a means to target and control certain populations—particularly people of color—has been a centerpiece of U.S. drug policy since the late 1800s, when the first drug prohibition laws in the United States targeted the Chinese community on the West Coast, outlawing the opiate use that was part of that community's culture.[78] The first laws against cannabis were passed in the early 1900s in the American Southwest, in response to Mexican immigration, to expand law enforcement tools for managing populations of Mexican workers. The first cocaine laws were passed in the South, as a way to target and attack black dock workers in the 1920s. The genesis of these laws—criminalizing specific populations of people of color— shapes how these laws are understood and carried out today.[79]

The United States formally launched the war on drugs as a global policy framework in 1914 with the passage of the Harrison Narcotics Control Act.[80] While it was not called a "war on drugs" at that time, the goals of the Harrison Act and the role of the United States in enforcing it abroad and at home are historically seen as the starting point for a national political framework of the criminalization of drug use and the elevation of law enforcement as a dominant response to drug use.

In 1971, the political framework developed in the earlier decades of the century was modernized when Nixon declared a war on drugs.[81] Consistent with the objectives of criminalizing particular populations, and especially people of color, a close aide and legal counsel to Nixon, John Ehrlichman, told a *Harper's* magazine reporter in 1994:

You want to know what this was really all about? The Nixon campaign in 1968, and the Nixon White House after that, had two enemies: the anti-war left and black people. You understand what I'm saying? We knew we couldn't make it illegal to be either against the war or black, but by getting the public to associate the hippies with marijuana and blacks with heroin, and then criminalizing both heavily, we could disrupt those communities. We could arrest their leaders, raid their homes, break up their meetings and vilify them night after night on the evening news. Did we know we were lying about the drugs? Of course we did.[82]

Nixon's war has had its intended effect. Racially discriminatory enforcement of drug possession laws has produced profound disparities at all levels of the criminal justice system.[83] Black people are far more likely to be criminalized for drug possession and use than white people, despite the fact that rates of reported drug use do not differ substantially among people of different races.[84] African Americans experience discrimination at every stage of the criminal justice system and are more likely to be stopped, searched, arrested, convicted, harshly sentenced, and saddled with a criminal record for mere possession.[85] Black people account for just 13 percent of the U.S. population but 30 percent of those arrested for drug law violations, nearly 40 percent of those incarcerated in state or federal prison for any drug law violations, and roughly 40 percent of those incarcerated in state prison for possession only.[86]

A racial equity framework will help all advocates understand how to address this history and the laws and practices that derive from it. Ending racial disparity in the criminal justice system is an essential component of taking on racial inequity in society generally. It is a moral imperative.

But for white people—including myself—taking on a racial equity framework can also simultaneously be an act of self-interest, in that it will help us to reclaim our humanity, which has been distorted, disfigured, and undermined through the system of white supremacy. In a policy context, such a framework will have protective effects for white people as well. Among the many problems with systemic racism in U.S. drug policies is how such policies also harm white people. Obviously, white people benefit from systemic racism in the drug war in a myriad of ways, including by not being the primary targets of criminalization—whites experience far lower rates of arrest and incarceration than people of color, even though drug use is relatively equal across racial categories. This is some of the fruit of white privilege.

But this fruit does not prevent addiction or eliminate the risk of overdose deaths. Today, when the crisis of opioid overdose is gripping low-income and middle-class white communities around the country, the health care infrastructure that could intervene and save lives is inadequate and largely ineffective. Why? Through the drug war, society made a massive investment in the criminal legal system as the primary mechanism of drug policy, rather than invest adequately in a health-based infrastructure to respond to drug problems and addiction. Thus, that vital public health infrastructure, including effective treatment, isn't there when Americans—of any race or ethnicity—need it. When it comes to drug use and addiction, Black folks are far more likely to go to jail or prison, and as a community do not generally receive the support or access to services necessary to address problems related to addiction. White folks, especially those who are poor and live in rural areas, are far less likely to go to jail or prison, but these days are too frequently headed to the morgue instead, because the health systems needed in every community have not yet been built. It's another example of how white people's collective buy-in to white supremacy is killing us—even those of us who despise and fight against racism.

A viable new drug approach must incorporate policies and practices for identifying and reporting on racial disparities, as well as develop mechanisms to address and eliminate those disparities and advance racial equity within institutions and systems. Both the drug war and mass incarceration serve the purpose of racial social control. Understanding and directly addressing racial inequity in criminal drug law enforcement equips advocates with one of the most important tools needed in efforts to end mass incarceration.

But it is not enough to correct our policies going forward. It is also necessary to address past harm. Beyond driving mass incarceration, the practice of punitive prohibition has created a legacy of harm perpetrated over generations. It has institutionalized practices related to racial disparities far beyond drug enforcement. Thus, ending the drug war will not address systemic racial bias without explicit efforts to do so. To end the drug war and mass incarceration, it is essential to account for the generational harms caused to communities, especially communities of color.

Many advocates, practitioners, and scholars have developed strategies for this kind of repair work. Frameworks for addressing systemically-perpetuated harm include truth and reconciliation, reparations, and restorative justice. Broadly speaking:

> Restorative justice acknowledges justice as honoring the inherent worth of all and is enacted through relationship. As such it affects all social structures. When something occurs that undermines the well-being of some, restorative justice provides a space for dialogue so that the humanity of all involved and affected can be restored and each person can once again become a fully contributing member of the community of which they are a part.[87]

In practice, restorative justice is increasingly used in the criminal legal system as an alternative approach to addressing harm that has been caused by individuals (see Chapter 7 in this book, by Danielle Sered, for examples of how this is used in cases of violence). While restorative justice has been used in this more interpersonal context, it—alongside its aligned strategies of truth and reconciliation and of reparations—can provide advocates with a conceptual framework for addressing harms that have been wrought by the drug war and mass incarceration, and help white people find our full humanity through accountability.

Cannabis policy reform serves here as an excellent example of where such practices of collective accountability and repair can be practically and tangibly utilized. Most of the new legalization laws include provisions that limit or exclude participation in the new multibillion-dollar industry by people who have criminal records for drug offenses. With comparatively few policy discussions about how new legal cannabis markets will address the implications of generations of racial discrimination, these new markets will almost surely serve to exacerbate racial disparities while enriching a majority group of white investors and businesspeople who, because they are white, were never the primary targets of the drug war in the first place. California's legalization initiative was among the first in the country to specifically address this issue and includes provisions to address the harms that had been caused to communities of color by prohibition and by nearly fifty years of a failed, racist drug war. As with any law, the effectiveness of this provision can be proven only through careful implementation.

The history of abuse, militarization, racism, and destruction of the war on drugs compels us to address it as a nation. We have to account for the fact that this war has harmed millions of people and disfigured our society. When political leaders say it's time to end the drug war, they're acknowledging that these policies and practice have caused harm. And the legacies of that harm live with us now, haunting our politics and distorting our policy debates, while continuing to impact millions of people through the collateral consequences of criminalization.

Americans must be truthful with each other about the impact of this war on our families, communities, and country. The mechanisms to address this harm are not new—truth and reconciliation processes have been implemented successfully in other nations, including Rwanda, South Africa, and Peru. And in the United States, truth and reconciliation processes have been used to address traumatic events such as the murder of community organizers in North Carolina by KKK members in 1979.[88]

In New York, the Center for Law and Justice, a thirty-year-old community organization led by the indomitable Dr. Alice Green, has called on New York State governor Andrew Cuomo to launch a truth and reconciliation commission for victims of the war on drugs.[89] Such a commission would

candidly and comprehensively [assess] the social, economic, and political impact of mass incarceration in New York State since 1970, including the extent to which the War on Drugs has impinged upon the civil and human rights of African Americans and Latinos, their families, and their communities; . . . [employ] a "truth and reconciliation" process to bring together law enforcement and the community at large to examine the impact of mass incarceration on those who have served time in prison, their families, and their communities; and . . . [provide] bold, systemic recommendations to halt the practice of mass incarceration in New York State, as well as redress grievances of those already harmed by this tragic policy.[90]

Such a framework gives advocates working to end the U.S. war on drugs and the phenomenon of mass incarceration—both of which can trace their roots to slavery—a tool to address the historic harms wrought by these failed, racist systems. This is especially important as the legal cannabis industry takes shape. The institutions, systems, and practices of the drug war and mass incarceration cannot be transformed without us also confronting that history and seeking to make right by it as much as possible.

Conclusion

Securing real change is hard to achieve, often requires making tough compromises, and is almost always difficult to implement. Anyone who has worked to build social movements and change policies knows that the work is long, arduous, and difficult. The work to end mass incarceration and the systems that feed it—including the drug war—is among the most urgent human and civil rights challenges of our time. It's my hope that these guidelines are useful toward that effort. The guidelines are not intended to be static or absolute. Applied together in an era of significant political upheaval and change, these guidelines will, I hope, help advocates, organizers, funders, and activists to advance substantive, system-oriented reforms, avoid being co-opted into the broken status quo, and contribute to building a movement that advances health, equity, and justice for everyone.

Notes

1. The author wishes to thank colleagues who read and provided feedback on this chapter, particularly Lorenzo Jones, Alexis Wilson Briggs, and Melody Lee.

2. Approximately one in five people are incarcerated for a drug offense. Prison Policy Initiative, "Mass Incarceration: The Whole Pie 2016," March 14, 2016, updated with a new 2017 version, https://www.prisonpolicy.org/reports/pie2016.html.

3. Roughly half of people in federal prisons are serving time for a drug offense, and the number of people in state prisons for drug offenses today is ten times greater than it was in 1980. Sentencing Project, "Issues: Drug Policy," 2017, http://www.sentencingproject .org/issues/drug-policy.

4. The Urban Institute analyzed the statistics relating to individuals under correction control across the United States and focused on policy changes in fifteen states to create an online tool called the Prison Population Forecaster. The Forecaster allows the user to recommend a variety of sentencing reform proposals to achieve decarceration. What becomes immediately clear to the user is that policy reforms principally relating to drug offenses will not at all be sufficient to end mass incarceration. See Ryan King et al., "The Prison Population Forecaster: State Prison Population," Urban Institute, 2015, http://webapp.urban.org/reducing-mass-incarceration.

5. Bureau of Justice Statistics, Department of Justice, "Prisoners, 1925–81," December 1982, https://www.bjs.gov/content/pub/pdf/p2581.pdf (198,061 in prisons in 1971); Bureau of Justice Statistics, Department of Justice, "Historical Corrections Statistics in the United States, 1850–1984," December 1986, https://www.bjs.gov/content/pub/pdf /hcsus5084.pdf (129,189 in jails per 1970 census).

6. Prison Policy Initiative, "Mass Incarceration." The population of Atlanta, Georgia, was roughly 460,000 in 2015, the latest year for which data is available: U.S. Census Bureau, "Quick Facts, Atlanta City, Georgia," https://www.census.gov/quickfacts/table /PST045215/1304000.

7. Ashley Nellis, "The Color of Justice: Racial and Ethnic Disparity in State Prisons," Sentencing Project, June 14, 2016, http://www.sentencingproject.org/publications/color -of-justice-racial-and-ethnic-disparity-in-state-prisons.

8. Michelle Alexander, *The New Jim Crow: Mass Incarceration in the Age of Color-blindness* (New York: The New Press, 2012); Carl Hart, *The High Price: A Neurologist's Journey of Self-Discovery That Challenges Everything You Know About Drugs and Society* (New York: HarperCollins, 2013); Johann Hari, *Chasing the Stream: The First and Last Days of the War on Drugs* (New York: Bloomsbury, 2016); Todd Clear, *The Punishment Imperative: The Rise and Failure of Mass Incarceration in America* (New York: New York University Press, 2013); National Academies of Science, *The Growth of Incarceration in the United States: Exploring Causes and Consequences* (Washington, DC: National Academies Press, 2014); L.B. Eisen et al., "How Many Americans Are Unnecessarily Incar-

cerated," Brennan Center, December 9, 2016; Christopher J. Coyne and Abigail R. Hall, "Four Years and Counting: The Continued Failure of the War on Drugs," Cato Institute, April 12, 2017.

9. See, e.g., Drug Policy Alliance, "Background on New York's Draconian Rockefeller Drug Laws," http://www.drugpolicy.org/sites/default/files/FactSheet_NY_Background%20on%20RDL%20Reforms.pdf.

10. See, e.g., Jazmine Ulloa, "Prop. 47 Got Thousands Out of Prison. Now, $103 Million in Savings Will Go Towards Keeping Them Out," *Los Angeles Times*, March 29, 2017.

11. See, e.g., Law Enforcement Assisted Diversion (LEAD) King County, http://leadkingcounty.org. See also LEAD Santa Fe, https://www.lead-santafe.org, and Paul Grondahl, "Albany Launches LEAD Diversion Program," Albany (NY) *Times Union*, March 31, 2016.

12. See, e.g., Baltimore City Health Department, "Substance Use and Misuse," http://health.baltimorecity.gov/programs/substance-abuse; Lisa W. Foderaro, "Ithaca's Anti-Heroin Plan: Open a Site to Shoot Heroin," *New York Times*, March 22, 2016; David Gutman, "Seattle, King County Move to Open Nation's First Safe Injection Sites for Drug Users," *Seattle Times*, January 27, 2017.

13. Mark Holden, "Criminal Justice Reform Is Ripe for Bipartisan Achievement" *The Hill*, January 17, 2017, http://thehill.com/blogs/congress-blog/judicial/312492-criminal-justice-reform-is-ripe-for-bipartisan-achievement. A prominent example of reform in action is the passage of the Fair Sentencing Act in 2010, a compromise law that reduced, but did not entirely fix, the unfair, racially biased, and unproductive disparity between sentences for crack and power cocaine. It is an example of drug policy and criminal justice reform advocates coming together, with bipartisan support, in a successful effort to reform injustice. For more analysis of the Fair Sentencing Act, see ACLU, "Fair Sentencing Act," https://www.aclu.org/feature/fair-sentencing-act.

14. I use "cannabis" throughout the text, rather than "marijuana." The term "marijuana" has its origins in the racist history of prohibition in America; "cannabis" is drawn from the botanical term for the plant.

15. Matt Ferner, "Man Who Was Serving More Than 13 Years over Two Joints' Worth of Marijuana Gets Sentence Reduced," *Huffington Post*, December 5, 2016.

16. ProCon.org, "Medical Marijuana Laws," http://medicalmarijuana.procon.org/view.resource.php?resourceID=000881.

17. Eight states (Connecticut, Delaware, Maryland, Mississippi, Nebraska, New York, Rhode Island, Vermont) consider simple possession of marijuana as an administrative or civil infraction. Four states (Minnesota, Missouri, North Carolina, Ohio) treat marijuana possession as a misdemeanor without jail time. And eight states (Alaska, California, Colorado, Maine, Massachusetts, Nevada, Oregon, Washington) plus Washington, D.C., have completely eliminated all penalties for personal possession of cannabis by adults. See NORML, www.norml.org.

18. The eight states with full legalization are Colorado and Washington State (2012); Alaska, Oregon, and Washington, D.C. (2014); and California, Nevada, Maine, and Massachusetts (2016). See National Organization to Reform Marijuana Laws (NORML), "State Info," http://norml.org/states.

19. Art Swift, "Support for Legal Marijuana Use Up to 60% in U.S.," Gallup, October 19, 2016, http://www.gallup.com/poll/196550/support-legal-marijuana.aspx.

20. See, e.g., Leon Neyfakh, "Obama Wants to End Mass Incarceration: Can He?," *Slate*, July 15, 2015.

21. See, e.g., Ames Grawert, "Analysis: Sen. Jeff Sessions's Record on Criminal Justice," Brennan Center for Justice, January 6, 2017, https://www.brennancenter.org /analysis/analysis-sen-jeff-sessions-record-criminal-justice. See also Alice Miranda Ollstein, "Under Jeff Sessions, Drug Legalization and Sentencing Reforms Will Go Up in Smoke," *Think Progress*, January 9, 2017.

22. See, e.g., Matthew Rozsa, "Jeff Sessions Is Reviving the War on Drugs, and It's Going to Hurt Minorities," *Salon*, April 10, 2017.

23. Justin McCarthy, "One in Eight U.S. Adults Say They Smoke Marijuana," Gallup, August 8, 2016.

24. FBI, Uniform Crime Report, "Crime in the United States 2013—Arrests," November 2014, 2.

25. Art Swift, "In U.S., 45% Say They Have Tried Marijuana," Gallup poll, July 19, 2007. http://www.gallup.com/poll/214250/say-tried-marijuana.aspx. It is important to consider that for years when these surveys have been taken, the respondents who admitted to using marijuana were admitting to a criminal offense. For this reason, it is likely that these polls actually undercount the number of Americans who have ever tried marijuana or regularly use marijuana.

26. Ernest Drucker, *A Plague of Prisons: The Epidemiology of Mass Incarceration in America* (New York: The New Press, 2011), 40–41. In a conversation between the author and Dr. Drucker about this insight from *Plague of Prisons*, Drucker noted, "If I was writing this now, I would add that the drug war has little to do with public safety, except to worsen it perpetuating illicit drug markets and increasing the profitability operating in those markets."

27. See Drug Policy Alliance, "Race and the Drug War," http://www.drugpolicy.org /race-and-drug-war. See generally Alexander, *The New Jim Crow*; Brian Stauffer, "Every 25 Seconds: The Human Toll of Criminalizing Drug Use in the United States," Human Rights Watch, October 2016.

28. See Radley Balko, *Rise of the Warrior Cop: The Militarization of America's Police Forces* (New York: Public Affairs, 2013). See also ACLU, "War Comes Home: The Excessive Militarization of American Policing," American Civil Liberties Union, June 2014, and Kevin Sack, "Door-Busting Drug Raids Leave a Trail of Blood," *New York Times*, March 18, 2017.

29. See Transform Drug Policy Foundation, "The War on Drugs: Threatening Public Health, Spreading Disease and Death," http://www.countthecosts.org/sites/default/files /Health-briefing.pdf.

30. Harry G. Levine and Craig Reinarman, "Alcohol Prohibition and Drug Prohibition: Lessons from Alcohol Policy for Drug Policy," Centre for Drug Research, University of Amsterdam, 2004, http://www.cedro-uva.org/lib/levine.alcohol.html.

31. For the proposition that it is a disease, see National Center on Addiction and Substance Abuse, "Addiction as a Disease," https://www.centeronaddiction.org/what -addiction/addiction-disease. For an opposing position, see Marc Lewis, *The Biology of Desire: Why Addiction Is Not a Disease* (New York: Public Affairs, 2015).

32. Maia Szalavitz, "Why We Should Decriminalize All Drugs," *Guardian*, July 5, 2016.

33. Peter J. Davidson et al., "Witnessing Heroin-Related Overdoses: The Experiences of Young Injectors in San Francisco," *Addiction* 97, no. 12 (2002). Also K.C. Ochoa et al., "Overdosing Among Young Injection Drug Users in San Francisco," *Addictive Behaviors* 26, no. 3 (2001); Robin A. Pollini et al., "Response to Overdose Among Injection Drug Users," *American Journal of Preventive Medicine* 31, no. 3 (2006); M. Tracy et al., "Circumstances of Witnessed Drug Overdose in New York City: Implications for Intervention," *Drug and Alcohol Dependence* 79, no. 2 (2005).

34. Drug Policy Alliance, "911 Good Samaritan Laws: Preventing Overdose Deaths, Saving Lives," February 2016

35. In 2014, voters in California made history by passing Prop 47, which reduced the penalties for simple drug possession, petty theft, shoplifting, forgery, writing a bad check, and receipt of stolen property, resulting in dramatic reductions to the state prison population and investments in drug and mental health treatment, school programs, and victims' services. See My Prop 47, http://myprop47.org. In 2012, California voters had approved Prop 36, which required that a "third strike" be a serious or violent felony (previously, a "third strike" could be any felony). See Aaron Sankin, "California Prop 36, Measure Reforming State's Three Strikes Law, Approved by Wide Majority of Voters," *Huffington Post*, November 7, 2012.

36. See Nick Wing, "Our Bail System Is Leaving Innocent People to Die in Jail Because They're Poor," *Huffington Post*, February 23, 2017.

37. Stauffer, "Every 25 Seconds."

38. Report of the Global Commission on Drug Policy, "War on Drugs," June 2011, 2.

39. The Global Commission emerged from another commission. In 2009, the Latin American Commission on Drugs and Democracy—a body made up of political leaders (including ex-presidents) and intellectuals from Latin American countries—published a report calling upon states to "establish the laws, institutions and regulations enabling those who have become addicted to drugs to stop being buyers in an illegal market and to become patients of the health care system." Statement by the Latin American Commission on Drugs and Democracy, "Drugs and Democracy: Toward a Paradigm Shift," 2009,

http://www.ungassondrugs.org/images/stories/towards.pdf. The commission's prestigious membership list is worth studying to appreciate the implications of such a call.

40. "Reforming International Drug Policy," *Lancet* 387, no. 10026 (April 2, 2016): 1347. "Drug policies intended to protect people, but based on prohibition and criminalisation, have had detrimental effects on public health in multiple ways and have undermined people's right to health."

41. Ban Ki Moon, "Message on International Day Against Drug Abuse and Illicit Trafficking," June 26, 2015, http://www.unis.unvienna.org/unis/en/pressrels/2015/unissgsm 645.html.

42. United Nations Office on Drugs and Crime, "Briefing Paper: Decriminalisation of Drug Use and Possession for Personal Consumption" (emphasis added), https://www .scribd.com/doc/285932597/UNODC-Briefing#fullscreen&from_embed. The paper was never officially released, and the draft itself was retracted and denounced by UN leadership after it was leaked to the public. But the mere fact that such a document was contemplated, then drafted and circulated within the UN, suggests that the evidence for decriminalization is so strong and so clear that even entities that are by design committed to the status quo have difficulty maintaining a position in favor of the drug war.

43. Ari Rosmarin and Niamh Eastwood, "A Quiet Revolution: Drug Decriminalisation Policies in Practice Across the Globe," Release (London), July 2012, https://www .opensocietyfoundations.org/sites/default/files/release-quiet-revolution-drug -decriminalisation-policies-20120709.pdf.

44. See Tom McKay, "One Year After Uruguay Legalized Marijuana, Here's What It's Become," *Mic*, December 9, 2014; David Reid, "Uruguay to Be First Country to Sell Cannabis in Drug Stores," CNBC, April 7, 2017.

45. Ian Austin, "Trudeau Unveils Bill Legalizing Recreational Marijuana in Canada," *New York Times*, April 13, 2017.

46. Special Session of the United Nations General Assembly on the World Drug Problem, "Achieving the 2019 Goals—A Better Tomorrow for the World's Youth," April 2016.

47. United Nations General Assembly, "Resolution Adopted by the General Assembly on 19 April 2016: Our Joint Commitment to Effectively Addressing and Countering the World Drug Problem," April 19, 2016. In March 2009, the United Nations Office on Drugs and Crime had issued "Political Declaration and Plan of Action on International Cooperation Towards an Integrated and Balanced Strategy to Counter the World Drug Problem," committing to meet a particular set of goals by 2019. In the months prior to the 2016 UN General Assembly special session, global organizations that work on drug policy reform, criminal justice reform, and related fields engaged their national leaders, in an attempt to influence their stance on drug policy reform and related issues and to advance the goals set out in the 2009 report.

48. "Public Health and International Drug Policy," *Lancet* 387, no. 10026 (April 2, 2016): 1427–80.

49. Sarah Boseley and Jessica Glenza, "Medical Experts Call for Global Drug Decriminalisation," *Guardian*, March 24, 2016.

50. It simply is not the case that the use of so-called hard drugs automatically leads to addiction. Though some drug users do become addicted, it is possible to use drugs recreationally and non-problematically. "Crack in itself doesn't make people violent, . . . methamphetamine alone will not make you look like one of those grisly 'after' photos in the public service ads, and cocaine and heroin are not as addictive as is commonly believed." Carl Hart, "Drug Myths Exposed." http://drcarlhart.com/drug-myths-exposed. As noted above, decriminalization is not the same as legalization. While there is little disagreement in the drug policy reform movement about legalizing, taxing, and regulating cannabis, there is a vigorous debate about decriminalization vs. legalization of all drugs. A major factor in the legalization question is how regulated a drug would be once legal. Among the best resources available to learn more about decriminalization, legalization, and regulation is *After the War on Drugs: Tools for the Debate*, a handbook produced by the U.K.-based drug policy reform group Transform, http://www.tdpf.org.uk/sites/default/files/Tools-For-The-Debate.pdf. See also "The Case for Reform" on the group's website, http://www.tdpf.org.uk/case-for-reform.

51. Christina Mehta and Marianne Mollmann, *Neither Justice nor Treatment: Drug Courts in the United States*, Physicians for Human Rights, June 2017, http://physiciansforhumanrights.org/library/reports/neither-justice-nor-treatment.html?referrer=https://medium.com/@PHR/how-drug-courts-are-falling-short-6b92e993cc3b.

52. "Labels Like 'Felon' Are an Unfair Life Sentence," *New York Times*, May 7, 2016. The *Times* editorial references Eddie Ellis and his "Language Letter": http://prisoneducation.nyu.edu/wp-content/uploads/2015/05/CNUS-lang-ltr_regular.pdf. Ellis, a pioneering founder and leader of the growing role of formerly incarcerated people in the movement to end mass incarceration, challenged the reform field to consider the implication of using terms like "offender" and "felon."

53. We also need to redefine what we mean by "public safety." "Public safety" has come to be synonymous, in common parlance, with "law enforcement." But true public safety requires a commitment to investing in the community support networks and services that make violent crime less likely. This topic is beyond the scope of this chapter, and requires further research.

54. Substance Abuse and Mental Health Services Administration, Center for Behavioral Health Statistics and Quality, "Treatment Episode Data Set (TEDS) 2002–2012: National Admissions to Substance Abuse Treatment Services," July 2014.

55. Ibid.

56. Carl Hart, "Neuroscientist: Meth Is Virtually Identical to Adderall—This Is How I Found Out," *The Influence*, http://theinfluence.org/neuroscientist-meth-is-virtually-identical-to-adderall-this-is-how-i-found-out.

57. Maia Szalavitz, "Why the Myth of a Meth-Damaged Brain May Hinder Recovery," *Time Magazine*, November 21, 2011. http://healthland.time.com/2011/11/21/why-the-myth -of-the-meth-damaged-brain-may-hinder-recovery.

58. Carl L. Hart, Caroline B. Marvin, Rae Silver, and Edward E. Smith, "Is Cognitive Functioning Impaired in Methamphetamine Users? A Critical Review," *Neuropsycho-pharmacology* 37 (2012): 586–608.

59. See, e.g., Join Together Staff, "Opioid Addiction Being Treated with Medical Marijuana in Massachusetts," Partnership for Drug-Free Kids, October 7, 2015.

60. A great reading list for this purpose would include Drucker, *Plague of Prisons*; Hart, *High Price*; Maia Szalavitz, *Unbroken Brain: A Revolutionary New Way of Understanding Addiction* (New York: St. Martin's, 2016).

61. Marsha Rosenbaum, "From Nancy Reagan's 'Just Say No' to Just Say 'Know,'" *USA Today*, March 11, 2016.

62. Harm Reduction Coalition, "Principles of Harm Reduction," http://harmreduc tion.org/about-us/principles-of-harm-reduction.

63. NYS Department of Health AIDS Institute, "Comprehensive Harm Reduction Reverses the Trend in New HIV Infections," March 2014, https://www.health.ny.gov /diseases/aids/providers/reports/docs/sep_report.pdf.

64. Gay Men's Health Crisis, "Syringe Exchange Programs around the World: The Global Context," 2009, http://www.gmhc.org/files/editor/file/gmhc_intl_seps.pdf.

65. David Gutman, "Seattle, King County Move to Open Nation's First Safe Injection Sites for Drug Users," *Seattle Times*, January 27, 2017. Lisa Foderaro, "Ithaca's Anti-Heroin Plan: Open Site to Shoot Heroin," *New York Times*, March 26, 2016.

66. Hartsfield Jackson International Airport, "Airport Amenities: Smoking Lounges," http://www.atl.com/about-atl/airport-amenities/#SmokingLounges.

67. Centers for Disease Control, "Smoking and Tobacco Use: Fast Facts," https://www .cdc.gov/tobacco/data_statistics/fact_sheets/fast_facts/index.htm#toll.

68. Jeff Ward, Wayne Hall, and Richard Mattick, "Role of Maintenance Treatment in Opioid Dependence," *The Lancet* 353 (1999): 221–226, http://www.sciencedirect .com/science/article/pii/S0140673698053562.

69. German Lopez, "The Case for Prescription Heroin," *Vox*, June 12, 2017, https:// www.vox.com/policy-and-politics/2017/6/12/15301458/canada-prescription-heroin -opioid-addiction.

70. John Strange, et. al, "Heroin on Trial: Systematic Review and Meta-Analysis of Randomised Trials of Diamorphine-Prescribing as Treatment for Refractory Heroin Addiction," *British Journal of Psychiatry* 207 (2015): 5–14, http://bjp.rcpsych.org/content /207/1/5.

71. Alex Stevens, *Drugs, Crime, and Public Health: The Political Economy of Drug Policy* (New York: Routledge, 2011), 128.

72. Gillian White, "The U.S. Ranks 23rd out of 30 Developed Countries for Inequality," *The Atlantic*, January 16, 2017, https://www.theatlantic.com/business/archive/2017/01/wef-davos-inequality/513185.

73. Stevens, *Drugs, Crime, and Public Health*, 128.

74. Chloe Cockburn, Daliah Heller, and gabriel sayegh, "Healthcare Not Handcuffs: Putting the Affordable Care Act to Work for Criminal Justice and Drug Policy Reform," American Civil Liberties Union and Drug Policy Alliance, December 2013.

75. A.E. Cuellar and J. Cheema, "Health Care Reform, Behavioral Health, and the Criminal Justice Population," *Journal of Behavioral Health Services & Research* 41(2014): 447–459. K. Patel, A. Boutwell, B.W. Brockmann, and J.D. Rich, "Integrating Correctional and Community Health Care for Formerly Incarcerated People Who Are Eligible for Medicaid," *Health Affairs* 33(2014): 468–473.

76. T. A. Eberly, Y. Takahashi, M. Messina, and P.C. Friday, "Chronic Offender Study: Final Report," Charlotte, NC: Mecklenburg County Sheriff's Office, Research and Planning Unit, 2007. M.C. Ford, "Frequent Fliers: The High Demand User in Local Corrections," *Californian Journal of Health Promotion* 3(2005): 61–71. A. B.Wilson, J. Draine, T. Hadley, S. Metraux, and A. Evans, "Examining the Impact of Mental Illness and Substance Use on Recidivism in a County Jail," *International Journal of Law and Psychiatry* 34(2011): 264–268, doi:10.1016/j.ijlp.2011.07.004. R. MacDonald, F. Kaba, Z. Rosner, A. Vise, D. Weiss, M. Brittner, M. Skerker, N. Dickey, and H. Venters, "The Rikers Island Hot Spotters: Defining the Needs of the Most Frequently Incarcerated," *American Journal of Public Health* 105, (2015):2262–2268

77. Boseley and Glenza, "Medical Experts."

78. See Richard L. Miller, *Drug Warriors and Their Prey* (Westport, CT: Praeger, 1996).

79. Ibid. *See also* Alexander, *The New Jim Crow*.

80. Harrison Narcotics Tax Act, 1914, text at http://www.druglibrary.org/schaffer/history/e1910/harrisonact.htm.

81. Richard Nixon, "Special Message to the Congress on Drug Abuse Prevention and Control," June 17, 1971, http://www.presidency.ucsb.edu/ws/?pid=3048.

82. Dan Baum, "Legalize It All: How to Win the War on Drugs," *Harper's*, April 2016.

83. Sentencing Project, "Reducing Racial Disparity in the Criminal Justice System: A Manual for Practitioners and Policymakers," 2016.

84. See, for example, National Research Council. *The Growth of Incarceration in the United States: Exploring Causes and Consequences* (Washington, DC: National Academies Press, 2014).

85. Latinos are also overrepresented among those imprisoned for personal drug possession, but the data concerning Latino overrepresentation in the criminal justice system are often inaccurate because of inaccurate reporting.

86. U.S. Census Bureau, "Quickfacts," https://www.census.gov/quickfacts/table
/PST045216/00; FBI, "Crime in the United States, 2014," table 49A, https://ucr.fbi
.gov/crime-in-the-u.s/2014/crime-in-the-u.s.-2014; E. Ann Carson, "Crime in the United
States, 2014," Appendix Tables 4 and 5, Bureau of Justice Statistics, U.S. Department of
Justice, 2015.

87. Howard Zehr, "A Needle for the Restorative Justice Compass," Zehr Institute for
Restorative Justice, Eastern Mennonite University, September 28, 2011 (quoting Doro-
thy Vaandering, "A Faithful Compass: Rethinking the Term Restorative Justice to Find
Clarity," *Contemporary Justice Review* 14, no. 3 [September 2011]: 307–28).

88. See the website of the Greensboro Truth and Reconciliation Commission, http://
www.greensborotrc.org.

89. Alice P. Green, "Begin with a Truth, Justice, Reconciliation Commission," Albany
Times-Union, December 14, 2014.

90. The Center for Law and Justice, "Petition to Governor Andrew Cuomo on Why
New York Needs a 'Truth, Justice and Reconciliation Commission' to End Mass Incarceration and the Legacy of the New Jim Crow," 2014.

PART II

Secondary Prevention

7

Transforming Our Responses to Violence

DANIELLE SERED

The United States faces two distinct but interconnected challenges: violence and mass incarceration. Ensuring safety from violence is an urgent and essential responsibility of a society and is core to the promise of justice. Society should protect its constituents from all forms of violence, but in particular it has a responsibility to both prevent and respond to violent crime. The United States has been remiss in fulfilling that responsibility because of its overreliance on incarceration as the primary pathway to address violent crime. Substantially reducing this form of violence will require acknowledging the limitations of prisons as a strategy to deliver safety or justice. And ending mass incarceration in America will require taking on the question of violence.

We cannot incarcerate our way out of violence. That is in part because incarceration is an inadequate and often counterproductive tool to transform those who have committed violence or protect those who have been harmed. It is neither the most effective way to change people nor the most effective way to keep people safe. Its standing in society is based largely on its role in protecting people from violence and those who commit it, but as a violence intervention strategy, it fails to deliver the outcomes all people deserve—at great human and financial cost. Increasingly, this message is being sounded not only by justice reformers but also by crime survivors themselves.

Prison is also limited as a tool because incarceration treats violence as a problem of "dangerous" individuals and not as a problem of social context and history. Most violence is not just a matter of individual pathology—it is created. Poverty drives violence.[1] Inequity drives violence.[2] Lack of opportunity drives violence.[3] Shame and isolation drive violence.[4] And like so many conditions known all too well to public health professionals, violence itself drives violence.[5]

In the United States, many policies have nurtured violence by exacerbating the very conditions in which violence thrives, including poverty, instability, substandard education, and insufficient housing.[6] Not only does incarceration fail to interrupt these drivers of violence, it intensifies them—interrupting people's education, rendering many homeless upon return from prison, limiting their prospects for employment and a living wage, and disrupting the social fabric that is the strongest protection against harm, even in the face of poverty.[7]

Nearly all poor communities bear the brunt of policy choices that have nurtured violence. In communities of color, the detrimental impact of these policies is amplified by historical and present injustices including colonization, slavery, convict leasing, and redlining.[8] These institutions and policies were supported by widespread violence (including lynchings, church burnings, and mob attacks) that was rarely met with punishment and often had the tacit or active sanction of government and police.[9] Exacerbating the divestment from, harm to, and underprotection of communities of color has been the concurrent investment in unevenly applied law enforcement—practices rife with disparities, from stop-and-frisk all the way through sentencing and parole. All this has meant that communities of color bear the brunt of the justice system's failure at strikingly disproportionate rates.[10]

Mass incarceration also fails to solve the problem of violence because it treats violence as a matter of good versus evil. The reality is far more complicated. Nearly everyone who commits violence has also survived it, and few have gotten formal support to heal.[11] Although people's history of victimization in no way excuses the harm they cause, it does implicate our society for not having addressed their pain earlier. And just as people who commit violence are not exempt from victimization, many survivors of violence have complex lives, imperfect histories, and even criminal convictions.[12] But in the same way that it would be wrong to excuse people's actions simply because they were previously victimized, it is also wrong to ignore someone's victimization because the person previously broke a law or committed harm in the past. Such a response to violence reinforces the notion that some people deserve to be hurt—the exact thinking about violence that should be uprooted.

Just as we cannot incarcerate our way out of violence, we cannot reform our way out of mass incarceration without taking on the question of violence. The United States sits at the crest of two rising tides. The 2016 presidential campaign brought a resurgence of "law and order" rhetoric and calls for harsher punishment. But at the same time (and in some cases even in the same place), a consensus and growing momentum have emerged to end the nation's globally unique overreliance on incarceration. This momentum is in response to a rising awareness of the devastating effects of jail and prison on people and communities. It is the product of decades of advocacy and organizing efforts—particularly on the part of those most impacted by the criminal justice system—which have commanded new allies and more energetic support in recent years. In 2016 alone, major strides in criminal justice reform were made, including victories such as Proposition 57 in California and State Questions 780 and 781 in Oklahoma, which stand to dramatically reduce the prison populations in those states.[13] Voters elected progressive candidates as local prosecutors and sheriffs in places including Illinois, Florida, Texas, and Arizona—outcomes that would have been unthinkable even five years earlier.[14] Although federal policy is influential in setting both law and tone, criminal justice remains largely a state-based and local issue— and often a bipartisan one. So there remains reason to be hopeful.

But there is a problem. As consensus and momentum to end mass incarceration have grown, the current reform narrative, though compelling, has been based on a fallacy: that the United States can achieve large-scale trans-formative change (that is, reductions of 50 percent or more) by changing responses to nonviolent offenses. That is impossible in a nation where 53 percent of people incarcerated were convicted of violent crimes.[15] In New York State, for instance, where some of the country's most substantial reductions in incarceration for drug offenses have already occurred, reducing by half either the number of people incarcerated for drug crimes or the time they serve would decrease the prison population by only 1 percent by 2021.[16] Although these types of reforms are essential, the country will not get anywhere close to reducing the number of people incarcerated by 50 percent—or, better, to 1970s levels—without taking on the issue that most of these campaigns avoid: the question of violence. It is not just a matter of morality and strategy, though it is both of those things. It is a matter of numbers.[17]

When efforts to reduce the nation's use of incarceration move beyond a focus on nonviolent crime, they face a wide range of deep-seated and well-known challenges, both political and practical. Such efforts come up against the continued salience of "tough on crime" and "law and order" rhetoric; the limited power of data as a tool to shape public opinion; deep misconceptions about who crime survivors are and what they want; the persistent tentativeness of even forward-thinking elected officials to enter this terrain; and the need to develop capacity to foster and demonstrate solutions that can take its place.

But crossing the line to deal with violence also opens up a range of possibilities not otherwise available—possibilities that will be even more essential in the current political landscape. It allows people to think holistically about the communities profoundly affected by violence and incarceration and not just about small segments of those neighborhoods. It allows people to envision a justice system that is not only smaller but also truly transformed into the vehicle for accountability, safety, and justice that everyone deserves. And it allows people to center the needs of crime survivors in their vision. This last is the dimension this chapter will explore.

Understanding why crime survivors would benefit from an end to mass in-carceration begins by grappling honestly with how violence impacts those who experience it.[18] Surviving violence can be life-changing. Exposure to trauma can significantly increase a person's chances of developing a variety of serious health issues ranging from cardiovascular problems to endocrine disease.[19] Common responses to traumatic experiences—including flash-backs triggered by sounds or smells, trouble sleeping, a sense of danger even in safe spaces, and panic attacks—can interrupt a student's education, con-tribute to disciplinary concerns, and diminish the chance of academic achieve-ment.[20] They can similarly affect a person's ability to function effectively or do one's best at work, and to obtain and retain a job.[21] Further, we know that some people who are harmed and do not get well are more likely to commit violence themselves.[22] And of course each of these factors carries not only a human cost but also a financial one. Without effective services and sup-port, these costs can deplete social service systems, including law enforce-ment, hospitals, and public aid.[23] Our set of responses raises the question of whether we would rather help people heal or pay for the cost of their ongoing pain. So far we have largely chosen the latter.

So what helps survivors come through that pain? Despite media portray-als that often emphasize their supposedly crippling irrationality (whether they are portrayed as vengeful or merciful, they are almost never portrayed as rational), survivors often act with enormous practicality, seeking precisely the things that will help them heal. First, *they want answers.* These answers, when they get them, contribute to a "coherent narrative," to use a term from the trauma recovery field—a story about what happened and why that the survivor can believe, make sense of, find some meaning in, and live with. *Survivors want their voices heard.* This desire is consistent with what research and practice teach about the importance of expression in forming a coherent narrative and in having it validated—both core elements of trauma recovery. *They want a sense of control relative to what happened to them.* Trauma is, most fundamentally, an experience of powerlessness, and experiences that counterbalance that with some degree of power and control, including over the story and the response to the harm they suffered, can contribute substantially to a survivor's healing process. *They want the person to repair the harm as best they possibly can.* It is a basic human desire to want what is broken to be fixed, and to want those who broke it to take responsibility for that repair however possible. Survivors who experience that repair are greatly aided in their healing processes. *They want something of use to come from their pain.* Our experience of being harmed is often one that isolates us, and we reconnect to the community from which the violence separated us in part by caring for and seeking the safety of others like us. Survivors know that harm done to them may be partially repaired, but it will never be fully undone. So many survivors seek meaning, power, and peace in the notion that the violence they survived could somehow be a force to protect others from the same pain. That impulse to make meaning is also supported in the literature about trauma recovery as a fundamental and useful element of coming through harm. *Finally—and most essentially—they don't want the person to hurt them or anyone else ever again.* If there is one common bottom line for all survivors, it is safety—theirs and others'.[24]

The problem is that our contemporary criminal justice system delivers far too few of these things to far too few survivors of crime, even when it metes out lengthy sentences for those responsible for harm. Most survivors do not report crime, much of reported crime does not result in arrest, many arrests do not result in convictions, and the end results of convictions—including incarceration—too often do not meet most survivors' needs. Survivors' voices are almost never heard or heeded in the process.[25] While trial may offer an opportunity for some to speak (even as many describe it as retraumatizing), in many jurisdictions across the country as many as 95 percent of convictions are arrived at by plea bargain, not trial, so virtually no survivors see a day in court.[26] All too often, survivors' questions are unanswered, their voices excluded, their input legally not required (with the exception of victim impact statements, which are not demonstrated to have a significant impact on sentencing outcomes), and their preferences frequently disregarded. What is more, the failure of incarceration to deliver public safety—as evidenced in part in the high rates of recidivism among those returning home from prison—runs contrary to survivors' fundamental need for the person who hurt them not to hurt anyone ever again. Many survivors are left with a set of responses that not only fail to meet many of their basic needs but also can block or supplant the very things that would.

Working with crime survivors, I have come to believe that despite our rhetoric and punitive policies, as a country we have not demonstrated a serious commitment to reducing violence. There are four primary things I believe we would do differently if we actually held that commitment.

First, if we were serious about reducing violence, we would regard the current rates of crime reporting as a moral crisis. In considering survivors' experience of the criminal justice system, we have to begin with their decision whether or not to engage it at all. From 2006 to 2010, a full 52 percent of violent victimizations in the United States went unreported.[27] Even in the cases of most serious violence, reporting rates were strikingly low: 43 percent of violent crime victimizations in which the victim was injured went unreported, as well as 42 percent of cases involving a weapon.[28] Even 29 percent of cases involving a serious injury (for example, when the victim was knocked unconscious or sustained a broken bone, a gunshot or stab wound, or internal injuries) went unreported to police.[29] The reasons victims give for not reporting to law enforcement include a belief that police could not or would not do anything to help; a belief that the crime—even a violent one—was not important enough to report; or, most common, a decision to handle the victimization another way, such as reporting it to someone else or addressing it privately.[30]

Even though people's experience of victimization varies based on their identity and where they live, these reporting patterns hold across demographic groups.[31] What is more, these estimates are widely regarded as understating the issue, as they reflect the participation of only those people reached by (and who decided to engage in) the National Crime Victimization Survey. Those who do not interact with or have access to systems of contact and care—or whose victimization is so minimized that they do not even identify it as such—are not represented in these already strikingly high numbers.

These numbers mean that we are in a nation where every year hundreds of thousands of people who survive violence prefer *nothing* to everything that the criminal justice system offers. When one considers the short- and long-term consequences of unaddressed violence—ranging from physical and emotional pain for people harmed to cycles of violence that result when harm is unaddressed—these rates point to a practical and moral crisis in addressing the needs of crime survivors as well as a substantial challenge to securing public safety.

Survivors make practical decisions about whether to engage law enforcement based in part on whether they believe that doing so will meet their needs for safety and justice. It has been widely documented and debated that these beliefs are based in part on survivors' views of the police. But another factor is likely underestimated: survivors' views of jail and prison. What if the barriers to survivors reporting crime involve a disbelief that the end result of the justice system's involvement—the incarceration of the person responsible—is right or will work? Thus far, debate about the causes of underreporting has focused almost exclusively on whether victims believe police involvement will make a difference. The discussion has not yet examined the degree to which survivors regard incarceration as an effective means of securing justice and safety. If survivors do not believe that incarcerating people who hurt them will result in greater safety or justice, why would they pick up the phone in the first place?

The second thing we would do differently if we were actually serious about reducing violence is to ask: who are crime survivors, what do they want, and what do they need to be safe? While the disparate impacts of mass incarceration are widely documented and understood, what is frequently underappreciated is the degree to which those *victimized* by violence are so often also disproportionately people of color, and young men of color in particular.

Although young men of all races between the ages of sixteen and twenty-four experience higher rates of violence, including assault and robbery, than any other age group, data collected by the Bureau of Justice Statistics at the U.S. Department of Justice from 1996 through 2007 show that young black men were the most likely to be victimized by violence overall in six of the eleven years.[32] For young men of color, this violence is also more likely to include homicide.[33] According to the Centers for Disease Control and Prevention, homicide is the leading cause of death for young black men ages ten to twenty-four.[34] The disparity can be especially acute in urban settings, where homicide is more common.[35] For instance, in New York City in 2015, 96 percent of shooting victims (fatal and non-fatal) were black or Latino.[36] Added to the challenge is the fact that the victimization that young men of color experience is likely to happen in a larger context of structural inequity, poverty, and disenfranchisement that diminishes their access to necessary supports; roughly three times as many black children, for instance, live in poverty as compared to white children.[37]

Young men of color are only one among many groups of survivors whose pain and preferences have been insufficiently heard and insufficiently heeded in the public conversation about crime and punishment. These other groups of survivors include women of color, people with disabilities, LGBTQ people, the working poor, undocumented immigrants, and more.[38] Together, they represent a substantial portion of those harmed, but they make up only a very small minority of the voices lifted up in the public debate about crime and punishment. Our national understanding of what survivors want is artificially monolithic and, because it draws from a largely nonrepresentative sample of crime survivors, often distorted.

If we truly listened to crime survivors, we would also find that many voices are excluded not just because of the survivors' identities but because of their views and preferences. Survivors who support draconian sentencing and punitive policies, while deserving of a voice, too, are given disproportionate space in the public discourse. Were we to listen to survivors more broadly, we would find that, across demographics, the vast majority of survivors, when asked what they want, answer with things that are entirely consistent with and supported by the literature about both trauma and recovery: validation, answers, voice, control, healing, and, above all, safety for themselves and others. Increasingly, for more and more survivors, safety does not mean—and certainly does not *only* mean—prison for the people who harmed them.

The criminal justice system fails to deliver to many survivors what they need and deserve—in part because we have not genuinely prioritized their well-being in our response to harm. What if instead of asking *Who should be punished and for how long?* we asked *What would it look like to build a criminal justice system in which the greatest portion of survivors experience a sense of justice and safety when they are harmed?* This is not a radical or partisan question. It is distinctly not an anti-law-enforcement question—quite the contrary. It is a practical question and a human question. And yet I believe we have abdicated our collective responsibility to answer it.

At Common Justice, the organization I direct, just over a decade ago we began asking this question—and rising to the responsibility of joining those who seek to answer it.[39] When asked, many survivors were for the development of alternatives to incarceration for violent crime—particularly for alternatives consistent with the principles and practices of restorative justice. Restorative justice brings together those most directly impacted by a given harm to reach a decision about how the responsible person can make things as right as possible. Restorative justice has been shown to leave those harmed more satisfied with outcomes: victims of crime who have taken part in restorative processes in the United States have reported 80 to 90 percent rates of satisfaction, compared with satisfaction rates around 30 percent for the traditional court system.[40] More recently, restorative justice programs have also been shown to significantly reduce post-traumatic stress symptoms in victims.[41]

Those impacts are in part attributable to the fact that these processes include precisely the things survivors want and do not get from the criminal justice process: answers, voice, control, repair, and a belief that others will be protected from the harm they survived. Their belief in these processes' contribution to safety is well founded: substantial research in the United States, Australia, Canada, and the United Kingdom has demonstrated that restorative justice can reduce recidivism rates by 34 percent and more[42]

Common Justice aims to make a new option available to survivors of violence in the adult court system in the United States. The project develops and advances solutions to violence that transform the lives of those harmed and foster racial equity without relying on incarceration. At the core of our work is an innovative victim service and alternative-to-incarceration program rooted in restorative justice principles for serious and violent felonies:

Based in Brooklyn and the Bronx, in New York, the program offers a response to serious harm such as assault, robbery, and burglary. If—and only if—both the harmed and responsible parties agree, these cases are diverted into a dialogue process that gives participants the power and opportunity to collectively identify and address impacts, needs, and obligations, in order to heal and put things as right as possible. In the dialogue process, all parties agree on sanctions other than incarceration to hold the responsible party accountable in ways meaningful to the person harmed. Staff closely monitor responsible parties' compliance with the resultant agreements, which replace the lengthy prison sentences they otherwise would have served. At the same time, the project provides wraparound services to the survivors of crime. The project works with a broad range of survivors of all demographics, but crucial among them are the young men of color currently excluded from most victim services—notably, a full 70 percent of Common Justice's harmed parties have been men of color.

One of the most important lessons we have learned in our work at Common Justice is what happens when survivors are presented with options. At Common Justice, we have found that survivors—even those who, before they were presented with alternatives, were eager to see the person who harmed them prosecuted and incarcerated—choose an option like Common Justice over prison, when given the choice, with far greater frequency than one might anticipate.

At Common Justice, the vast majority of survivors—in fact, *a full 90 percent*—across race, class, and gender who have been given the choice between seeing the person who harmed them in the Common Justice program or seeing them in prison have chosen Common Justice. It is essential to note that the overwhelming support among survivors for these processes is not just about the promise of restorative justice, nor is it about mercy; it is about the failure of incarceration to meet survivors' needs. While some certainly choose Common Justice out of compassion, most choose it for sheer self-interest and pragmatism: because they believe Common Justice stands a better chance than prison of meeting their short- and long-term needs for safety and justice and for ensuring that others do not experience the same suffering they did. While incarceration certainly provides some people with a temporary sense of safety from the person who harmed them and/or satisfies a desire to see someone punished for wrongdoing, it does not in itself deliver the healing that those harmed deserve. What is more, many survivors find that the incarceration of the person who hurt them makes them feel less safe.[43] For some, this is because they fear others in the community may be angry with them for their role in securing the responsible person's punishment. For others, it is because they know that the person who harmed them will eventually come home and they do not believe that he or she will be better for having spent time in prison; to the contrary, they often believe that incarceration will make the person worse. Many victims who live in communities where incarceration is common are frequently dissatisfied with its results. And even those victims who *do* want the incarceration of those who hurt them are often disappointed by what it delivers in practice.[44] Many survivors seek incarceration only to find later that it did not make them safe and did not heal them in the way they had anticipated.[45]

We do not believe Common Justice is right for all survivors. Some survivors will continue to want the people who hurt them incarcerated, and meeting the needs of the full range of survivors will require the development of a wide range of strategies and interventions. That said, we have heard survivors' resounding demand to create options that address the underlying causes of harm and generate resolutions that bring people peace in both the short and long term. Developing survivor-centered responses to violence will require far more listening of the kind that produced Common Justice, and that listening will generate a far wider range of options and solutions than have existed thus far.

The third thing we would do differently if we were truly committed to reducing violence is to align our responses to violence with the best knowledge about what actually reduces it. That is not currently what we do.

All too often, we talk about violence in isolation without an appreciation for the context in which it takes place, the people responsible for it, the needs of those harmed by it, the opportunities for intervention, and the long-term impacts of our strategies. A domestic violence homicide in a small rural town and a shooting related to an open-air drug market in a large city are unquestionably not the same, nor are they the same as a robbery and mugging committed by a group of teenagers, a sexual assault committed by someone known to the survivor, or a stabbing resulting from a long-standing dispute between former friends. Yet regardless of the type of violence, we as a nation have chosen to rely on incarceration as the single blunt instrument in our toolbox—all without any data-driven indication that it is the tool most likely to secure the short- and long-term safety of the survivors and others with a stake in the outcome.

In fact, we know a good deal about what causes violence. The four core causes are shame, isolation, exposure to violence, and diminished ability to meet one's economic needs.[46] (These are on the individual level, not the community level, though they are unquestionably aggravated by the structural factors described above.) One might argue that the core defining features of prison are shame, isolation, exposure to violence, and diminished ability to meet one's economic needs. That means we rely almost exclusively on an intervention for violence that we know is characterized by precisely the factors that drive it. Using prison to reduce violence is therefore like trying to put out a house fire by throwing a Molotov cocktail through the window. That is not what people who are serious about quelling the flames do.

Studies in fact demonstrate that prison can have a criminogenic effect—meaning it is likely to cause, rather than prevent, further crime.[47] To put it simply, prison is a risk factor for violence. This is especially problematic because virtually all incarcerated people—a full 95 percent—come home.[48] Securing the safety of survivors and communities impacted by violent crime will therefore require an honest reckoning with the degree to which our current approach delivers safety in the short and long term to survivors and communities impacted by violence. And it will require developing interventions rooted in the best and most current understanding about the drivers of violence so that we are poised to reduce it.

Fourth, if we were serious about reducing violence, we would commit to reducing one of the single greatest drivers and products of violence—racial inequity. Violence is not distributed equally. Research in the field demonstrates the disproportionate impact of violence in communities of color, even when other factors, such as poverty, are accounted for. It is also widely documented that not just poverty but *inequity* is a key driver of violent crime rates.[49] When we understand this reality in the historical context of intergenerational racial inequity in the United States, we become poised to develop responses to violence that are informed by, rather than blind to, this context.[50] Addressing these inequities will require, in part, recasting a persistent and pervasive narrative that overrepresents young men of color as aggressors or criminals, and often erases the experiences of women of color entirely.[51] The narrative about men of color, age-old and still prevalent in the media and public discourse, includes portraying young men of color almost exclusively—and disproportionately to actual crime rates—in their capacity as people committing crime, not as victims of it. This distortion, which excludes such a substantial portion of young men of color's experience and humanity, nurtures the misperception that violence and pain somehow impact young men of color less profoundly than other victims. This is not without consequence—failing to see young men's vulnerability clearly may limit our ability to recognize accurately symptoms of trauma (such as being overly reactive to perceived threats) as natural human responses to pain and fear rather than as signs of character flaws or moral failure.[52] This distorted narrative can also powerfully shape how others see and treat young men of color, with serious implications for social services, the criminal justice system, and the development of an equitable society more broadly.[53]

And while we tell dehumanizing stories about young men of color, all too often we do not talk about women of color at all. The stories of women of color who experience violence are largely excluded from mainstream white public consciousness about harm and healing. The absence of these stories—like the absence of any stories that constitute a substantial portion of a situation we are trying to understand—demonstrates and perpetuates a failure to respond to women of color's experiences of violence with the gravity and respect they deserve. When people do tell these stories, the public narrative can portray women of color as uncommonly, even superhumanly, resilient—to the point of obscuring their human vulnerability and diminishing their continued need for healing and care. This story is as old as our country. It conceals our history from us. It allows us to ignore the pain of women of color and to abdicate our responsibility to provide what they need and deserve to heal. Whether through erasure or distortion, our failure to tell and hear the stories of women of color's pain compromises our ability to develop solutions that will help make all survivors whole.

The call to transform these long-standing and interlocking racial narratives is an urgent one. These narratives hide immense suffering from view; in their different ways, they deny the validity of the pain of black and brown men and women. And when society discounts their pain, public policies will necessarily fail to include what survivors of violence want and need, and to create sound criminal justice policy that can truly keep people safe.

If our nation is going to rise to the challenge of reducing violence, we will have to pay attention to the actual impact that incarceration has on survivors, listen to the full range of people who survive harm, center racial equity in our responses, and become honest about the profound limitations of prisons as a method of delivering safety or healing. And if we are going to end mass incarceration, we must include crime survivors in the process—because their lives are at stake in our success.

What we have learned at Common Justice is that when we demonstrate care for the full range of survivors of crime, two things happen. First, we can begin, finally, to meet the needs of all survivors, regardless of their race, class, and gender, and begin to repair an extraordinary, long-standing, and damaging inequity in the criminal justice system. And second, that in a broad and honest listening to the full range of survivors of crime, one thing emerges with surprising commonality and clarity: the need to end mass incarceration—so much so, and with such consistency, that it begins to become clear that any truly survivor-centered criminal justice reform platform will have to have ending mass incarceration at its center.

Notes

1. "Patterns of Violence in American Society," in *Understanding and Preventing Violence: Panel on the Understanding and Control of Violent Behavior*, vol. 1, ed. Albert Reiss and Jeffrey Roth (Washington, DC: National Academy Press, 1993), 70.

2. See Bruce Kennedy, Ichiro Kawachi, Deborah Prothrow-Stith, Kimberly Lochner, and Vanita Gupta, "Social Capital, Income Inequality, and Firearm Violent Crime," *Social Science and Medicine* 47, no. 1 (1998): 7–17; and Cleopatra H. Caldwell, Laura P. Kohn-Wood, Karen H. Schmeelk-Cone, Tabbye M. Chavous, and Marc A. Zimmerman, "Racial Discrimination and Racial Identity as Risk or Protective Factors for Violent Behaviors in African American Young Adults," *American Journal of Community Psychology* 33 (2004): 91–105.

3. "Perspectives on Violence," in *Understanding and Preventing Violence: Panel on the Understanding and Control of Violent Behavior*, vol. 1, ed. Albert Reiss and Jeffrey Roth (Washington, DC: National Academy Press, 1993), 145.

4. James Gilligan, *Violence: Our Deadly Epidemic and Its Causes* (New York: Putnam, 1996).

5. Li-yu Song, Mark Singer, and Trina Anglin, "Violence Exposure and Emotional Trauma as Contributors to Adolescents' Violent Behaviors," *Archives of Pediatric and Adolescent Medicine* 152 (1998): 531–36.

6. Kara Williams, Lourdes Rivera, Robert Neighbours, and Vivian Reznik, "Youth Violence Prevention Comes of Age: Research, Training and Future Directions," *Annual Review of Public Health* 28 (2007): 195–211.

7. Urban Institute, *The Challenges of Prisoner Reentry: Facts and Figures* (Washington, DC: Urban Institute, 2008).

8. Redlining is the practice of refusing loans or insurance to people because they live in areas deemed to be "poor financial risks"—a practice applied almost exclusively in communities of color. See Michelle Alexander, *The New Jim Crow: Mass Incarceration in the Age of Colorblindness* (New York: The New Press, 2012), 20–26; Douglas A. Blackmon, *Slavery by Another Name: The Re-Enslavement of Black Americans from the Civil War to World War II* (New York: Anchor Books, 2009); Ta-Nehisi Coates, "The Case for Reparations," *Atlantic*, June 2014; and Alex F. Schwartz, *Housing Policy in the United States* (New York: Routledge, 2010), 332.

9. Equal Justice Initiative, *Lynching in America: Confronting the Legacy of Racial Terror, Second Edition* (Montgomery, AL: Equal Justice Initiative, 2015).

10. Christopher Hartney and Linh Vuong, *Created Equal: Racial and Ethnic Disparities in the US Criminal Justice System* (Oakland, CA: National Council on Crime and Delinquency, 2009), 3.

11. See Randy Borum, "Assessing Violence Risk Among Youth," *Journal of Clinical Psychology* 56, no. 10 (2000): 1263–88; and Jennifer N. Shaffer and R. Barry Ruback, *Vio-*

lent Victimization as a Risk Factor for Violent Offending Among Juveniles (Washington, DC: U.S. Department of Justice, Office of Justice Programs, Office of Juvenile Justice and Delinquency Prevention, 2002), 6, 8; Kenneth V. Hardy and Tracey A. Laszloffy, *Teens Who Hurt: Clinical Interventions to Break the Cycle of Adolescent Violence* (New York: Guilford Press, 2005); John A. Rich and Courtney M. Grey, "Pathways to Recurrent Trauma Among Young Black Men: Traumatic Stress, Substance Use, and the 'Code of the Street,'" *American Journal of Public Health* 95, no. 5 (2005): 816–24; Erika Harrell, *Black Victims of Violent Crime*, Bureau of Justice Statistics, Department of Justice, NCJ 214258, 2007.

12. *Beyond Innocence: Toward a Framework for Serving All Survivors of Crime* (New York: Vera Institute of Justice and Common Justice, 2015), 1–9.

13. See *Ballotpedia*, "California Proposition 57, Parole for Non-Violent Criminals and Juvenile Court Trial Requirements (2016)," https://ballotpedia.org/California_Proposition_57,_Parole_for_Non-Violent_Criminals_and_Juvenile_Court_Trial_Requirements_(2016); and *Ballotpedia*, "Oklahoma Reclassification of Some Drug and Property Crimes as Misdemeanors, State Question 780 (2016)," https://ballotpedia.org/Oklahoma_Reclassification_of_Some_Drug_and_Property_Crimes_as_Misdemeanors,_State_Question_780_(2016).

14. See Hal Dardick and Matthew Walberg, "Kim Foxx Declares Win in Cook County State's Attorney's Race," *Chicago Tribune*, November 8, 2016; Elyssa Cherney, "Aramis Ayala Upsets Jeff Ashton for State Attorney," *Orlando Sentinel*, August 31, 2016; Brian Rogers, Margaret Kadifa, and Emily Foxhall, "Anderson Defeated in Harris County DA Race," *Houston Chronicle*, November 8, 2016; and Fernanda Santos, "Sheriff Joe Arpaio Loses Bid for 7th Term in Arizona," *New York Times*, November 9, 2016.

15. Leah Sakala, *Breaking Down Mass Incarceration in the 2010 Census: State-by-State Incarceration Rates by Race/Ethnicity* (Northampton, MA: Prison Policy Initiative, 2014).

16. Ryan King, Bryce Peterson, Brian Elderbroom, and Elizabeth Pelletier, "Reducing Mass Incarceration Requires Far-Reaching Reforms," Urban Institute, 2015, http://webapp.urban.org/reducing-mass-incarceration.

17. Justice Policy Institute, *Defining Violence: Reducing Incarceration by Rethinking America's Approach to Violence* (Washington, DC: JPI, 2016), 4.

18. Crime victims show much higher incidences of PTSD than people not victimized by crime. Research shows that 25 percent of crime victims experienced lifetime PTSD and 9.7 percent had current PTSD (PTSD within six months of being surveyed), whereas 9.4 percent of people who had not been victims of crime had lifetime PTSD and 3.4 percent had current PTSD; D. Kilpatrick and R. Acierno, "Mental Health Needs of Crime Victims: Epidemiology and Outcomes," *Journal of Traumatic Stress*, 2003, 1612. "Studies of children at risk of violence show high rates of PTSD. As many as 100 percent of children who witness a parental homicide or sexual assault, 90 percent of sexually

abused children, 77 percent of children exposed to school shootings, and 35 percent of children exposed to community violence develop PTSD"; National Center for Post-Traumatic Stress Disorder, *PTSD in Children and Adolescents* (Washington, DC: Department of Veterans Affairs, 2004). See also PTSD Alliance, "Post Traumatic Stress Disorder Fact Sheet," published by the Sidran Institute (2004), available online at http://www.sidran.org/sub.cfm?contentID=76§ionid=4.

19. Joseph A. Boscarino, "Posttraumatic Stress Disorder and Physical Illness: Results from Clinical and Epidemiologic Studies," *Annals of the New York Academy of Sciences* 1032 (2004).

20. T. Mathews, M. Dempsey, and S. Overstreet, "Effects of Exposure to Community Violence On School Functioning: The Mediating Role of Posttraumatic Stress Symptoms," *Behaviour Research and Therapy* 47, no. 7 (2009): 586–91; S. Kataoka et al., "Responding to Students with PTSD in Schools," *Child and Adolescent Psychiatric Clinics of North America* 21, no. 1 (2012): 119–33.

21. M.W. Smith, P.P. Schnurr, and R.A. Rosenheck, "Employment Outcomes and PTSD Symptom Severity," *Mental Health Services Research* 7, no. 2 (2005): 89–101.

22. R. Borum, "Assessing Violence Risk Among Youth," *Journal of Clinical Psychology* 56, no. 10 (2000): 1263–88; S.N. Jennifer and R.B. Ruback, "Violent Victimization as a Risk Factor for Violent Offending Among Juveniles," *Juvenile Justice Bulletin*, Office of Juvenile Justice and Delinquency Prevention, Department of Justice, December 2002.

23. According to the Cost-Benefit Knowledge Bank for Criminal Justice, a 2010 study by McCollister et al. offers the most current estimate of victim costs, using the cost-of-illness and jury-compensation approaches. According to the study, the estimated costs related to *victimization* for aggravated assault are $96,254; $24,211 for robbery; and $1,653 for burglary. Cost-Benefit Knowledge Bank for Criminal Justice, "Victim Costs," http://cbkb.org/toolkit/victim-costs (accessed June 20, 2014).

24. Judith Herman, *Trauma and Recovery: The Aftermath of Violence—from Domestic Abuse to Political Terror* (New York: Basic Books, 1997).

25. See Mary P. Koss, "Restoring Rape Survivors," *Annals of the New York Academy of Sciences* 1087, no. 1 (2006): 206–34; Judith L. Herman, "The Mental Health of Crime Victims: Impact of Legal Intervention," *Journal of Traumatic Stress* 16, no. 2 (2003): 159–66; American Civil Liberties Union, *Responses from the Field: Sexual Assault, Domestic Violence, and Policing* (New York: ACLU, 2015), 11–23, 29–31; Rhissa Briones-Robinson, Ràchael A. Powers, and Kelly M. Socia, "Sexual Orientation Bias Crimes: Examination of Reporting, Perception of Police Bias, and Differential Police Response," *Criminal Justice and Behavior* 43, no. 12 (2016): 1688–709; and Edna Erez and Nawal Ammar, *Violence Against Immigrant Women and Systemic Responses: An Exploratory Study*, Kent State University and National Network on Behalf of Battered Immigrant Women, May 2003, available at www.ncjrs.gov/pdffiles1/nij/grants/202561.pdf.

26. Only approximately 5 percent of federal criminal prosecutions, or 8,612 out of 68,533, go to trial. See Bureau of Justice Statistics, Department of Justice, *Sourcebook of Criminal Justice Statistics 2003*, 31st ed. (2005), Table 5.17. And only approximately 5 percent of all state felony criminal prosecutions go to trial. See ibid., Table 5.46.

27. Bureau of Justice Statistics, Department of Justice, *Victimizations Not Reported to the Police, 2006–2010*, NCJ 238536, 2012, 1.

28. Ibid., 5.

29. Ibid.

30. Ibid., 7, 8.

31. See Robert J. Sampson and Janet L. Lauritsen, "Racial and Ethnic Disparities in Crime and Criminal Justice in the United States," *Crime and Justice* 21 (1997): 311–74; Harrell, *Black Victims*, 2007.

32. Bureau of Justice Statistics, National Crime Victimization Survey, Table 10: "Number of Victimizations and Victimization Rates for Persons Age 12 and Over, by Race, Gender, and Age of Victims and Type of Crime, 1996–2007," http://www.bjs.gov /content/pub/sheets/cvsprslts.cfm (accessed August 13, 2014). When these numbers are broken down by crime type, there are types of crime, e.g., domestic violence, in which other groups are significantly more likely to be victims.

33. K.F. Parker, *Unequal Crime Decline: Theorizing Race, Urban Inequality, and Criminal Violence* (New York. New York University Press, 2008).

34. Centers for Disease Control and Prevention, "Youth Violence: National Statistics," http://www.cdc.gov/violenceprevention/youthviolence/stats_at-a_glance/national _stats.html (accessed August 13, 2014).

35. M.S. Eberhardt and E.R. Pamuk, "The Importance of Place of Residence: Examining Health in Rural and Nonrural Areas," *American Journal of Public Health* 94, no. 10 (2004): 1682–6.

36. R.W. Kelly, *Crime and Enforcement Activity in New York City (Jan. 1—Dec. 31, 2015)*, 1–16, http://www.nyc.gov/html/nypd/downloads/pdf/analysis_and_planning/year _end_2015_enforcement_report.pdf .

37. *Data Book: State Trend in Child Well-Being* (Baltimore: Annie E. Casey Foundation, 2013).

38. J. Bonderman, *Working with Victims of Gun Violence* (Washington, DC: Office for Victims of Crime, 2001); M. Govindshenoy and N. Spencer, "Abuse of the Disabled Child: A Systematic Review of Population-Based Studies," *Child: Care, Health and Development* 33, no. 5 (2007), 552–58; R.A. Hibbard, L.W. Desch, and the Committee on Child Abuse and Neglect and the Council on Children with Disabilities, "Maltreatment of Children with Disabilities," *Pediatrics* 119, no. 5 (2007):1018–25; J.E. Kesner, G.E. Bingham, and K.A. Kwon, "Child Maltreatment in United States: An Examination of Child Reports and Substantiation Rates," *International Journal of Children's Rights* 17,

no. 3 (2009), 433–44; Y. Baba and S.B. Murray, *Racial/Ethnic Differences Among Battered Women in a Local Shelter* (San Jose, CA: San Jose State University, 2003); M.E. Wolf, U. Ly, M.A. Hobart, and M.A. Kernic, "Barriers to Seeking Police Help for Intimate Partner Violence," *Journal of Family Violence* 18, no. 2 (2003): 121–29; J.M. Zweig, K.A. Schlichter, and M.R. Burt, "Assisting Women Victims of Violence Who Experience Multiple Barriers to Services," *Violence Against Women* 8, no. 2 (2002): 162–80; and L. Langton, *Use of Victim Service Agencies by Victims of Serious Violent Crime, 1993–2009* (Washington, DC: Bureau of Justice Statistics, 2011).

39. Some of the most powerful examples in the restorative justice field include Restorative Justice for Oakland Youth, in Oakland, California; Community Works, also in Oakland; Impact Justice and its partners nationally; the Community Conferencing Center, in Baltimore; the Community Justice for Youth Institute, in Chicago; and the Insight Prison Project, in San Quentin, California.

40. Mark S. Umbreit, Robert B. Coates, and Betty Vos, "The Impact of Victim-Offender Mediation: Two Decades of Research," *Federal Probation* 65, no. 3 (December 2001).

41. Caroline M. Angel, "Crime Victims Meet Their Offenders: Testing the Impact of Restorative Justice Conferences on Victims' Post-Traumatic Stress Symptoms," Ph.D. dissertation, University of Pennsylvania, 2005. This study examined restorative justice programs in Australia and the United Kingdom and found that robbery, assault, and burglary victims who took part in the programs reported 37 percent fewer symptoms of post-traumatic stress than those who participated in standard court processes.

42. See Mark S. Umbreit, Robert B. Coates, and Betty Vos, "Victim-Offender Mediation: Three Decades of Practice and Research," *Conflict Resolution Quarterly* 22, nos. 1–2 (2004): 279–303; and *Scaling Restorative Community Conferencing Through a Pay for Success Model: A Feasibility Assessment Report* (Oakland, CA: National Council on Crime and Delinquency, 2015), 9.

43. Alliance for Safety and Justice, *Crime Survivors Speak: The First-Ever National Survey of Victims' Views on Safety and Justice* (Oakland, CA: Alliance for Safety and Justice, 2016).

44. Christopher Bromson, Erin Eastwood, Michael Polenberg, Kimberly Sanchez, Danielle Sered, and Susan Xenarios, "A New Vision for Crime Victims," *Huffington Post*, November 4, 2016.

45. Ulrich Orth, "Does Perpetrator Punishment Satisfy Victims' Feelings of Revenge?," *Aggressive Behavior* 30, no. 1 (2004), 62–70.

46. Gilligan, *Violence*; Song, Singer, and Anglin, "Violence Exposure"; "Patterns of Violence," 70; "Perspectives on Violence," 145; Kennedy et al., "Social Capital"; Caldwell et al., "Racial Discrimination."

47. Francis T. Cullen, Cheryl Lero Jonson, and Daniel S. Nagin, "Prisons Do Not Reduce Recidivism: The High Cost of Ignoring Science," *Prison Journal* 91, no. 3 suppl.

(2011): 48S–65S; Paul Gendreau, Claire Goggin, Francis T. Cullen, and Donald A. Andrews, *Forum on Corrections Research* 12, no. 2 (2000): 10–13; Paula Smith, Claire Goggin, and Paul Gendreau, *The Effects of Prison Sentences and Intermediate Sanctions on Recidivism: General Effects and Individual Differences*, JS42-103/2002 (Ottawa: Public Works and Government Services Canada, 2002); Patrice Villettaz, Martin Killias, and Isabelle Zoder, *The Effects of Custodial vs. Noncustodial Sentences on Reoffending: A Systematic Review of the State of Knowledge* (Philadelphia: Campbell Collaboration Crime and Justice Group, 2006); Daniel S. Nagin, Francis T. Cullen, and Cheryl Lero Jonson, "Imprisonment and Reoffending," in *Crime and Justice: A Review of Research* 38, no. 1 (2009): 115–200; Cheryl Lero Jonson, "The Impact of Imprisonment on Reoffending: A Meta-Analysis," Ph.D. diss., University of Cincinnati, 2010, 45–65; Anthony Petrosino, Carolyn Turpin-Petrosino, and Sarah Guckenburg, *Formal System Processing of Juveniles: Effects on Delinquency* (Oslo: Campbell Collaboration, 2010); Ted Chiricos, Kelle Barrick, William Bales, and Stephanie Bontrager, "The Labeling of Convicted Felons and Its Consequences for Recidivism," *Criminology* 45, no. 3 (2007). 547–81; Michael Mueller-Smith, "The Criminal and Labor Market Impacts of Incarceration," Department of Economics, Columbia University, 2015.

48. Bureau of Justice Statistics, Department of Justice, "Reentry Trends in the U.S.," updated December 2, 2016, www.bjs.gov/content/reentry/reentry.cfm.

49. See Kennedy et al., "Social Capital", Caldwell et al., "Racial Discrimination."

50. See Khalil Gibran Muhammad, *The Condemnation of Blackness: Race, Crime and the Making of Modern America* (Cambridge, MA: Harvard University Press, 2010); and David M. Kennedy, 2009.

51. Linda G. Tucker, *Lockstep and Dance: Images of Black Men in Popular Culture* (Jackson: University Press of Mississippi, 2007); Robert M. Entman and Andrew Rojecki, *The Black Image in the White Mind: Media and Race in America* (Chicago: University of Chicago Press, 2000); Robert M. Entman and Kimberly A. Gross, "Race to Judgement: Stereotyping Media and Criminal Defendants," *Law and Contemporary Problems* 71 (2008): 98, citing Travis L. Dixon and Daniel Linz, "Race and the Misrepresentation of Victimization on Local Television News," *Communication Research* 27, no. 5 (2000); M. Rich et al., "Aggressors or Victims: Gender and Race in Music Video Violence," *Pediatrics* 101 (1998); and Robert M. Entman, *Young Men of Color in the Media: Images and Impacts* (Washington, DC: Joint Center for Political and Economic Studies, 2006).

52. Opportunity Agenda, *Social Science Literature Review: Media Representations and Impact on the Lives of Black Men and Boys* (New York: Opportunity Agenda, 2011).

53. Toni Schmader et al., "An Integrated Process Model of Stereotype Threat Effects on Performance," *Psychological Review* 115, no. 2 (2008); Joshua Aronson and C.M. Steele, "Stereotypes and the Fragility of Human Competence, Motivation and Self-Concept," in *Handbook of Competence and Motivation,* ed. A. Elliot and C. Dweck

(New York: Guilford Press, 2005); T.A. Rahhal et al., "Instructional Manipulations and Age Differences in Memory: Now You See Them, Now You Don't," *Psychology and Aging* 16 (2001); A. Smith-McLallen et al., "Black and White: The Role of Color Bias in Implicit Race Bias," *Social Cognition* 24, no. 1 (2006); Entman, *Young Men of Color.*

8

Minimizing the Impact
of Parental Incarceration

ELIZABETH GAYNES AND TANYA KRUPAT

America's incarceration policies have led to the greatest separation of families since the end of chattel slavery and quite possibly the greatest separation of children from their parents in human history.[1] Exact numbers are scarce since children of incarcerated parents are rarely counted and do not often choose to advertise their parent's criminal justice involvement, but estimates are that up to 10 million children have experienced parental incarceration or have had a parent under some form of correctional supervision, and that there are roughly 2.7 million children with an incarcerated parent on any given day.[2] Available statistics reveal that more than half of those in prison are parents of minor children, most of them living with their children and/or contributing financial and/or emotional support.[3] In a country with thirteen million arrests each year, and a jail and prison population exceeding any other worldwide—more than two million people—it is clear that tens of millions of children have been affected during America's forty years of mass incarceration. And as is true throughout the criminal justice system, these children will predictably and disproportionately be children from low-income families and children of color. The risk of parental imprisonment for

African American children whose fathers did not complete high school is over 50 percent.[4]

The fact that most people incarcerated in our jails and prisons are parents to minor children remains largely hidden from public view. This is not surprising given that the criminal justice system responds to individuals in its custody only as criminals, not as parents, sons, daughters, siblings, partners, or members of families or neighborhoods. The discussion of mass incarceration—even among progressives—is typically about individual people who have committed crimes and are being punished for their individual behavior.

Nowhere is this more obvious than in the endless focus of reformers on "nonviolent drug offenders" versus "violent offenders"—a distinction that is inconsequential to children and loved ones. While it is important that parents take responsibility for their actions and circumstances, apologize for the impact on their victims and their families, and take steps to make amends and change their lives, the violent/nonviolent distinction can be detrimental to children. It is wrong to assume, for example, that the children of "white-collar" or "nonviolent" criminals love their parents more or would experience more trauma from the separation. From a child's perspective, a parent who was convicted for robbery that turned into assault with a weapon (a violent crime) may be a loving, actively involved parent whose crime was out of his/her children's view, and a parent convicted of a nonviolent drug offense who was battling his or her own addiction may be an inconsistent or unavailable parent who is still loved deeply by his or her children. This is neither an endorsement of any crime nor a judgment of parents, but rather a rejection of the classification of people and their worthiness as parents based on the classification of a crime, which tells us little about whether a person is dangerous, and nothing about the parent-child relationship or the parent's importance to his or her children. In any case, the criminal justice system is particularly unsuited to judging the importance of attachment and family relationships. By focusing on punitive measures such as long sentences and harsh prison environments rather than rehabilitative measures that sustain family ties, the criminal justice system bears significant responsibility for the conditions of both these parents and their children.

Advocates for decarceration need to be careful: claiming that criminal justice reforms will result in fewer people in prison but that those incarcerated will be "the worst of the worst" demonizes incarcerated parents and their families even more than they are now. The criminal justice system creates these distinctions and then reinforces them. A campaign that humanizes parents and all people involved in the justice system is a key component of decarceration, but it must be very careful not to create classes of unworthy people based on their crime. Drug law reform is a separate (and important) component and should not be conflated with the need to reduce incarceration on its own merits.[5]

While the most efficient way to reduce the number of children directly affected by parental incarceration and parental arrest is to arrest, detain, and incarcerate fewer individuals, that approach alone will not be effective in shifting the paradigm of punishment. It will not reduce the demonization of the parents who remain incarcerated, continuing to serve extremely long sentences, and the shaming of the children and families whose loved ones have been characterized as "the worst of the worst."[6] A more humane and rehabilitative approach to justice (not "criminal" justice) would also consider the pathways to crime and the growing body of research revealing that those who have committed acts of violence were often victims of crime first, and it would need to confront racism and anti-poor sentiments as among the intricate and fertile roots of our current punitive stance.[7]

A growing body of research has linked parental incarceration with several adverse effects on children. Some of these effects are economic: incarceration can diminish parents' economic support for their children and lead to material hardship, ultimately contributing to an increased risk of housing instability and homelessness.[8] Unsurprisingly, these impacts of parental incarceration are better recognized in health circles than by those in the justice system: parental incarceration is one of ten adverse childhood experiences (ACEs) recognized by the Centers for Disease Control and Prevention that are associated with health and social problems as an adult. The ACE Study, a landmark in epidemiological research, also demonstrates that the more ACEs a person has as a child, the more likely he or she will be to experience negative health outcomes as an adult.[9] For most children with an incarcerated parent, and particularly for children of incarcerated mothers, the incarceration was preceded by other challenges and other ACEs.[10] As a result, it can be difficult or impossible to distinguish causality of negative outcomes for children of incarcerated parents. For example, was it the parent's incarceration or the preceding domestic violence, parental unemployment, and substance abuse that led to the negative outcome?

Parental incarceration has been linked to effects on children's educational outcomes: for young children, parental incarceration has been found to lead to behavioral problems and diminished school readiness.[11] According to a study in Law and Society Review, having a mother imprisoned at any point between birth and the age of eighteen is associated with a roughly 0.35-point decrease in cumulative high school GPA.[12] However, many of these negative effects can be linked to the stigma associated with parental incarceration; in other words, the negative external response to a parent's incarceration is also damaging to children and families.

The stress of parental incarceration has effects on children's health and health behaviors. For girls, paternal incarceration is linked with an increased body mass index and obesity, due to girls' distinctive internalizing behaviors.[13] Children of incarcerated mothers have also been found to show increased depressive symptoms.[14] Paternal incarceration is associated with significantly higher illegal drug use among young adult children, likely a response to high levels of stress.[15]

The significant costs associated with incarceration—extended to the health and well-being of both the incarcerated and their families—is well documented in a report issued by the Ella Baker Center in 2015, Who Pays? The True Cost of Incarceration on Families.[16] Of the people surveyed for the report, about one in every two formerly incarcerated people and one in every two family members experienced negative physical and psychological health impacts related to their own or a loved one's incarceration. Families, including their incarcerated loved ones, frequently reported post-traumatic stress disorder, nightmares, hopelessness, depression, and anxiety. Yet families have little institutional support for addressing and healing this trauma and becoming more emotionally and financially stable during and after periods of a family member's incarceration.

And while the increased risks associated with parental incarceration are primarily associated with children's health and *not* with delinquency, future criminality, or incarceration, many are unfortunately quick to make that assumption and treat children of the incarcerated as "criminals in waiting." How much this contributes to increasing the risk for children's negative outcomes is worthy of pause and consideration. One study examining teachers' responses to students revealed that when they learned that a student had an incarcerated mother, the teacher's expectations for the student went down.[17] Is it any wonder that many families choose not to disclose the incarceration of a loved one, even to a teacher or health care provider? And is it any wonder that there is little support for maintaining a relationship—between a child and his or her incarcerated parent—that is assumed to be harmful?

Over the last decade, however, the number of children affected by a parent's arrest and incarceration and the increasing volume of their voices have garnered attention beyond the systems typically associated with the well-being of children (e.g., health and mental health, child welfare, and education). More and more, the justice system is buzzing with phrases such as "family engagement," and research is demonstrating that justice-involved people show better outcomes when they are able to make, mend, and maintain family connections. As a result, these children are now getting some attention from law enforcement, courts, corrections, and community supervision.

Yet even the systems that are charged with the responsibility of children's well-being and protection have largely failed to support relationships between incarcerated parents and their children. Family Court and child welfare systems nationally have leaned away from keeping families together when a parent is or has been incarcerated. The ACE study and other research can be easily misinterpreted to suggest that a child's attachment to a parent and the critical nature of this relationship following an arrest or during incarceration should be discouraged or ignored. Even neutral interventions such as mentoring can appear to suggest that the parent needs to be replaced, not reattached.

In no other context is the parent-child relationship so easily dismissed. In fact, elsewhere it is recognized as essential for a child's healthy development. According to the American Academy of Pediatrics: "Any intervention that separates a child from the primary caregiver who provides psychological support should be cautiously considered and treated as a matter of urgency and profound importance."[18] In recognition of that fact, the U.S. military goes to great lengths to support children's relationships with their deployed parents, including providing Skype programs and life-size photos of the parent for their children to "live with" while Mommy or Daddy is away.[19]

In part, the lack of attention to what mass incarceration has meant for children—unprecedented parent-child separation and ruptured attachments—comes from equating lawbreaking with bad and even abusive parenting. The ACE study, for example, asks adults to reflect on their childhood experiences to identify factors that might correlate with current deficits and challenges. This includes abuse or neglect at the hands of others as well as factors that do not constitute child maltreatment (parental mental illness, death, or incarceration). When factors such as parental incarceration are confused with experiences that constitute child maltreatment, the natural impulse is to remove the cause (i.e., the parent), interfering with attempts to support children in maintaining their relationships with their parents, during and following incarceration.

The most persuasive counterargument to the view that children are better off when kept away from their incarcerated parents has come from the children themselves. While few, including the courts, seem to respect the right of parents in prison to have a relationship with their children, the children have asserted that the right is their own.[20] "Viewed through the lens of a child's experience, it threatens a right so central as to be not merely civil but human: the right to family."[21] And these children (plus those who care for them and about them) claim that along with their status come some basic human rights.

In 2005, young people in San Francisco, with help from the San Francisco Children of Incarcerated Parents Partnership (SFCIPP), created a bill of rights for children of incarcerated parents. From its inception, this groundbreaking document, entitled "Children of Incarcerated Parents: A Bill of Rights," resonated powerfully with children and youth across the country, and it also provided a road map for much of the policy advocacy that has been most relevant and most successful.

Children of Incarcerated Parents

A Bill of Rights

1. I have the right to be kept safe and informed at the time of my parent's arrest.
2. I have the right to be heard when decisions are made about me.
3. I have the right to be considered when decisions are made about my parent.
4. I have the right to be well cared for in my parent's absence.
5. I have the right to speak with, see, and touch my parent.
6. I have the right to support as I struggle with my parent's incarceration.
7. I have the right not to be judged, blamed, or labeled because of my parent's incarceration.
8. I have the right to a lifelong relationship with my parent.

There are many examples across the country of children and youth speaking up to claim their right to have a relationship with their incarcerated parent. Perhaps one of the first young people to speak out about her experience as a child of an incarcerated parent was Emani Davis, who—more than two decades ago, while still a teenager—was asked to speak during a federal videoconference called "Children of Prisoners, Children at Risk" about having a father in prison.[22] She agreed to speak—if the conference organizers reframed and renamed "children at risk" as "children of promise," shifting the narrative about children with incarcerated parents from a negative one imposed upon them to a positive one they claimed for themselves. The name was changed, demonstrating the power of young voices to generate solutions. Another example, Project WHAT, a program for and by youth leaders and advocates in San Francisco with incarcerated parents, exemplifies this; the program title stands for "We're Here and Talking."

Echoes of Incarceration, a group of young filmmakers in New York City who have direct experience with parental incarceration, are claiming rights for themselves and other children through their powerful films.[23] Their work addresses the Bill of Rights for children of incarcerated parents and provides a forum for young people to share not only the nuances and details of their diverse experiences but also their recommendations for policy change. In partnership with Sesame Street and Upworthy, they made a film solely about the importance of visiting an incarcerated parent, addressing the issue from children's perspectives. Daniel Beaty, a talented actor, writer, and director whose father was incarcerated for most of his childhood, also broke ground close to ten years ago with his spoken-word piece "Knock Knock."[24] In three short minutes, Beaty describes loving memories of his father, then a confusing visit through glass, followed by years of the painful absence of his father. At the end he proclaims, "We are our fathers' sons and daughters, but we are not their choices."

Not only film and theater but books have come from directly affected children of those in our prisons. Tony Lewis Jr. recently published *Slugg: A Boy's Life in the Age of Mass Incarceration* (2015), in which he shares his experiences and his insights about how his father's long-term incarceration has changed his life in profound and multifaceted ways.

Recently Ebony Underwood, a Soros Justice Fellow and daughter of a father who has been incarcerated for almost thirty years in federal prison, is creating a national online platform for youth to communicate with each other, for professionals working with children of incarcerated parents to find one another and share resources, and for caregivers to locate resources and support. Like most of the others who have stepped forward, she has gone beyond arguing for policies to end mass incarceration, acknowledging the role of peers in her journey: #WeGotUsNow.

These and other powerful and brave actions by young people about what they experience, need, have a right to, and deserve provide the solutions that are urgently needed. We need only to consult the *Bill of Rights* to see their inventory of what needs to change. The next section delves more deeply into policy changes that are needed and under way.

Six Ways to Improve the Lives of Children with Incarcerated Parents

Aligned with the *Bill of Rights* for children of incarcerated parents are thoughtful policy recommendations and concrete reforms (several of which are discussed below) that manifest the principles embedded in them. Many of these proposals have been adapted and adopted to varying degrees in one or more jurisdictions. They have also demonstrated their potential to support the well-being and future prospects of children whose parents are incarcerated. These policies span the entire continuum of the criminal justice spectrum, including a parent's arrest, detention, incarceration, community supervision, parole, and reintegration.

Child-Sensitive Arrest Policies

Whether a child is physically present at the time a parent is taken into police custody, comes home to find a missing parent, or learns of the arrest later, children experience the arrest of a parent to whom they have an attachment as a traumatic and potentially life-changing event. To actually see a parent arrested—frisked, handcuffed, placed in a patrol car, and taken away—is akin to witnessing a parent assaulted. Exposure to violence, as the arrest may be experienced, contributes an additional adverse childhood experience, and the cumulative effect is even more powerful. When the arrested parent is also the custodial or primary caregiving parent, the arrest may create a downward spiral regarding where and how the children will survive. A study in California published in 2007 found that

> in the absence of [police] protocols or planning, 70 percent of children who are present at a parent's arrest watch that parent being handcuffed. Nearly 30 percent are confronted with drawn weapons. Many go on to demonstrate the symptoms of post-traumatic stress syndrome. Smaller

children may respond by becoming unable to eat or to sleep, losing the ability to speak, or even reverting from walking to crawling.[25]

Most police departments have few guidelines or regulations—and virtually no training—regarding the arrest of a parent or person responsible for children. And yet, when presented with information about the trauma of a parent's arrest for children, several police departments expressed interest in adopting policies and protocols that would reduce the trauma. Police officers also expressed an interest in addressing the secondary trauma for themselves of witnessing the pain experienced by the children present, and they worried about how the children would fare when their parent was taken away in handcuffs. As protests are erupting about police shootings, and police and community relations seem to be at a very low point, several law enforcement agencies have realized the opportunity to build trust with community members if children and families are well cared for when a loved one is arrested.

While several jurisdictions, such as San Francisco and New Mexico, have already begun developing guidelines for arresting parents in a child-sensitive manner, advocates for children of incarcerated parents raised the issue to a broader level.[26] In June 2013, the White House honored twelve Champions of Change for Children of Incarcerated Parents, and deputy U.S. attorney general James M. Cole delivered remarks announcing that the "International Association of Chiefs of Police (IACP) with funding support from the Department of Justice (DOJ), is developing a model protocol and training on protecting the physical and emotional well-being of children when their parents are arrested."[27] In August 2014, IACP and the Bureau of Justice Assistance (BJA) released its model protocol, which is an important read for anyone concerned with minimizing the impact of a parent's justice involvement on children.[28] At the same time, as law enforcement leaders recognized the benefits to children of the model protocol, they also were mindful of the benefits to police. As the model policy suggests, minimizing the trauma of children "is directly linked to community perception of law enforcement, which translates into an officer safety issue . . . and a clear component of principles of community policing, problem solving and conflict resolution."[29]

One year later, the Albany Police Department (in New York) implemented its slightly adapted Children of Arrested Parents protocol.[30] This included training and a detailed examination of practice, as well as data collection. Implementing this protocol fit with the department's own strategic plan, which included improving community relations and "winning over a generation" (building improved relationships with young people). Implementing the protocol also led to a more detailed approach to the execution of warrants, one that attempts to ensure that children will not be home when a warrant is executed.[31] The New York State Association of Chiefs of Police is now recommending including information on whether there are children in the home in the planning for executing a warrant.[32] In October 2015, IACP and BJA released a roll call training video to prepare officers on how to respond when arresting a child's caregiver when children are either present or away.[33]

Family Impact Statements Prior to Sentencing

Advocates have been working toward establishing family impact statements that take into account the impact on children and family of various sentencing options. (In New York, in order not to confuse these with victim impact statements, they are called family responsibility statements.)

Some jurisdictions (and the federal courts) have made an effort to formally gather and consider information about the defendant's familial role and responsibilities prior to sentencing and to consider the impact on children of sentencing decisions.[34] Questions typically include whether a parent is the primary caregiver, the extent of the parent's involvement in the child's life and home, and the level of financial and emotional support provided; these aid in determining the degree to which the well-being of minor children is dependent on the parent's continued presence in the home. Oklahoma has a statute that requires judges to ask if the sentenced individual is a single custodial parent and to inquire about child care arrangements. While this post-sentencing inquiry is not a family impact statement, it does require the courts to ensure that the child of a single custodial parent who is sentenced to incarceration has an adequate care plan.[35]

While the acknowledgment of parenthood status in an impact statement does not automatically lead to an alternative to incarceration, it may lead the court and prosecutor to consider a sentence that does not punish the children. If those making decisions about options for responding to criminal convictions (including discharge, treatment, fines, or community-based alternatives to jail and prison) consider the defendant's role in the lives of those who depend on him or her, judges, prosecutors, and probation departments might question whether incarceration is the best way to hold the defendant accountable for his or her actions.

There are several high-profile precedents for considering a parent's role, responsibilities, and importance to children in sentencing decisions. One such example is the conviction of Andrew and Lea Fastow:

When Andrew Fastow and his wife Lea were both charged in connection with the Enron scandal, they and their lawyers made their children's needs central to plea negotiations. The result was staggered sentences, so that the children would not be left parentless. Rather than being decried as special treatment, similar consideration should routinely be extended to children of lawbreakers whose collars are other than white.[36]

In 2013, former congressman Jesse Jackson Jr. and his wife were accorded sentences to be served at different times. As reported in the *New York Times*, "The judge granted a request from the couple, who have two children, ages 9 and 13, that they be allowed to serve their sentences one at a time."[37] A more recent example is that of the high-profile couple from *The Real Housewives of New Jersey*, Teresa Giudice and her husband, Joe Giudice. The nation watched and seemed to support that the couple was being sentenced to prison consecutively, so that one of the parents would remain with the children at all times.

In each of these cases, the defendants were wealthy or famous. Does this suggest that rich and famous parents are needed by their children, but poor parents are not?

Proximity and Visiting

Even if a parent is sent to prison despite the fact that the child would fare better with that parent remaining at home or in the community, the relationship can be maintained if it is acknowledged and respected by the corrections department. A child's right to speak with, see, and touch his or her parent is dependent on access to jails or prisons. Access is abridged in county jails (located in the county of arrest, which is often the county where the children and family reside) due to a lack of visiting hours, a requirement that visits involve no physical contact, and few if any provisions for children. If a parent is sentenced to prison (for sentences that are more than one year), distance is almost always a barrier. Prisons are largely located in distant, rural areas, constructed to provide jobs for the people who live nearby. The sites are typically more than a hundred miles from the cities where most families live, and a fair distance from public transportation. Unfortunately, in most states, proximity to children and family is still not considered in correctional prison assignment and transfer policies. This is discussed further below.

Improving Communication Between Incarcerated Parents and Their Children

A recent analysis of the 2011–12 National Survey of Children's Health data suggests that the trauma and stigma experienced by children of incarcerated parents can be reduced in part by improving communication between the child and the incarcerated parent and by making visits with incarcerated parents more child-friendly.[38] Maintaining these connections from behind bars has been shown not only to be beneficial to the well-being of children but also to be one of the most crucial factors in success for parents returning to the community.[39] A large 2011 study of the effects of visiting on people in Minnesota prisons demonstrated that visiting has a statistically significant effect on recidivism.[40] The report stated that visiting "can sustain or broaden [incarcerated parents'] networks of support," which was important to lowering recidivism; even one visit lowered the likelihood that an individual would commit future felonies or violate the conditions of their release (by 13 and 25 percent, respectively).[41] Yet virtually all prison assignments ignore the location of children and families. Security levels, program availability, and medical or mental health needs are all part of the algorithm in determining which prison is assigned, even if it is farthest from the children. In fact, little information about the prisoner's status as a parent is even collected in most jurisdictions.

Visits are hard to navigate, are expensive, and may involve long waits, invasive searches, rude prison staff, crowded visiting rooms, and difficult conversations. And yet most people who are able to visit find it more satisfying than the alternative of not visiting. For those who cannot afford the high costs, the effects are dire. In the Ella Baker Center report *Who Pays?*, the authors illustrate how incarceration "damages familial relationships and stability by separating people from their support systems, disrupting continuity of families, and causing lifelong health impacts that impede families from thriving."[42] The report goes on to say:

> The high cost of maintaining contact with incarcerated family members led more than one in three families (34%) into debt to pay for phone calls and visits alone. Family members who were not able to talk or visit with their loved ones regularly were much more likely to report experiencing negative health impacts related to a family member's incarceration.[43]

If prisons continue to be in remote areas, there must be accommodation to reduce costs and increase access for families. This would begin with a fundamental acceptance that in the vast majority of cases it is beneficial to the child to be able "to speak with, see, and touch" his or her parent. The denial of contact is harmful to children and does nothing to make prisons safer or saner (and actually makes them less safe and less sane), nor does it make incarcerated people better prepared to return to the community.

In some correctional facilities, email and video visiting are available, though video visiting sometimes requires traveling to the jail or to another site. Video visiting can increase parent-child contact when offered as a *supplement* to in-person visiting, but in many jails in particular, it is being used to replace face-to-face visits. In some cases, the technology companies require jails to sign a contract agreeing to eliminate face-to-face visits when they sign up for the video technology. Washington, D.C., eliminated in-person visits in their jails for men, until a lawsuit eventually mandated the restoration of face-to-face visits. In 2015, the Texas state legislature passed HB 549, ensuring that incarcerated people receive a minimum of two 20-minute in-person, face-to-face visits per week at Texas's county jails. Sadly, these visits are non-contact, and this is very little time, especially for a child to visit a parent. Unfortunately, there is also a grandfather clause that excludes jails where creating the infrastructure for in-person visits (such as for jails recently constructed without visiting room capacity) would impose a financial "burden."

Many of the methods used to increase communication (phone calls and video visiting, for example) are part of the ever-expanding "private prison" business that drives enormous profits—not only to those who operate private prisons and detention centers, but also to a wide range of companies that sell their products to law enforcement agencies, from police to parole. This is true for video visiting, where in addition to the business deals, families are often charged for video visits. Private prisons, commissaries, and phone calls have always generated profits for the private sector, but now there are security cameras, debit release cards, electronic bracelets, electronic reporting systems, tablets designed for jails, and all manner of goods and services that feed off the punishment paradigm, during and after incarceration. And the companies that profit directly by operating prisons have assured their shareholders that despite the "bipartisan" rhetoric about criminal justice reform, they are looking to a strong economic future and little danger of reduced contracts or profits.

Despite the profit, convenience (for correctional staff), and technology-as-new-toy draws toward video visiting, we need only to go to a visiting room or speak with children to understand how in-person, face-to-face contact visits in a child-friendly environment are critically important. With the exception of those who are very young, children want to decide whether, when, and how often they visit their parents. This is true regardless of the crime for which a parent was convicted, or the length of sentence—or even if the child didn't know the parent prior to incarceration. As Emani Davis pointed out, "Many people think we're doing a service to children, when a parent is doing life, in having them sever contact. But as children, we understand who we are as human beings by understanding who our parents are."[44]

Through visits, children can learn to appreciate that their parents have both strengths and deficiencies, *like all parents*. Cecily Carr, whose father was incarcerated for more than twenty years, including most of her childhood, mentions this in the many trainings she facilitates. She says while she loves her father, visits helped her "pick up the apple and throw it far from the tree," deciding what about her father she wanted to replicate and how she wanted to be different, while also maintaining a lifelong relationship with him.[45]

Family Centers, such as those the Osborne Association offers in seven New York State prisons, provide the quality experience that nurtures parent-child communication, healing, and active parenting during visits.[46] Hour Children runs a children's center in the Bedford Hills correctional facility that is a national model for mother-child visiting.[47]

Reentry and Reintegration

Returning home would not be so difficult if people could remain meaningfully connected to their families during incarceration. Yet many of our policies are backward. For example, in New York, incarcerated people are initially placed far away from home and have to "earn" their way closer to home as they near their release. At this point, many relationships will have been severed because of distance, cost, and time. This policy certainly does not consider children's attachment needs and the need for families to adjust to the separation by being able to see each other.

While the most frequently asked question by children of an incarcerated parent may be "When are you coming home?" (with the answer given setting off an eager countdown), both children and families are often unprepared for what "coming home" really means. Despite increasing investment (or at least plans for future investment) in "reentry programs" and government focus on employment, housing, and treatment needs upon release, the actual reentry program of first and last resort is the family.

As is documented in *Who Pays?*:

Despite their often-limited resources, families are the primary resource for housing, employment, and health needs of their formerly incarcerated loved ones, filling the gaps left by diminishing budgets for reentry services. Two-thirds (67%) of respondents' families helped them find housing. Nearly one in five families (18%) involved in our survey faced eviction, were denied housing, or did not qualify for public housing once their formerly incarcerated family member returned. Reentry programs, nonprofits, and faith-based organizations combined did not provide housing and other support at the levels that families did.[48]

Children—especially older children—anticipating the release of their incarcerated parents think about larger community-level challenges that their parents will face, such as trying to find work. They understand that sustaining their relationship will be dependent on their parents' ability to sustain themselves after release. This will require more than simply releasing more people or releasing them sooner (although these are good ideas, too).

In addition to changing policies, such as public housing restrictions and parole conditions, there also needs to be support for families that now have another mouth to feed. One recommendation put forth by the Osborne Association is to implement "kinship reentry support," similar to kinship foster care, which would temporarily compensate families who make a home for returning citizens.[49]

Although criminal justice officials (and the politicians who appoint them) may bear the major responsibility for the four-decade run-up of the prison population, the solutions may lie largely outside the justice system. Many parents returning home fear being judged and do not know how to navigate their children's schools and other bureaucracies, which can be daunting even without the stigma of a criminal conviction. Engaging schools, mental health providers, employers, and landlords to support children and their families during the reentry period would also go a long way toward promoting positive outcomes.

For any and all of the reforms mentioned here to be meaningfully and sustainably achieved, the leadership of those directly affected will have to be nurtured and supported. Only when this happens can we truly begin to shift the current punishment paradigm that drives overincarceration toward one that embodies the realization of the *Bill of Rights* for the children of incarcerated parents and supports positive outcomes for the individuals inside our correctional facilities as well as for their children and families,

We—policy makers, researchers, and service providers—should not think that we know what people need. We should ask them and support them in developing their own solutions. Young people with incarcerated parents are experts on what they need to succeed. Yet much research has not included them and has been deficit-focused, outlining the risks associated with having an incarcerated parent, not the resilience. Lifting up the voices and leadership of youth means shifting away from a currently very negative narrative—authored by others, not themselves—which actually serves to increase the risk of negative outcomes, not mitigate it. We need research that involves them, values them as experts on their own lives and experiences, and includes knowing more about what helps them succeed and be so resilient.

This can increase their hopes for a bright future driven by their own talents and desires, not the decisions of their parents. If we focus on, support, nurture, and build upon the leadership of youth who have experienced parental incarceration, and if we truly embrace them when they say "Nothing about us without us," we may succeed in rolling back decades of harm inflicted by mass incarceration.

Notes

1. M. Alexander, *The New Jim Crow: Mass Incarceration in the Age of Colorblindness* (New York: The New Press, 2010).

2. Sentencing Project, *Incarcerated Parents and Their Children: Trends 1991–2007* (Washington, DC: Sentencing Project, 2009); Pew Charitable Trusts, *Collateral Costs: Incarceration's Effect on Economic Mobility* (Washington, DC: Pew Charitable Trusts, 2010).

3. L.E. Glaze and L.M. Maruschak, *Parents in Prison and Their Minor Children*, Bureau of Justice Statistics, Department of Justice, March 30, 2010.

4. C. Wildeman, "Parental Imprisonment, the Prison Boom, and the Concentration of Childhood Disadvantage," *Demography* 46, no. 2 (May 2009): 265–80.

5. For a recent discussion of the need to address violent crime as part of decarceration efforts, see J. Pfaff, "A Better Approach to Violent Crime," *Wall Street Journal*, January 27, 2017.

6. State Senator Jim Hughes, Columbus, Ohio, quoted in T. Jackson, "Kasich Signs Bill Targeting Violent Criminals," *Sandusky Register*, June 16, 2016.

7. Common Justice, *Accounting for Violence*, 2017.

8. A. Geller, I. Garfinkel, and B. Western, "Paternal Incarceration and Support for Children in Fragile Families," *Demography* 48, no. 1 (February 2011): 25–47; O. Schwartz-Soicher, A. Geller, and I. Garfinkel, "The Effect of Paternal Incarceration on Material Hardship," *Social Service Review* 85, no. 3 (September 2011); A. Geller and A. Franklin, "Paternal Incarceration and the Housing Security of Urban Mothers," *Journal of Marriage and the Family* 76, no. 2 (April 2014): 411–27; S. Wakefield and C.J. Wildeman, *Children of the Prison Boom: Mass Incarceration and the Future of American Inequality* (Oxford: Oxford University Press, 2014).

9. The Adverse Childhood Experiences questionnaire asks about ten types of childhood trauma that occurred in a child's life before s/he reached eighteen, including three types of abuse (sexual, physical, emotional), two types of neglect (physical, emotional), and five types of family-related challenges (a parent who was incarcerated, a caregiver who was abused, a household member with a mental illness, a household member who abused alcohol or drugs, or parents who separated or divorced). See https://www.cdc.gov/violenceprevention/acestudy/about.html.

10. S. Wakefield and C.J. Wildeman, *Children of the Prison Boom*.

11. T.A.L. Craigie, "The Effect of Paternal Incarceration on Early Childhood Behavioral Problems: A Racial Comparison," *Journal of Ethnicity and Criminal Justice* 9, no. 3 (2011): 179–99; K. Turney and A.R. Haskins, "Falling Behind? Children's Early Grade Retention After Paternal Incarceration," *Sociology of Education* 87, no. 4 (2014): 241–58.

12. J. Hagan and H. Foster, "Children of the American Prison Generation: Student and School Spillover Effects of Incarcerating Mothers," *Law and Society Review* 46, no. 1 (March 2012): 37–69.

13. M.E. Roettger and J.D. Boardman, "Parental Incarceration and Gender-Based Risks for Increased Body Mass Index: Evidence from the National Longitudinal Study

of Adolescent Health in the United States," *American Journal of Epidemiology* 175, no. 7 (2012): 636–44.

14. H. Foster and J. Hagan, "Maternal and Paternal Imprisonment in the Stress Process," *Social Science Research* 42, no. 3 (2013): 650–69.

15. M.E. Roettger, R.R. Swisher, D.C. Kuhl, and J. Chavez, "Paternal Incarceration and Trajectories of Marijuana and Other Illegal Drug Use from Adolescence into Young Adulthood: Evidence from Longitudinal Panels of Males and Females in the United States," *Addiction* 106, no. 1 (2011): 121–32). Foster and Hagan, "Maternal and Paternal Imprisonment."

16. S. deVuono-Powell, C. Schweidler, A. Walters, and A. Zohrabi, *Who Pays? The True Cost of Incarceration on Families* (Oakland, CA: Ella Baker Center, 2015).

17. D.H. Dallaire, A. Ciccone, L.C. Wilson, "Teachers' Experiences with and Expectations of Children with Incarcerated Parents," *Journal of Applied Developmental Psychology* 31, no. 4 (2010): 281–90.

18. American Academy of Pediatrics, "Developmental Issues for Young Children in Foster Care: Committee on Early Childhood, Adoption, and Dependent Care," *Pediatrics* 106, no. 5 (2000): 1146.

19. K. Zezima, "When Soldiers Go to War, Flat Daddies Hold Their Place at Home," *New York Times*, September 30, 2006.

20. C. Boudin, "Children of Incarcerated Parents: The Child's Constitutional Right to the Family Relationship," *Journal of Criminal Law and Criminology* 101, no. 1 (2011).

21. Nell Bernstein, *All Alone in the World: Children of the Incarcerated* (New York: The New Press, 2005), 269–70.

22. Emani Davis is a nationally recognized advocate for children of incarcerated parents and also the daughter of Liz Gaynes.

23. See the website of Echoes of Incarceration, www.echoesofincarceration.org.

24. Beaty's website is www.danielbeaty.com.

25. G. Puddefoot and L.K. Foster, *Keeping Children Safe When Their Parents Are Arrested: Local Approaches That Work* (Sacramento: California Research Bureau, 2007).

26. J. Lang and C. Bory, "A Collaborative Model to Support Children Following a Caregiver's Arrest: Responding To Children Of Arrested Caregivers Together (REACT)," Connecticut Center for Effective Practice and Child Health and Development Institute of Connecticut, Inc., September 2012.

27. M. Defraites, "Lowering Incarceration Rates, Honoring Children of Incarcerated Parents," June 12, 2013, https://obamawhitehouse.archives.gov/blog/2013/06/12/lowering -incarceration-rates-honoring-children-incarcerated-parents.

28. Office of Public Affairs, Department of Justice, "Department of Justice and the International Association of Chiefs of Police Release Groundbreaking Model Policy: Safeguarding Children of Arrested Parents," press release, July 31, 2014.

29. International Association of Chiefs of Police and Department of Justice, *Safeguarding Children of Arrested Parents: A Model Protocol*, 2014, 11.

30. International Association of Chiefs of Police and Bureau of Justice Assistance, "Spotlight on Albany Police Department," in *Implementing a Parental Arrest Policy to Safeguard Children: A Guide for Police Executives*, August 2016, 12.

31. Albany police chief Brendan Cox, personal communication, August 2, 2016.

32. *The New York State Chief's Chronicle* (New York State Association of Chiefs of Police), June 2016.

33. The use of training videos during roll call when officers report for their shifts each day is not unprecedented. IACP also uses these tools to train officers on responding to other high-need groups, such as people living with Alzheimer's and other dementias.

34. Senator Carol Liu SCR 20 Fact sheet, 2009. SCR20 can be accessed at http://www.leginfo.ca.gov/pub/09-10/bill/sen/sb_0001-0050/scr_20_bill_20090901_chaptered.pdf; D.N. Newell, personal communication, April 11, 2012.

35. Oklahoma Statute Title §22-20.

36. Bernstein, *All Alone in the World*, 260.

37. A. Southall, "Jesse Jackson, Jr., Gets 30 Months, and His Wife 12, to Be Served at Separate Times," *New York Times*, August 14, 2013.

38. D. Murphey and P.M. Cooper, *Parents Behind Bars: What Happens to Their Children?* (Bethesda, MD: ChildTrends, 2015).

39. M.T.Berg and B.M. Huebner, "Reentry and the Ties That Bind: An Examination of Social Ties, Employment and Recidivism," *Justice Quarterly* 28, no.2 (2011): 382–410; C.Shapiro and M. Schwartz, "Coming Home: Building on Family Connections," *Corrections Management Quarterly* 5, no. 3 (2001): 52–61.

40. G. Duwe and V. Clark, "Blessed Be the Social Tie That Binds: The Effect of Visitation on Offender Recidivism," *Criminal Justice Policy Review* 24, no. 3 (2011): 271–96.

41. Ibid., 29.

42. DeVuono-Powell et al., *Who Pays?*

43. Ibid., 9.

44. Bernstein, *All Alone in the World*, 95.

45. C. Carr, personal communication, 2014.

46. The Osborne Association's website is www.osborneny.org.

47. The Hour Children website is www.hourchildren.org.

48. DeVuono-Powell et al., *Who Pays?*, 9.

49. In 2017, the Osborne Association circulated a concept paper describing kinship reentry to city and state legislators. There was interest, but to date this has not been implemented.

9

Health and Decarceration

ROSS MACDONALD AND HOMER VENTERS

There can be no more compelling case for decarceration than a look inside the walls of American jails and prisons. Here there is ample evidence of failed management strategies, unmet community needs, and often a mismatch between the needs and abilities of almost everyone involved. While it is certainly true that jails and prisons house very sick and high-needs inmates, it is equally important to realize that these settings also create new health risks for the incarcerated. These risks are not spread evenly across the population, much like the risk of incarceration itself. The large disparities in class and race that play into arrest and conviction continue inside the walls of jails and prisons, with even less transparency. In addition, the inability of criminal justice systems to break the cycles of repeated incarcerations has created a cohort of high-needs people with substance use histories and housing problems that are largely unaddressed.

As these people repeatedly cycle through jails, homeless shelters, inpatient psychiatric settings, and street homelessness, the arc of their lives rarely is bent toward any improvement, despite the expenditure of enormous resources at every point of contact. This is in part because the considerable health services that are provided in jails and prisons lack consistent oversight or accountability in terms of access or quality.

The mandate to provide health care to the incarcerated makes prisoners the only group of American civilians who are guaranteed a "right" to health care. This right is linked to the Eighth Amendment of the U.S. Constitution via prohibition against "cruel and unusual" punishment, however, meaning that very common and broadly defined types of malpractice or unintentional lapses in care do not constitute a breach of this right. In addition, the funding of this care is local, as is the oversight, leading to many inconsistent and narrowly focused correctional health services.

Not all the examples of prison health care are negative. In some settings, efforts to establish teams that plan for an inmate's discharge from prison have improved health and other outcomes after incarceration. In addition, data from prior incarcerations can be leveraged to divert people after arrest toward treatment and away from jail or prison.

Such examples notwithstanding, in the discussion of how to decarcerate the United States, an examination of the health risks of incarceration provides ample evidence of the specific failures of mass incarceration, as well as guidance about which groups of currently incarcerated people can be better served in alternate settings. In addition, the expansion of health insurance and coordinated case management created by the Affordable Care Act drew community health systems and insurance corporations into the discussion of the human and financial costs of mass incarceration. Prior to the 2016 election, there was some hope that this involvement could be leveraged for positive changes in correctional health care and coordination with aftercare upon reentry. But at the time of this writing (2017) no assumptions can be made about the future of most health care policies in America.

Health Risks of Incarceration

In the United States, we have come to accept the narrative that jails and prisons receive an increasingly sick and high-needs cohort of people. However, as incarceration has evolved to focus on those with nonviolent charges and with behavioral health problems, there has been relatively little analysis of the de novo health risks that these settings confer on the incarcerated. Adverse outcomes among the incarcerated, from missed medications to injury from violence or overdose death after release, reflect an interaction between inmates' own characteristics and the risks that come from their surroundings. Understanding how these health issues interact is key to improving outcomes for the incarcerated, but also for designing alternatives that might improve community outcomes and avoid the need for incarceration.

The most reliably reported health outcome in jails and prisons is death, with the U.S. Department of Justice's Bureau of Justice Statistics (BJS) receiving and aggregating basic death statistics. While most deaths in custody are linked to long-standing chronic illness, failures in provision of medications or other types of care can precipitate early death in jail or prison. Rates of suicide are far greater in jails, where people are typically held before they are convicted or for sentences of less than one year, than in prisons, and reflect the chaos of new criminal charges as well as the relative lack of knowledge about the people cycling through jail settings. In the most recent BJS report, covering 2000–2013, suicide was the leading cause of death in jails for every year of the reporting period, accounting for 34 percent of all jail deaths in 2013. In prison, natural causes of death predominate, with illness-related deaths such as heart and liver disease and cancer accounting for 89 percent of deaths in 2013. It is difficult to compare the rates of mortality between jail and prison because the data included by BJS are measured per 100,000 inmates and there are dramatic differences in length of stay and the age of inmates between the two types of settings.[1]

Another important health risk of incarceration is injury. Unlike deaths, injuries in jail and prison are not collected or analyzed in a standardized way, despite their extremely high prevalence. We conducted an analysis of injuries

Table 9.1. Top Five Causes of Death, Overall Trend 2008–2013

Jail:	Suicide ↑	Heart disease ↑	Alcohol/ drug ↑	Accident/ homicide ↑	AIDS-related ↓
Prison:	Heart disease ↑	Cancer ↑	Liver disease ↑	AIDS-related ↓	Respiratory ↓

in the New York City jail system in 2011, which revealed that rates of injury among inmates were over 736 per 1,000 person-years, far in excess of community rates (which span approximately 90–300 per 1,000 person-years). In subsequent years, we have further refined our injury-tracking efforts to gather more information about the intentionality, cause, and circumstances of injuries to our patients. A major feature of this work has been to modify our electronic health record to allow for aggregate collection of health outcomes alongside variables that can be analyzed as part of these health outcomes, such as individual patient characteristics, environmental characteristics, mechanisms of injury, and so forth. For example, we are able to track injuries that include blows to the head and examine the percentage of inmate fights versus uses of force with security staff that cause this sort of injury.[2]

Our analyses of injuries led us to examine the relationship between self-harm and potential predictive factors. We observed that the incidence of self-harm was increasing dramatically in 2011 and 2012. Clinical staff reported that this was often a function of the stress of being placed in solitary confinement, especially for adolescents and patients with mental illness. In order to better characterize these observations, we analyzed approximately 225,000 patient admissions in our electronic health record. We found that being adolescent, having serious mental illness, and exposure to solitary confinement were all risk factors that increased the likelihood of being in the group that self-harmed by six to eight times. Another way of looking at this data was that only about 7 percent of people who entered the jail ever went into solitary confinement. Nonetheless, more than half (53 percent) of all the self-harm occurred in this small group, as did almost half (45 percent) of the potentially lethal self-harm.[3] We followed this analysis with another that examined approximately fifty thousand first-time jail admissions and revealed significant racial and age disparities in who received punishment (via solitary confinement) and who received treatment (in the jail mental health service). In this analysis, African American men were 2.4 times more likely to be confined in solitary than white men, even when adjusting for length of stay.[4] These analyses reveal the physical harm and associated trauma that is a component of incarceration. They also reveal that the same racial disparities that are associated with incarceration may compound the adverse health consequences conferred by incarceration itself.

Aside from the human toll on individuals and their families, a great deal of expense is incurred by these health outcomes. For example, in our self-harm analysis, we calculated that every 100 acts of self-harm (there were more than 2,000 in this three-year analysis) entailed 36 transfers to a higher level of care and 3,760 hours of escort time by security staff, usually on overtime.

These data, along with favorable political circumstances and concerted collaboration between mental health and security staff, have led to virtual elimination in the use of solitary confinement for adolescents and people with serious mental illness in the New York City jail system. But few systems have the political will, the local resources, or the capital necessary to implement alternative models to safely house those with significant behavioral challenges.

Supportive Housing and Incarceration

Another aspect of the folly of mass incarceration involves those who cycle through jails repeatedly. In New York City, we have identified a group of eight hundred frequently incarcerated individuals who together accounted for more than eighteen thousand incarcerations over approximately six years, making up only 0.3 percent of the population incarcerated in New York City jails over that time but accounting for 3.5 percent of all incarcerations at an estimated cost of approximately $129 million.[5] Incarcerations in this group were marked by their short duration and minor charges such as petty larceny, possession of trace amounts of controlled substances, trespassing, and jumping the subway turnstile. Assault charges are less common in this group than in a cross section of the jail population. With a mean age of forty-two years, this population was significantly older than the cross-sectional jail population.

Here we find a population for whom incarceration is serving no apparent purpose. They are not incapacitated, because they stay briefly and spend most of their time in the community. They are not deterred or rehabilitated, as evidenced by their repeated engagement in the same behavior that returns them to jail. And jailing does not represent retribution for their crimes because these are so minor as to not require retribution. The criminal justice system moves to release them from jail as soon as it becomes aware that they have been incarcerated again (median length of stay eleven days), but the cycle persists.

A look at the medical and mental health needs of these people sheds more light on this phenomenon. Significant substance use in this group was 97 percent prevalent, with 19 percent meeting criteria for serious mental illnesses and 37 percent having ever been prescribed an antipsychotic in jail. The prevalence of chronic disease such as HIV, hepatitis C, diabetes, and epilepsy was higher in this group than in the cross-sectional jail population, which is already known to outpace the community in these measures.

More than half had evidence of homelessness in their medical charts, though the study design was not sensitive to this. Indeed, with a mean of twenty-three incarcerations per person over the approximately six-year study, the vast majority likely struggled with housing instability. We hypothesize that homelessness is the medium by which substance use disorders, often in conjunction with significant mental illness, come to the attention of the public and thus the criminal justice system. Living on the street leads this group to interact with the public in ways that are uncomfortable or unacceptable, such as public intoxication (leading perhaps to the trace possession charges), trespassing, or subsistence petty theft. Though they may be eligible for public services such as food stamps and even supportive housing, qualitative evidence suggests that they are profoundly disabled by substance use, limited bureaucratic literacy, mental illness, and frequent incarceration itself, such that they cannot consistently access these supportive services. In this framework, their minor charges can then be viewed more as a pretense to remove them from untenable public situations rather than as the actual target of policing efforts. The same degree of substance use or mental illness in a person with stable housing would more often be managed in the treatment arena without coming to the attention of the public, and thus the criminal justice system. Just as housing is known to be a key social determinant of health, here it represents a social determinant of incarceration.

Thus, the routine of repeated incarceration and release of this subgroup represents a set of disruptive and traumatic transitions that could be addressed through a focus on supportive housing—if it were more widely available. First, we must understand that this population is not disengaged from services broadly; rather, the natures of the services they access do not address the underlying housing problem. In New York City, 96 percent of the frequently incarcerated had at some point had a Medicaid number—far higher than the cross-sectional jail population. Qualitative work suggests that these patients are so engaged in services that various institutions often *become* their housing. They cycle through jails, but also emergency departments, inpatient hospitalization, psychiatric hospitalization, nursing homes, shelters, and inpatient drug rehab centers, such that these coalesce to become their housing, a phenomenon described by medical anthropologist Kim Hopper as the institutional circuit.[6] At the same time, supportive housing interventions often require involved application processes that this disabled population cannot successfully navigate, and incarceration often interferes. Further, eligibility for supportive housing may be broad, such that those in the pool with best control of their mental illness or substance use secure placement to the exclusion of those most in need, who remain too disabled to navigate the bureaucracy.

Approaching supportive housing as a decarceration intervention requires a novel strategy. Localities can identify their most frequently incarcerated populations using modern data systems and define this group of specific individuals as the group eligible for a reserved set of supportive housing slots. These same data systems can be used to identify the frequently incarcerated when they are next arrested and can expedite their warm handoff into supportive housing directly from jail discharge. Though it should not preclude other supportive housing efforts, this targeted approach is fundamentally different from investing in supportive housing efforts with broad eligibility criteria. With per-bed annual costs exceeding $160,000 in a large urban jail, such efforts could readily reduce public outlay, or at least represent a highly cost-effective health intervention.[7]

Barriers to such a cost-effective policy, however, are powerful. Costs are relatively invisible to the public when the criminal justice system or police consign the homeless to jail, whereas no-cost scatter-site housing for this marginalized group could be met with public scrutiny. Budgetary silos make the savings garnered from reduced jail populations difficult to redirect to supportive housing. Such savings also represent loss to the vested interests that defend criminal justice spending.

The criminal justice system itself should have access to supportive tools rather than just punitive ones. The balance of evidence suggests that supportive housing as an intervention for the frequently incarcerated would be more effective than frequent jailing in addressing criminal justice outcomes—protecting public safety, reducing petty crime and public nuisance—and at markedly lower cost.[8] This approach could improve community safety and quality of life while saving taxpayer money, but it requires a cultural frame shift on the part of judges, prosecutors, and legislators. These stakeholders must also release drug urine screening back to the purview of medical professionals and accept that community-dwelling adults must be allowed to struggle with drug relapse without returning to jail based on use alone. Such supportive interventions might be best housed within dedicated decarceration courts.[9]

Employment and Incarceration

In addition to addressing housing status, the project of more rapid decarceration will require examination of other traditional social determinants of health, including poverty and race. The frequently incarcerated group we have described has a very different set of needs than a young man caught up in the entrepreneurship of the drug trade and the crime organizations that operate this industry. For such a young man, the prospect of viable employment in the mainstream economy is the common pathway that might protect him from years of life lost to incarceration and to gun violence. For the two groups, the appropriate interventions that impact social determinants of both health and incarceration can be doubly cost-effective investments for society.

Correctional Health Care and Decarceration

Substance use and mental health disorders represent the two most common types of diagnoses among the incarcerated. They also reflect how poor and minority people with these problems come to be incarcerated, and reveal the importance of correctional health care in undoing the American error of mass incarceration. The United States has more beds allocated to incarceration than to substance treatment and inpatient psychiatric care combined. With 2.3 million people incarcerated, the United States has approximately 720 beds of incarceration per 100,000 people. The total number of inpatient psychiatric beds in the United States has declined from 550,000 in 1960 to about 43,000 in 2011, yielding a rate of 13 beds of inpatient psychiatric care per 100,000 people.[10] A 2012 review of inpatient substance use disorder facilities in 2012 revealed approximately 1.2 million people in care for drug or alcohol use disorder, reflecting a rate of 480 per 100,000 people.[11] Taken together, this reflects a rate of approximately 493 per 100,000 for treatment of these concerns. While this reflects about 32 percent fewer beds dedicated to treatment versus incarceration, it is important to remember not only that incarceration is much more expensive than treatment but also that treatment is associated with financial savings to the community and incarceration is associated with increases in overdose and death immediately after release.

At the same time, the need to reduce American incarceration rates is also widely acknowledged. There are two important areas where both goals can be pursued together. First, the scope of correctional health services should be expanded, especially to support diversion efforts before incarceration and also to include medication-assisted therapy (e.g., opioid maintenance treatment with methadone or buprenorphine) during incarceration, thereby reducing risk of death after release. In the case of diversion, comprehensive health data for frequently incarcerated people can help formulate an alternative to detention.

A second nexus between improving correctional health and decarceration is the funding mechanism of correctional health. Currently, correctional health is funded almost exclusively by local tax levy of cities, counties, and states. In jails and prisons, spending priorities and quality measurement usually fall to sheriffs and departments of correction instead of the Centers for Medicare and Medicaid Services (CMS) and the Joint Commission. As a consequence, the care delivered during twelve million incarcerations each year is essentially hidden from the rest of American health care quality assessment and improvement.

In order to integrate evidence-based practices into correctional health, states should be allowed to utilize some Medicaid funds to reimburse for care inside jails and prisons. The most pressing case for this approach is for treatment of hepatitis C. New drug regimens make treatment and cure of hepatitis C realistic for millions of Americans, many of whom also have criminal justice involvement. However, most correctional settings lack the funds to pay for these medications, which cost approximately $60,000 for a twelve-week regimen. For community health systems and CMS, the prospect of treatment interruption, failure, and restarting during incarceration is likely more costly than simply continuing treatment.

Funding this work would bring in the robust quality assessment and improvements that are standard in virtually every other American health care setting. This approach, and other similar efforts, would allow community health systems to understand the true costs of incarceration and take the dual approach of promoting continuity of care for their incarcerated patients and also weighing in on the core decisions that lead so many people with mental health and substance use problems to end up incarcerated.

Discharge Health Planning

The weeks immediately following incarceration in jails or prisons represent a high-risk time for death, most commonly due to overdose, followed by suicide and homicide.[12] The magnitude of the increased risk for death is variable across different studies but has been demonstrated across a wide range of geographic locations and populations and in both prisons and jails.[13] The World Health Organization identifies access to opioid substitution therapy (e.g., methadone or buprenorphine) as an essential element of a strategy to combat this health risk of incarceration.[14] However, most American jails and prisons appear not to offer this evidence-based treatment except in limited circumstances.[15] Afflicting substance users most prominently, post-release death demonstrates how drug war policy aimed at mitigating the consequences of illicit drug use can have the opposite effect.

Though in-custody death is widely tracked and reported, post-release death has traditionally been described only in epidemiologic terms. Modern data systems could track post-release deaths, which could help interested localities to improve jail-based health services and discharge planning.[16] Such investigations could draw attention to the high rates of post-release overdose death and may lead to implementation of new jail- or prison-based opioid treatment programs, or quality improvement initiatives within those programs that already exist. For example, every person with serious mental illness or substance abuse concerns should be linked to community health resources. This linkage requires much more than simply making an appointment and should include medications dispensed at the time of the intervention; transportation to home, social service hubs, or other initial points of reentry; and communication of essential health information with patient consent. Because the length of stay in jail is relatively short and hard to predict, effective reentry work requires notification of local health homes, care coordinators, or other community health partners when incarceration begins. This would allow for a shared plan of care that could involve coordinated reentry but is also poised to react to the unexpected discharge of people from jail. Our own efforts in these areas have shown that comprehensive discharge planning can promote improved health outcomes as well as decreased homelessness, food insecurity, and use of emergency services.[17]

The documentation of the health risks of incarceration is an important component of the decarceration movement. Incarcerated people experience new health risks that contribute to death, injury, and other adverse health outcomes both during and after incarceration—especially in jails. In addition, the repeated incarceration of some groups (e.g., people with substance use and housing concerns) is a costly and ineffective use of resources. Increasing supportive housing must be an essential part of ending American mass incarceration if the cycling of individuals from jail to homeless shelters to inpatient psychiatric settings is to be broken. Correctional health services will also need to come into the modern age of evidence-based addiction treatment, including methadone and buprenorphine, as a means to improve survival and reduce recidivism. Finally, making fundamental reforms in the provision of health care in prisons and jails will bring improved health outcomes for the incarcerated, and allow those health systems to join with community partners at key decision points along the criminal justice pipeline.

In order to realize this potential, correctional health services in jail and prison will need to develop robust reentry teams that can also partner with drug, decarceration, and mental health courts to facilitate diversion as well as reentry.

Notes

1. L. Glaze and D. Kaeble, *Correctional Populations in the United States*, Bureau of Justice Statistics, Department of Justice, NCJ 248479, December 19, 2014.

2. S. Glowa-Kollisch, K. Andrade, R. Stazesky, P. Teixeira, F. Kaba, R. MacDonald, Z. Rosner, D. Selling, A. Parsons, and H. Venters, "Data-Driven Human Rights: Using the Electronic Health Record to Promote Human Rights in Jail," *Health and Human Rights* 16, no. 1 (2014): 157–65.

3. F. Kaba, A. Lewsi, S. Glowa-Kollisch, J. Hadler, D. Lee, H. Alper, D. Selling, R. MacDonald, A. Solimo, A. Parsons, and H. Venters, "Solitary Confinement and Risk of Self-Harm Among Jail Inmates," *American Journal of Public Health* 104, no. 3 (2014): 442–47.

4. F. Kaba, A. Solimo, J. Graves, S. Glowa-Kollisch, A. Vise, R. MacDonald, A. Waters, Z. Rosner, N. Dickey, S. Angell, and H. Venters, "Disparities in Mental Health Referral and Diagnosis in the NYC Jail Mental Health Service," *American Journal of Public Health* 105, no. 9 (September 2015): e27–e34.

5. R. MacDonald, F. Kaba, Z. Rosner, A. Vise, M. Skerker, D. Weiss, M. Brittner, N. Dickey, and H. Venters, "The Rikers Island Hot Spotters: Defining the Needs of the Most

Frequently Incarcerated," *American Journal of Public Health* 105, no. 11 (November 2015): 2262–8.

6. K. Hopper, J. Jost, T. Hay, S. Welber, and G. Haugland, "Homelessness, Severe Mental Illness, and the Institutional Circuit," *Psychiatric Services* 48, no. 5 (1997): 659–65.

7. Independent Budget Office of the City of New York, "NYC's Jail Population: Who's There and Why?," August 22, 2013, http://ibo.nyc.ny.us/cgi-park2/2013/08/nycs-jail-population-whos-there-and-why.

8. A. Aidala, W. McAllister, M. Yomogida, and V. Shubert, New York City Frequent User Service Enhancement (FUSE) Initiative, "New York City FUSE II Evaluation Report," http://www.csh.org/wp-content/uploads/2014/01/FUSE-Eval-Report-Final_Linked.pdf , accessed July 23, 2017.

9. A.M. McLeod, "Decarceration Courts: Possibilities and Perils of a Shifting Criminal Law," *Georgetown Law Journal* 100 (2012): 1587–674.

10. *No Room at the Inn: Trends and Consequences of Closing Public Psychiatric Hospitals 2005–2010*, Treatment Advocacy Center, July 19, 2012, available at http://www.treatmentadvocacycenter.org/storage/documents/no_room_at_the_inn-2012.pdf.

11. *National Survey of Substance Abuse Treatment Services (N-SSATS): 2012*, Substance Abuse and Mental Health Services Administration, Department of Health and Human Services, SMA 14-4809, 2013.

12. J. Zlodre and S. Fazel, "All-Cause and External Mortality in Released Prisoners: Systematic Review and Meta-analysis," *American Journal of Public Health* 102, no. 12 (December 2012): e67–75.

13. On prisons: I.A. Binswanger, M.F. Stern, R.A. Deyo, P.J. Heagerty, A. Cheadle, J.G. Elmore, and T.D. Koepsell, "Release from Prison—A High Risk of Death for Former Inmates," *New England Journal of Medicine* 356, no. 2 (January 11, 2007): 157–65, erratum in *New England Journal of Medicine* 356, no. 5 (February 1, 2007): 536. On jails: S. Lim, A.L. Seligson, F.M. Parvez, C.W. Luther, M.P. Mavinkurve, I.A. Binswanger, and B.D. Kerker, "Risks of Drug-Related Death, Suicide, and Homicide During the Immediate Post-Release Period Among People Released from New York City Jails, 2001–2005," *American Journal of Epidemiology* 175, no. 6 (March 15, 2012): 519–26.

14. *Prevention of Acute Drug-related Mortality in Prison Populations During the Immediate Post-Release Period* (Copenhagen: World Health Organization, 2010).

15. A. Nunn, N. Zaller, S. Dickman, C. Trimbur, A. Nijhawan, and J.D. Rich, "Methadone and Buprenorphine Prescribing and Referral Practices in US Prison Systems: Results from a Nationwide Survey," *Drug and Alcohol Dependence* 105, nos. 1–2 (November 1, 2009): 83–88, erratum in *Drug and Alcohol Dependence* 113, nos. 2–3 (January 15, 2011): 252.

16. B. Alex, D.B. Weiss, F. Kaba, Z. Rosner, D. Lee, S. Lim, H. Venters, and R. Mac-Donald, "Death After Jail Release," *Journal of Correctional Health Care* 23, no. 1 (January 2017): 83–87.

17. P.A. Teixeira, A.O. Jordan, N. Zaller, D. Shah, and H. Venters, "Health Outcomes for HIV-Infected Persons Released from the New York City Jail System with a Transitional Care-Coordination Plan," *Am J Public Health* 105, no. 2 (February 2015):351–7.

10

Release Aging People in Prison

MUJAHID FARID AND LAURA WHITEHORN

Mass incarceration in the United States has emerged as one of the most urgent human rights issues of the twenty-first century. The United States is
the most incarcerated nation on the planet, bar none—a reality rendered
all the more demoralizing because this country holds itself out as the bea-
con of democracy for the rest of the world. Whatever democracy really means
in America, it cannot be overlooked that at the root of mass incarceration
is the long-standing issue of racism. Black people are incarcerated at a rate
six times higher than whites, and Latinos are nearly twice as likely to be incarcerated as whites.

Also largely inspired by race is the propensity to punish. This is a driving force behind mass incarceration, and it has become so pervasive that
some researchers note it has metastasized into a "carceral state," infecting
almost every other social institution with negative collateral consequences and turning the United States into a nation defined by its repres-
sive apparatus.[1]

Public health scholars have begun classifying mass incarceration as a
public health crisis because of its widespread and devastating social impact.[2]

Noting that it has developed epidemic proportions, some have employed an epidemiological framework to study its causes and consequences.

Though it is widely recognized that mass incarceration in the United States portends a bleak future for the society as a whole, and bipartisan commissions have arisen to address the crisis, there has been strong resistance to credible initiatives that could substantially contribute to solutions. The failure to consider and implement concrete solutions to the crisis of mass incarceration has caused the number of people aging in prison to continue to skyrocket, confining thousands of seniors in cruel and degrading conditions.

In New York State, as a result of a failure to confront the punishment paradigm, the number of people over fifty years of age who are confined increased by more than 84 percent between 2004 and 2014, even as the total number of people locked up fell by 23 percent during the same period.[3]

What Needs to Change

To commence the process of ushering in real change, government leaders and policy makers must accept that it is not possible to substantially reduce the deadly impact of this "disease" through strategies that focus solely on releasing people confined for low-level crimes—that is, people who are imprisoned for nonviolent, nonsexual, and nonserious drug-related offenses.

To promote this acceptance by policy makers, advocates need to adopt a two-pronged strategy: offering viable approaches to downsizing jail and prison populations, and educating the public and officials about the need to quench the endless desire to punish—a desire that has produced a vast rise in the prison population in the past four decades, adversely affecting all our social institutions and communities.

For a start, New York State and other jurisdictions that routinely deny parole, compassionate release, and clemency to medically challenged, low-risk, and aging people in prison must shift direction and begin employing a rational policy centered in public safety concerns.

In sum, the task we must undertake involves the design, proposal, and execution of widespread projects and campaigns that will have a substantial impact on diminishing the carceral state—and that will have a reasonable chance of convincing the public and policy makers to adopt them. One of the elements of this strategy is to release elderly people in prison.

The Struggle Before Us

By 2012, when years of work by thousands of incarcerated people and other social activists, together with Michelle Alexander's book *The New Jim Crow*, had made the term "mass incarceration" widely familiar, the United States prison population of more than 2.4 million had finally begun to slowly decline.[4]

Whether one thought the penal system was broken or operating as planned for the marginalization and control of Black and Latino people, a significant number of people were coming to realize that the current situation was not viable. And beginning with the fiscal crisis of 2008, policy makers were forced to face the rising costs of the swollen prison system. Both progressives and conservatives were pushing for various forms of decarceration and reform, making for strange bedfellows. While conservatives and many politicians were motivated by financial constraints rather than by concern for social justice, the impact was clear. In New York State, for example, the prison population fell by 23 percent between 2008 and 2017, a result of things such as modest reforms to the Rockefeller-era drug laws that had filled the state's prison and jails to overflowing capacity.

At the same time, many journalists and public officials noted the escalating population of elderly people in prison. Attention was being paid—but it was devoted to creating geriatric prison wards, hospices, and other ways to accommodate elders behind bars.

And some activists noticed a problem in the new reforms.[5] Language like "low-level, nonserious, nonviolent, nonsexual" was creeping into the discussion, and only one national reform (a Supreme Court decision barring the use of mandatory life-without-parole sentences for juveniles)[6] seemed at all likely to undermine a primary pillar of mass incarceration: the system's commitment to permanent punishment and revenge against people convicted of crimes that were not "victimless"—and even some that were.

One popular initiative that has drawn much attention is Cut 50, a project initiated by a number of bipartisan criminal justice reform organizations and politicians to reduce the prison population by 50 percent within the next ten to fifteen years.[7] Although this plan may be perceived as bold, much more will be required to bring the United States out of the quagmire of being a carceral state.

With 2.2 million people confined in United States prisons and jails, a 50 percent reduction would mean reducing the prison population by at least 1 million within the time period projected. Such a task would require establishing initiatives to address both ends of the penal system—reducing the number of people entering the system (and the amount of time they will have to spend behind bars) and increasing the number of people coming out.

Quoting a former New York City corrections and probation official, a 2015 article published by the Marshall Project poses an important question: "When does mass incarceration become regular incarceration?"[8] To bring the U.S. incarceration rate into line with that of European nations—or with the rate of the United States in the early 1970s—requires reducing the current incarceration rate of 700 per 100,000 to about 150 per 100,000. That would be a reduction of about 80 percent. Consequently, although the bipartisan effort to reduce the numbers of incarcerated people by 50 percent is considered bold, it would arguably still leave the United States with an incarceration-related public health crisis and still in need of a public health cure.

In addition, more than 50 percent of the prison population consists of people convicted for violent offenses. In New York State, for example, approximately 65 percent of the total incarcerated population are serving sentences for violent offenses.[9] Thus, even if it were possible to release all of the nonviolent drug offenders in the next ten to fifteen years, it is impossible to reach a 50 percent reduction without including people convicted of violent offenses in the plan. Professor Marie Gottschalk notes that, "even if every drug offender were released today, the U.S. would still have a sky-high incarceration rate."[10] Such an approach would also fail to shift us away from the fundamental problem at the root of the mass incarceration crisis: the belief in revenge and permanent punishment as the path to public safety.

A Grassroots Approach to Disbanding the Carceral State

Formerly incarcerated people in New York created the Release Aging People in Prison (RAPP) campaign to meet these issues head-on. This approach is rational, based on reams of evidence relating to public safety, prison populations, and recidivism. It also allows us to attack two pillars of mass incarceration, both rooted in racism. RAPP's strategy tackles the ideology of permanent punishment and the thinking that people convicted of violent crimes should spend their entire lives in prison. These two foundations of mass incarceration grow from and perpetuate the criminalization of Black and Latino people.

RAPP is a popular effort to mobilize advocates, legislators, formerly incarcerated people, men and women who are currently confined, family members, and concerned citizens to demand that state officials, prison administrators, and parole authorities release incarcerated elders who have already served considerable time behind prison walls and who would pose little or no threat to public safety upon release. We cite clear statistical evidence:

- Elders pose the lowest risk to public safety if released. While overall recidivism rates hover near 40 percent in New York State, people over fifty return to prison for a violation of parole or for committing a new offense at a rate of 5.2 percent, and for those over sixty-five the recidivism rate falls to less than 1 percent.
- The recidivism rate of people who have served long sentences for serious felonies is 1.3 percent—lower than any other category of those released.[11]

Noting that people over fifty pose an extremely low risk of recidivism, we argue, "If the risk is low, let them go."[12] The way to address the problem of increasing numbers of elders behind bars is not to make prison elder-friendly, we maintain, but to release older people. If we can make a dent in the reliance on permanent punishment for that group, we hope we can advance the push for decarceration and fundamental change on a broader scale as well.

RAPP was designed specifically to embrace a large segment of people in prison who are often ignored or excluded from policies and laws implemented to reduce mass incarceration: long-termers convicted of serious offenses, including murder. These people constitute the bulk of the over-fifty prison population. As formerly incarcerated people ourselves, we are perhaps uniquely aware that many of these human beings have taken responsibility for their actions, transformed their lives, developed skills and abilities they lacked before incarceration, and could be released from prison with no threat to public safety. In fact, the current movement for prison reform receives much of its impetus and vigor from the leadership and participation of formerly incarcerated people, who serve as experts not only on what the problems are but also on how to solve them.

RAPP argues that accelerated release mechanisms for aging incarcerated people must be created or, where they already exist, utilized. Our platform includes those seeking compassionate release (medical parole) and clemency. Because our campaign launched in New York, this approach immediately brought us face-to-face with the parole board, which releases fewer than a quarter of all people who are eligible for parole, no matter their age or risk to public safety. The board consistently fails to rely on rational standards that measure a person's readiness for release, turning instead again and again to the "nature of the offense"—the crime for which a person was incarcerated, something that will never change.

The work of RAPP combines public education, direct policy proposals, and evidence-based advocacy to promote the release of aging men and women through executive law, regulatory reforms, and legislation. We work together with other groups and advocates who are challenging current release practices and arguing for the use of validated and proven evidence-based tools to guide release decisions.

RAPP also works in coalition with groups and agencies that provide reentry services for people released from prisons. At the outset we were asked: *If long-term incarcerated people are released, where will they go, and how will they acclimate to society after such long absence?* We responded to this concern by joining others to initiate an Aging Reentry Task Force of government and private organizations and agencies, some providing geriatric advocacy and services, others providing advocacy and services for formerly incarcerated people. The task force has created what we believe is the country's first pilot project for discharge planning and reentry (better called reintegration) services for aging people released from prison.[13]

The crisis within parole and other prison release mechanisms in New York State has been mounting for the past twenty-five years. Back in the early 1990s these systems became co-opted by the encroaching punishment paradigm spreading across the United States, part of what is now recognized as a misguided attempt to be "tough on crime." Consequently, a process commenced of routinely denying parole and release applications regardless of the applicant's personal change, rehabilitation, time already served, infirmities, or other humane considerations. This was especially the case for those who had been convicted of serious or violent offenses.

Arguably, this shift in the back-end release processes played a major role in building what is now being called mass incarceration. In a 1999 article, a former chair of the New York State Board of Parole wrote, "While the criteria for parole eligibility have not changed by legislative enactment, an examination of the current release practice of the Board of Parole reveals that the current parole system has been at the forefront of an ideological revolution."[14]

Confronting Concrete Walls of Resistance to Change

RAPP organizers have learned that the ideology and structures put in place to support the constructing of mass incarceration and a carceral state were essentially etched in stone, and eradicating them requires intense organizing energies and efforts.

As the prison population in New York State began to expand, in conjunction with a paradigm shift that paved the way for cursory parole reviews with rubber-stamp denials, management challenges were presented to the parole commissioners responsible for carrying out their daily duties. Given the number of days on which parole hearings are held each month and the number of hearings being held, the average time that can be allotted to each parole hearing is less than five minutes.[15] This structural shift in the way in which the parole board goes about its daily operations has put the agency in the unenviable position of sometimes having to openly resist and defy judicial decisions and court orders. An example is *Harris v. N.Y.S. Division of Parole*.[16]

The New York State Division of Parole, in addition to providing regular hearings for people scheduled for release consideration (parole, compassionate release, and clemency), is also responsible for providing reviews of administrative appeals submitted by people when release is denied. Outside of their duties to conduct the hearings, the board's commissioners are responsible for reviewing and making decisions on the voluminous appeals submitted through the administrative process. According to the regulations governing administrative appeals, the appeals are to be conducted by three commissioners sitting in conference, and none of them should have participated on the original panel that considered and denied release.

In 1995, Theodore Harris, who had been denied parole and thereafter filed an administrative appeal, noted that the official decision he received from the Appeals Unit denying his appeal indicated that each commissioner had signed and dated the decision and notice on different dates. Harris challenged that process when he ultimately submitted his judicial challenge to the local court upon exhausting his administrative remedies.

The local court held that Harris was correct in that the parole board appeal process he received was severely flawed. The parole board appealed the decision but eventually lost there too. The Appellate Division, Third Department, agreed that the administrative appeal was in violation of lawful procedure and found that the commissioners must meet "collectively" to render a proper decision.[17]

What happened following the *Harris* decision is most interesting and instructive. Likely driven by its utter reliance on mass production processes and an inability, given its limited time and resources, to provide lawful administrative appeals even if it desired to do so, the Division of Parole began issuing notices of its administrative appeal decisions that were identical to the earlier version except for the removal of the section that previously showed the date of each commissioner's signature.[18] The objective clearly was to make it difficult for an applicant to mount a challenge on the basis that the decision was not rendered by a committee sitting collectively.

To compound matters, some years later when parole applicants whose administrative appeals were similarly denied submitted freedom-of-information requests to the Board of Parole seeking the dates that their decisions were made, the answers were always along the lines of "Please be advised that there is no document or other information indicating the actual date each of the members of the Board of Parole signed the Administrative Appeal Decision Notice."[19]

More Than a Decade of Struggle to Reorient Parole Board Practice

In 2011, after many years of frustration on the part of community groups and legislators seeking to rein in parole board practices that seemed to be without executive oversight, the New York State Legislature passed a revision of Executive Law Sec. 259-c ("State Board of Parole; functions, powers, and duties") that requires the parole board to establish and apply "risk and needs principles to measure the rehabilitation of persons appearing before the board" and to gauge the likelihood of success should the applicant be released.[20] The amendment was intended to correct the board's practice of focusing solely on the nature of crimes committed perhaps decades earlier. Risk and needs assessments use objective, scientific standards—rather than the subjective viewpoints of individual parole commissioners—to guide the board in its key task: predicting whether a parole applicant will, if released, commit crimes.[21]

Basing release on such a standard reflects New York's mandate to protect public safety as well as to honor the rehabilitative goals of the penal system. New York adopted an actuarial assessment model called COMPAS for use in its decision-making. This approach creates an individualized picture of how the incarcerated person has changed since the original crime, what risks there are for future criminal behavior, what support is necessary for the individual's successful reentry, and, critically, what kind of skills, attitudes, and capacities the individual developed during incarceration. As of 2014, at least twenty states had adopted similar models.[22]

For about three years after the new law passed, community advocates, incarcerated people, and lawyers urged the board to draft new regulations, as required by the law, but to no avail. Trying to remedy the problem, Assembly member Daniel O'Donnell, then chair of the Committee on Corrections, convened a public hearing on parole practices in Albany in early December 2013. Along with dozens of community members and advocates, representatives of the Department of Corrections and Community Supervision, including parole board chair Tina Stanford, testified at what turned into an all-day hearing. In her testimony Stanford made no mention of new regulations. Later in the day, however, community members learned that the board had in fact finally posted new draft regulations just one day earlier.

The new proposed regulations were not good. Instead of responding to the spirit and letter of the new law, they once again attempted to smother the use of risk and needs assessment amid a mountain of additional factors to be weighed in making release decisions.

In a joint statement responding to the board's draft regulations, O'Donnell and Kenneth Zebrowski, chair of the Assembly's Administrative Regulations Review Commission, wrote:

> We were extremely disappointed to see that the proposed rules contain no substantive change to the working requirements of the Parole Board. Indeed, they fail to achieve any change in the status quo, much less the significant change envisioned at the time we negotiated the amendments (to the executive law).
>
> The proposed rules treat the requirements of 259-c (4) of the Executive Law as mere additional factors for consideration by the Parole Board.

Had the legislative wanted to add additional factors we would have done so. . . .

We believe the intent of the Legislature was to modernize and make more objective a parole process that has been overly subjective in the past. The proposed rules do not do that.[23]

During the subsequent ninety-day public comment period, formerly and currently incarcerated people, their families, legal and civil rights organizations, and other concerned groups and individuals echoed Assembly members O'Donnell and Zebrowski, filing letters criticizing the newly proposed regulations. Normally, according to those who monitor public comments for the state, a new regulation garners at most thirty to sixty comments. In contrast, the parole regulations drew some three hundred comments. The overwhelming majority of comments asserted that the board's proposed regulations were inadequate to address the core problem: that parole decisions currently function more as retrials of parole applicants than as assessments of the individual's readiness for release.

Ignoring the community took less than three minutes for the parole board. At their April 21, 2014, meeting, the board dismissed the three hundred public comments that urged the use of objective and consistent criteria in release decisions. With no discussion, and without a single mention of any of the myriad community and legislative concerns, the board unanimously passed the new regulations as they had originally proposed them.

When Governor Andrew Cuomo wrote in his 2016 agenda for the New York State of the State address that only one in five applicants for parole was granted release and that he wanted to expand that number, he was responding to these years of community pressure and demands for a more functional parole system in New York State, as well as to the growing national consensus that reform of the criminal justice system is urgently required if we are ever to solve the problem of mass incarceration.[24] Sadly, the governor's agenda did not provide a clear direction on how to remedy the problem. In addition, the commissioners of the Board of Parole have not responded to the national and statewide cry for parole justice. That is why intervention by other prominent authorities is desperately needed.

Unremitting Contemptuous Behavior by the Parole Board

Since their adoption of new, faulty regulations, the board has exhibited a similarly dismissive attitude toward community sentiment and the law, consistently ignoring the real meaning of Executive Law Sec. 259-i ("Procedures for the conduct of the work of the state board of parole") and continuing a practice of granting only about one in five parole applications.

Parole applicants, their lawyers, and the community have not let the board's intransigence pass without a fight. More significant is that some courts have also taken note of the board's insistence on continuing business as usual and have taken the board to task, a number even going so far as to hold the board in contempt.

A parole applicant who is denied release must first file an administrative appeal, and then, when that is either denied or ignored (after 120 days the appeal is considered "constructively denied"), can file an Article 78 petition, the means by which New York law permits an individual to challenge an administrative action. An Article 78 petition is heard by a court, as opposed to being decided by the parole board itself.

Since the parole board's new regulations went into effect in April 2014, numerous Article 78 petitions have been granted. Even when such an appeal is granted, however, the courts consistently maintain that the only power they have is to order the board to grant the applicant a new (de novo) hearing. All too often, such hearings merely repeat the error of the original hearing.

While it may or may not be correct that the courts do not have jurisdiction to order the release of a petitioner, it has long been established that a court of record has the power to "punish, by fine or imprisonment, or either, a neglect or violation of duty, or other misconduct, by which a right or remedy of a party to a civil action or special proceeding, pending in the court may be defeated, impaired, impeded, or prejudiced."[25] The parole board should have an arbitration process employing an expert group which reviews each such case—after the Article 78 petition when the prisoner has been released. To assure that the Article 78 release does not compromise public safety, all such cases should be reviewed regularly and make any climbs of evidence of misconduct that adversely affects public safety. In such cases the prisoner may go before the board (with legal counsel) to argue their case.

The Courts Attempt to Take on the Parole Board

Recently several courts have severely criticized the parole board—in some cases citing the board for contempt—in these situations. When contempt citations have been issued, courts have ordered the board to pay attorney fees and a penalty to the litigant until a new and fair hearing is held.

In a case in Sullivan County, New York, after the court ordered a de novo hearing and the board failed to schedule one in timely fashion, the attorney representing the litigant petitioned the court to order the board to pay a "daily fine of $250.00 directly to Petitioner Dempsey Hawkins every day until its contempt is purged." The court's original order for a de novo hearing in this case was based on the failure of the board to consider anything other than the nature of the original offense, including the age at which Hawkins had committed the murder.[26]

In another recent case, brought by petitioner Alejo Rodriguez, Orange County judge Sandra Sciortino ruled that the board had "issued a boilerplate decision" in Rodriguez's case. She continued:

> The instant matter, like so many others, arises from the Board's failure to abide by statutory mandates. The Board is without authority to ignore the command of the Legislature. In continuing to issue such manifestly inadequate decisions despite a clear Legislative mandate, and in the face of so many cases in the courts of this state which reinforce that mandate, the Board is essentially thumbing its nose at the Legislature and the courts. Such behavior cannot be condoned. . . .

The courts will continue to enforce the requirement announced by the Legislature as long as it remains necessary. However, for the courts of this state to repeatedly entertain petitions and issue decisions ordering *de novo* hearings because the Board fails to follow a clear statutory standard is wasteful of the time of all involved and of the resources of the State.[27]

In *Cassidy v. New York State Board of Parole*, an Orange County Supreme Court judge ordered the board to pay the attorney representing Michael Cassidy $3,000 and grant a new hearing within sixty days.[28] When the board denied parole again at the return hearing, focusing on Cassidy's criminal offense, the court held the board in contempt, ruling that under executive law the determination had to be based on "future-focused risk assessment procedures." This decision was recently overturned on government appeal. However, the reasons given by the reversing court focused on Cassidy's mediocre risk assessment scores, thus distinguishing his case from the central issue more clearly present in most other cases.

On May 24, 2016, the Dutchess County Supreme Court held the board in contempt in the case of John MacKenzie and levied a fee of $500 a day against the board until a new and proper hearing could be held and "a decision is issued in accordance with Executive Law 259-i."[29] MacKenzie had filed a motion for contempt following a string of parole appearances and denials stretching over fifteen years. In 2015, the court had ordered a de novo hearing after one such denial, citing the board's failure to do more than rehash the details of the original crime. When the new hearing once again merely echoed the earlier ones, MacKenzie sought the contempt citation.

In her decision granting MacKenzie's motion, Justice Maria G. Rosa wrote, "It is undisputed that it is unlawful for the Parole Board to deny parole solely on the basis of the underlying conviction. Yet the court can reach no other conclusion but that this is exactly what the Parole Board did in this case." She also wrote, "It is undisputed that this petitioner has a perfect institutional record for the past 35 years. This case begs the question, if parole isn't granted to this petitioner, when and under what circumstances would it be granted?"

Upon issuing her order and decision on May 24, 2016, Rosa specifically "ORDERED that none of the members of either the 2014 or 2015 parole boards that denied parole shall participate in the de novo hearing."[30] The obvious implication of this specific prohibitory order is the court's recognition that some members of the parole board had exhibited an apparent inability to afford the petitioner a fair parole hearing.

On June 21, 2016, MacKenzie was interviewed by a parole board panel consisting of parole board chair Tina Stanford along with commissioners Christina Hernandez and Kevin Ludlow. This short pseudo-hearing included some very strange occurrences. First, at the start of the hearing, John MacKenzie made a point of noting that, according to the standing order of contempt, Commissioner Ludlow should have been prohibited from sitting on the hearing. MacKenzie began: "What I am saying is, my de novo was a court order and I'm pretty sure it said that you couldn't sit on the panel, you or Ms. Elovich."[31]

Commissioner Ludlow responded, "You object to my presence do you?"

Then Stanford indicated that the current meeting would *not* be the de novo hearing; rather, that day's panel intended to postpone the hearing in order to secure other records and documents. Stanford went on to state:

We'll review in the interim the records to make sure that the panel that interviews you is the appropriate composition *based on any court orders that we feel we have to abide by*, okay, so we are going to see you again in July, and we will review the records in the meantime to make sure that the panel that sees you is a panel that can see you.[32]

John MacKenzie was scheduled for another parole board hearing on July 26, 2016. Present on that panel was Commissioner William Smith, who also was prohibited from participating according to the contempt order. During the hearing MacKenzie noted this fact, to no avail. This panel once again denied John MacKenzie's parole application, leaving him to wait another two years before reconsideration. Tragically, on August 3, 2016, MacKenzie—feeling there was no hope against an intransigent parole board that could not be contained in its thirst for vengeance and was not answerable to any public authority—died by suicide.[33]

Even in the face of a standing order of contempt forbidding specified commissioners from participating in a de novo hearing, the parole board did not "feel" it had to abide by the order. The circumstances of this case are truly indicative of the monumental task presented in the work of deconstructing the carceral state. Those of us who work energetically to confront a system focused on a paradigm of punishment, revenge, and abuse will come face-to-face with actors wielding authority and power who will resist by all means the implementation of progressive change.

The roots of mass incarceration are so diverse that no one initiative could address their full scope. RAPP focuses on "back-end" methodologies to reduce the prison population. We concentrate on removing impediments to release for aging people in prison, highlighting the fact that this makes fiscal sense (in New York State the average annual cost to incarcerate one person over the age of fifty rises to between $120,000 and $240,000, compared with about $60,000 for those under fifty years of age) as well as moral and social sense.[34] We emphasize the human right to grow old with dignity, and we urge communities to take back control over the way we deal with and heal from violence, ending the reliance on police and prisons and moving toward making our society safe and healthy.

In 2014, University of California–Berkeley law professor Jonathan Simon wrote, "There are far better ways to spend money on reducing violence than incarcerating aging prisoners who once did something violent. But for now, few even in the anti-mass incarceration community are ready to take on that fight."[35] RAPP has taken on that fight and, in the few years of our existence, we've seen others join us, increasing our hopes of success.[36]

If mass incarceration can be classified as a health crisis and even an epidemic, then real healing requires the "patient" to accept the diagnosis and assent to properly prescribed treatments. These critical times will require much more than a placebo. Attempting to take on this gargantuan calamity with subclinical solutions will keep us tethered to what children's advocate Marian Wright Edelman refers to as a "cycle of infection" that perpetuates "one of the most damaging health problems in America today."[37]

Indeed, it would be tragic if the emerging movement were to succumb to what writer and activist James Kilgore outlined as a looming possibility: "measur[ing] success solely by the volume of Congressional hearing invitations and the number of foundation grants scored rather than the extent of genuine movement building."[38]

Ernest Drucker, a national public health scholar, writes, "We must develop new models and methods for our criminal justice system that value the lives and dignity of all of our people—even those who transgress."[39] We consider RAPP to be the prototype of the kind of initiatives that must be developed if we are to succeed in fundamentally decarcerating our system of government.

Elsewhere Drucker concludes, "Our failed drug policies have for decades undermined our ability to deal effectively with both our drug problems and related public health problems—e.g., the AIDS epidemic, which continues to spread at a very high rate in the U.S."[40] Likewise, unless there is a recognition that ending mass incarceration requires radical reforms that attack permanent punishment, release many elders serving long sentences for violent crimes, and reverse the "law and order" fever that produced sentences such as life without parole, in the coming days we will be making the same observation about the failures caused by focusing on so-called low-risk individuals.

RAPP arises from the belief that whatever reforms are instituted in this period will either weaken the stranglehold of this ideology of punishment—and therefore move us toward a healthy system—or will merely pretty up the system as it exists and render it even more impervious to change. Given the deeply rooted intensity of the opposition to real and fundamental change to the carceral system, it is crucial that groups and organizations working on related issues began connecting the dots and developing a more in-depth understanding of the relatedness of all the various prongs of the carceral state—in particular, how each is rooted in racism and the propensity to punish and deprive—and begin providing mutual support to advance this important work.

One direct route to confronting the punishment paradigm is to initiate a focus on the population of "political prisoners" being held behind bars in the United States. However, the United States government is loath to admit that there are such people under confinement in this country, mainly because many of them, having aged, are still in America's prisons after more than forty-five years, and their cases show how America's prisons serve primitive desires for vengeance and torture, rather than notions of correction or public safety. By focusing on elderly long-termers and political prisoners (people who can be likened to canaries in the coal mine as advocates begin focusing on accelerated punishments) and by arguing for an end to the paradigm of punishment and deprivation witnessed throughout the entire social structure, we hope to contribute to a real advance in social justice.

This, we hold, is the treatment that will allow us to become the physician who can "heal thyself."[41]

Notes

1. See, for example, M. Gottschalk, *Caught: The Prison State and the Lockdown of American Politics* (Princeton, NJ: Princeton University Press, 2014).

2. See, for just a few examples, E. Drucker, *A Plague of Prisons: The Epidemiology of Mass Incarceration in America* (New York: The New Press, 2011); Columbia University, Mailman School of Public Health, "Incarceration and Public Health Action Network," www.mailman.columbia.edu/research/incarceration-and-public-health-action-network, and "Public Health Approach to Incarceration," www.mailman.columbia.edu/incarceration-prevention-program/public-health-approach-incarceration.

3. Department of Corrections and Community Supervision (DOCCS), Under Custody Reports, 2004 to 2014, retrieved from www.doccs.ny.gov/Research/annotate.asp#pop.

4. Michelle Alexander, *The New Jim Crow: Mass Incarceration in the Age of Color Blindness* (New York: The New Press, 2010). Alexander's book was preceded by years of organizing and education by advocates and academics such as Angela Davis and Joy James, incarcerated journalist Mumia Abu-Jamal, organizations such as Critical Resistance and the Jericho Movement, the journal *Prison Legal News*, and thousands if not millions of incarcerated people.

5. Tony Fabelo and Michael Thompson, "Reducing Incarceration Rates: When Science Meets Political Realities," *Issues in Science and Technology* 32, no. 1 (Fall 2015); Andrew Gargano, "Federal Sentencing Reform Can Reduce Prison Overcrowding and

Save Money," *The Hill*, April 29, 2015; Nathan James, "The Federal Prison Population Buildup: Options for Congress," Congressional Research Service, May 20, 2016.

6. *Miller v. Alabama*, 2012. *Miller*'s ban on life-without-parole sentences for juveniles was rendered retroactive by *Montgomery v. Louisiana* (2016).

7. See Cut 50's website: www.cut50.org.

8. Dana Goldstein, "How to Cut the Prison Population by 50 Percent," Marshall Project, March 4, 2015.

9. DOCCS, Under Custody Report, 2014.

10. Gottschalk, *Caught*, 261.

11. Ryang Hui Kim, "2010 Inmate Releases: Three-Year Post Release Follow-up," DOCCS, June 2014.

12. Since we coined this phrase in 2013, it has been widely adopted by prison reform groups and progressive politicians.

13. See Aging Reentry Task Force, "Community Re-Integration Pilot Case Management Model," in *Aging in Prison: Reducing Elder Incarceration and Promoting Public Safety*, ed. Samuel K. Roberts (New York: Center for Justice at Columbia University, 2015), 84.

14. Edward R. Hammock and James Seelandt, "New York's Sentencing and Parole Law: An Unanticipated and Unacceptable Distortion of the Parole Board's Discretion," *Journal of Civil Rights and Economic Development* 13 (Spring 1999): 527–28.

15. See RAPP, "It Is Important to Understand Structural Barriers in Parole Advocacy," http://rappcampaign.com/wp-content/uploads/It-is-Important-to-Understand-Structural-Advocacy-to-Parole-Advocacy.pdf.

16. *Harris v. N.Y.S. Div. of Parole*, 628 N.Y.S.2d 416; 211 A.D.2d 205 (1995).

17. Ibid.

18. RAPP, "It Is Important to Understand Structural Barriers to Parole Advocacy."

19. Ibid.

20. New York Consolidated Laws, Executive Law—EXC § 259-c, "State board of parole; functions, powers and duties," http://codes.findlaw.com/ny/executive-law/exc-sect-259-c.html.

21. Daniel O'Donnell and Kenneth Zebrowski, "Re: Proposed Rule on Parole Decision-Making, I.D. No. CCS-51-13-00013-P," www.correctionalassociation.org/wp-content/uploads/2014/01/Assemblymember-Daniel-ODonnell.pdf.

22. Sonja B. Starr, "Evidence-Based Sentencing and the Scientific Rationalization of Discrimination," *Stanford Law Review* 66, no. 4 (April 2014): 809.

23. O'Donnell and Zebrowski, "Re: Proposed Rule."

24. "More than 10,000 people are denied parole annually in New York State and only one in five have it granted." Andrew Cuomo, 2016 State of the State, www.governor.ny.gov/sites/governor.ny.gov/files/atoms/files/2016_State_of_the_State_Book.pdf, 194.

25. New York Judiciary Law § 75.

26. *Matter of Hawkins v. New York State Department of Corrections and Community Supervision*, 521536, Index No. 0011-15, Sullivan County (2016).

27. *Alejo Rodriguez v. New York State Board of Parole*, Decision and Order, Index No. 8670/2015, returnable January 14, 2016, Orange County.

28. *Matter of Cassidy v. New York State Board of Parole*, Index No. 2255/14 2015-06927 28 NY.3rd 1128 (2017); 68 NY.3rd 97; 45 N.Y.S.3rd 368; 2017 NY Slip Op 60593.

29. *John MacKenzie v. Tina M. Stanford*, Decision and Order, Index No. 2789/15, Dutchess County.

30. Ibid.

31. From transcript of hearing provided to the authors by MacKenzie.

32. Ibid. Emphasis added.

33. See Victoria Law, "Suicide of 70-Year-Old John MacKenzie After Tenth Parole Denial Illustrates Broken System," *Village Voice*, August 9, 2016.

34. Samuel K. Roberts, ed., *Aging in Prison: Reducing Elder Incarceration and Promoting Public Safety* (New York: Center for Justice at Columbia University, 2015).

35. Jonathan Simon, "Proposition 47: A Simple Step Toward Reducing Mass Incarceration," *Governing Through Crime*, October 21, 2014, quoted in Jean Trounstine, "A Moral Imperative: Releasing Aging and Long-Term Prisoners," *Truthout*, February 10, 2015 (an article that profiles RAPP).

36. In June 2017, again in response to community pressure, the governor appointed six new parole commissioners and declined to reappoint three of the most intransigent current commissioners. Simultaneously, the Board of Parole promulgated new regulations directing commissioners to consider risk and needs assessments as an overarching element, rather than one item on a list (those regulations will be made public by the end of September). While these steps indicate progress, it remains to be seen what impact the changes will have on parole release rates.

37. Marian Wright Edelman, "The Cradle to Prison Pipeline: An American Health Crisis," *Preventing Chronic Disease* 4, no. 3 (July 2007): A43.

38. James Kilgore, "What the Movement Against Mass Incarceration Can Learn from the Struggle for Climate Justice," *Truthout*, September 24, 2014.

39. Drucker, *A Plague of Prisons*, 189.

40. Ernest Drucker, "Drug Law, Mass Incarceration, and Public Health," *Oregon Law Review* 91 (2013): 1097–128.

41. Contact RAPP c/o Correctional Association of New York, 22 Cortlandt Street, 33rd Floor, New York, New York 10007, office: (646) 793-9082 ext. 1014, cell: (347) 395-9700, email: nyrappcampaign@gmail.com, website: http://www.rappcampaign.com.

PART III

Tertiary Prevention

11

Health Care as a Vehicle
for Decarceration

DALIAH HELLER

The case for health care as a vehicle for decarceration is rooted in a public health vision for the health care system. It emerges in part from the history of psychiatric deinstitutionalization and the subsequent (though unrelated) war on drugs. It recognizes that the carceral consequences of these shifts in the public health and criminal justice landscape were both exacerbated and facilitated by economic displacement and a shrinking social safety net during this era. A public health vision counteracts these historical social forces. It prioritizes wellness over sickness, addresses mental illness and addiction[1] as chronic health conditions, and orients to the social determinants of health—the conditions in which people live and work—at its core. This vision of health care is a strategy for decarceration because it promotes health and social equity.

Making the Case

In context, the U.S. plan for psychiatric deinstitutionalization after World War II was well-intended. A shrinking mental health care system, based on a network of antiquated psychiatric hospitals, was to be replaced by an expanded community-based system. But as this plan was executed in practice it became an example of the squishy-balloon effect: when you squeeze the air in one part of the balloon, it simply puffs up in another place. During the 1970s and 1980s, the last of the psychiatric hospitals closed, but sufficient investment never materialized for the proposed community-based system. Without it, people with mental illness have been placed at great risk for incarceration, as the scarcity of health supports expanded to become a problem of unattended mental illness and homelessness. Public behaviors viewed as antisocial, threatening, or inappropriate attract the attention of law enforcement: first responders who are equipped with criminal justice tools, and acting in the absence of mental health care resources. The criminal justice system became the destination for many people with mental illness.

Coincident with the final wave of state hospital closures, in 1971, President Richard M. Nixon declared drug abuse "public enemy number one," and the decades-long national war on drugs was launched. Over the years, the war on drugs provided the foundation and rationale for a tough-on-crime approach, and the investments followed. Intensifying law enforcement activity and escalating criminal penalties were accompanied by the introduction of lengthy sentences, including mandatory minimums and truth-in-sentencing laws. Under these conditions, the criminal justice system experienced massive growth. Low-income Black and Latino communities became sites of hyperincarceration, the geographic concentration of mass incarceration.[2]

These developments were accompanied by the stunted development of public health care systems and the further unraveling of the social safety net, with profound effects on the nation's poorest populations and serious implications for people with mental illness. Reductions in federal aid to cities combined with the loss of manufacturing jobs to cheaper foreign markets to increase local poverty rates. In the mid-1990s, federal income support effectively ended with welfare reform, while funding for many critical social programs continued to be systematically cut. It was no coincidence that the communities most affected by these changes—low-income, predominantly Black and Latino— also experienced higher rates of preventable injury, disease, and death. Health inequalities are preserved and reinforced by punitive social policies under inequitable conditions in a form of structural violence.[3] For more than four decades, the combination of hyperincarceration and vanishing public resources has contained and perpetuated these conditions in affected communities.[4]

In 2008, a combination of forces propelled Barack Obama to the presidency with a strong mandate for social change. While his administration didn't foreground the problem of mass incarceration until well into Obama's second term, the Patient Protection and Affordable Care Act of 2010 became an early and signature accomplishment of his presidency. This successful effort incorporated a public health vision for health care, unlike the Clintons' attempt to reform the U.S. health care system fourteen years earlier,[5] albeit with continued reliance on a private health insurance marketplace and a system that remains largely for-profit. Elements of the act, however, suggested opportunities for decarceration, with significant investments in broader coverage, including for behavioral health care, and in supportive services. Beyond the act, other developments in health care have further strengthened these opportunities, including the promotion of health information technology via 2009 legislation, and capacity expansion for substance use disorder treatment and mental health services via 2016 legislation.

A comprehensive, sustained effort to develop a robust, public-health-oriented health care system could help to reverse-engineer the squishy-balloon effect. By expanding and improving coverage and care in the community, we could shrink the criminal justice system as a consequence. The rationale, therefore, for this notion that health care is a vehicle for achieving decarceration is reflected through the practical experience of mass incarceration and the potential of a public health imperative to redress some of the health care failings it has exposed. At a minimum, this health care decarceration vehicle must include three features:

- *Universal health insurance coverage, and targeted enrollment and retention in coverage for justice-involved individuals and their families.* Research shows that as many as nine out of ten people entering jail are uninsured,[6] and at least 80 percent lack health care coverage at the time of their release.[7]

- *Investment in mental health and substance use disorder care and treatment—behavioral health care—as a core component of the general health care system.* Approximately half of prisoners and two-thirds of jail inmates, respectively, meet clinical criteria for alcohol and/or drug abuse or dependence. The prevalence of diagnosed mental illness among the incarcerated hovers around 50 percent; among jail inmates, the rate may be as high as two-thirds of the population. Not surprisingly, serious mental illness is also disproportionately high, affecting at least one in ten prisoners in the United States. Among jail inmates with serious mental illness, an estimated 70 percent have a co-occurring substance use disorder.[8]
- *Supportive services to address the social determinants of health.* A wealth of evidence demonstrates that housing, legal, family, income, and employment issues can make or break a successful return to community life after incarceration. Problems in one or more of these domains increase the risk of arrest, and also exert a considerable influence on health outcomes.

This vision of health care interrupts the negative feedback loops created by individual unmet health problems and worsening social conditions, and saves lives and money with early, preventive, community-oriented interventions. Aside from these broader benefits to population health, if such health care investments are directed, for the long term, to those same communities suffering the dominance of the criminal justice paradigm, they offer considerable potential for dismantling the carceral state. From a systems perspective, this health care decarceration vehicle offers a transformative conceptual and practical framework for improving health and social equity in the United States.

Universal Health Insurance Coverage

Because the incarcerated are excluded from official poverty statistics, the scale of economic disadvantage in this population is not routinely reported.[9]

Studies suggest that between one-third and one-half of people held in federal, state, and local jails earned incomes prior to incarceration no higher than the federal poverty level.[10] Health care coverage could help to counteract some of the negative consequences of incarceration by facilitating access to health care and services, and securing a social safety net that could prevent future incarceration.

While the U.S. health care system has not yet embraced a universal coverage model, government-led programs have offered some semblance of this approach, beginning with Medicare and Medicaid in 1965, and more recently with the health care marketplaces and Medicaid expansion provided by the Affordable Care Act in 2010. For current and former prisoners, many of whom are single adults, this latest development was particularly notable: for the first time, low-income, nondisabled individuals without dependents became eligible for Medicaid coverage. Federal guidance released in 2016 clarified how, when, and where correctional authorities could facilitate access to Medicaid coverage and health care for individuals transitioning back to their communities. Some jurisdictions already recognized this opportunity; as of January 2015, sixty-four programs provided Medicaid enrollment in correctional settings. Most were located in states opting for Medicaid expansion, and the vast majority of these programs were implemented in jails.[11]

The intricacies of establishing Medicaid eligibility and enrollment were simplified with policy changes incorporated into the act, and accompanied by additional federal funding for upgrading state information systems and automating eligibility and connectivity processes for the jail population. For correctional agencies, establishing eligibility could produce internal cost savings, because revised federal policies under the act allowed Medicaid payment to cover hospitalizations occurring during the period of incarceration.[12] Several states reported annual savings of up to $19 million with this arrangement.[13]

Although federal law already allowed states to suspend rather than terminate Medicaid coverage during the period of imprisonment, few chose to implement this option due to limitations in their information-sharing capacity. These limitations made their systems vulnerable to inappropriate payments to insurance companies, because they were unable to verify patient status in real time. Among the sixty-four criminal-justice-based Medicaid enrollment programs in January 2015 mentioned earlier, two-thirds were suspending instead of terminating Medicaid coverage upon incarceration. This arrangement simplifies the process for ensuring coverage upon release, because it requires simple reactivation rather than the more complex, time-consuming steps of reapplication. For health plans, it suggests the longer-term promise of health care cost containment, because individuals who are incarcerated for shorter periods of time will be more easily retained in care.

In a true public-health-oriented health care system, these provisions would be unnecessary. Health insurance should remain active through any period of incarceration and available to cover all health care delivered inside. In addition to improving the continuity of care for individuals detained in prisons and jails, this alignment would reduce expenses to the criminal justice system, and likely also improve the care delivered in these settings.

The quality of health care inside prisons and jails remains unacceptable by modern standards, and legal judgments seeking to improve it go largely unenforced. Because there is no national accreditation mandate or oversight monitoring, there is no assurance that prisoners will receive preventive health care during their incarceration, or even care that is sufficiently timely for addressing chronic health conditions. In 1976, the U.S. Supreme Court established in *Estelle v. Gamble* that failure to address the medical needs of a prisoner constitutes "cruel and unusual punishment," a violation of the Eighth Amendment, but this case law has not produced a U.S. prison health care system. Obtaining coverage before leaving the criminal justice system does nothing to address the problem of underinvestment in prison health care, where effective and meaningful health interventions are still lacking. In 2016, the Centers for Disease Control released findings from the first-ever report on prison health care in the United States, including results from correctional authorities in forty-five participating states.[14] This information could help to set an agenda for future improvements in the structure and delivery of health care to the incarcerated, and a basis for preserving coverage through the period of incarceration.

Under a single-payer plan, universal coverage facilitates the sharing of health information among providers, which is crucial to ensuring the continuity and coordination of care. In the absence of a single-payer model, electronic health records provide a functionally similar method for achieving this arrangement, if implementation is sufficiently widespread. In 2009, a federal law offered incentives for providers instituting such health information technology to promote this approach, including in correctional health care settings. Health care connectivity between criminal justice and community-based settings is a critical step toward health care engagement and retention for individuals who have been justice-involved. But for this to occur, health plans need to work with criminal justice settings to develop procedures for record-sharing. The Affordable Care Act created health information exchanges—networks of providers agreeing to share patient electronic health records—to structure this type of relationship.

Ultimately, the participation of prisons and jails in health insurance exchanges provided a critical opportunity for improving health care connectivity and coordination between the criminal justice setting and community-based care. As systems prepare for or undergo larger structural changes, correctional agencies can help to carve the relational pathways for building these kinds of partnerships. In Connecticut, state agencies representing both the health and human services and the criminal justice systems, respectively, established an agreement to accept each other's release-of-information forms in order to authorize the sharing of health—including behavioral health—information.[15] Ideally, policy standards for data collection and information exchange between the health care and criminal justice systems are established in a data governance structure.[16]

In the absence of a single-payer plan, who are the health care providers with whom jails and prisons should develop information-sharing agreements and foster technological connectivity? In Multnomah County, Oregon, 80 percent of health care providers are using the same electronic health record as the jail.[17] Achieving this level of integration could be a goal for some jurisdictions, but community health centers, known as federally qualified health clinics, offer a natural starting place for building this relationship. These sites are structured to provide safety net care and are located in many of the same neighborhoods experiencing hyperincarceration.

The transitions clinic model formalizes this role by explicitly identifying itself as a primary-care-coordinated care service for formerly incarcerated individuals with chronic health conditions, and incorporates community health workers with similar lived experience.[18] Participants in this model have lower rates of emergency room visits in comparison with their counterparts receiving regular primary care, demonstrating effective care engagement and suggesting improved health outcomes.[19]

Investment in Behavioral Health Care as a Core Component of the General Health Care System

Coverage brings the opportunity for health care access. Given the prevalence of mental illness and addiction among prisoners in the United States, improving access to behavioral health care is a significant opportunity for reducing and preventing incarceration. In a public health vision, behavioral health care is part of general health care. This represents an approach distinctly different from its historical relegation to the realm of specialty care, where it has remained isolated and underfunded, in contrast to the enormous investment made in a criminal justice response to drug use. Through the process of psychiatric deinstitutionalization, the mental health care system lost critical funding that could have developed a community-based approach.

The introduction of mental health managed care in the 1980s led to indirect cost-shifting from health care to jails. As people with mental illness were incarcerated, their managed care coverage was terminated as they moved out of the domain of community mental health care and into the separate universe of the criminal justice system. With the health of these individuals no longer under their purview, providers and insurers realized system-level cost savings as a consequence.[20] Community-based models were not adequately financed, nor were they structured to address the integrated health and social needs of people with mental illness and their families.[21] Advances in psychosocial treatment, medication-assisted addiction treatment, psychopharmacology, and mental health services over the past two decades have introduced opportunities for considerable improvement, but coverage and capacity have remained out of reach.

The segmentation and starvation of behavioral health care in the specialty model gained some relief with the passage of a mandate for parity coverage with medical and surgical care in 2008 legislation. This mandate was reinforced by the Affordable Care Act in 2010, which named behavioral health care as one of ten essential health benefits for coverage. Because the act also expanded coverage, individuals could actually gain access to behavioral health care via the parity requirement, and meet their treatment needs. Medicaid expansion began generating improvements in the quality of behavioral health care delivered by safety net providers, including the integration of behavioral health care with medical care and medical-legal partnerships and community-based services to address the social determinants of health.[22]

A series of studies tracked the effect of enrollment in Medicaid upon release from jail on behavioral health care and subsequent rearrest among justice-involved people with serious mental illness. This research was conducted several years before the 2010 Affordable Care Act and examined Medicaid coverage linked to disability benefits for people with serious mental illness. Investigators found that the group with Medicaid at release was more likely to use community-based services, to access them quickly, and to participate for longer periods of time. Importantly, they also experienced less reincarceration: a 16 percent reduction in the average number of subsequent detentions.[23]

Despite the expansion of coverage and the reinforcement of parity provided by the Affordable Care Act, the problem of behavioral health care capacity has remained a barrier to treatment on demand, especially for substance use disorders. In 2016, the Comprehensive Addiction and Recovery Act and the subsequent 21st Century Cures Act responded to this gap with investments to improve treatment access and quality and to augment community mental health services.

Another study describes the effect of expanding publicly funded substance use disorder treatment on treatment utilization and arrest rates in a jail-involved population. From 2005 to 2009, Washington invested in a massive treatment expansion on the basis of projected cost savings in medical and long-term care, which the study found were subsequently realized. The expansion also resulted in significantly lower arrest rates in the year following treatment, with arrests declining by 17 to 33 percent across three differently insured groups under the expansion.[24]

Taken together, the effects documented in these studies suggest that, in combination, coverage for people with behavioral health conditions and capacity expansion for care and treatment will both reduce incarceration as a preventive effect, and reduce the potential for recidivism after reentry. Whether national legislative efforts to develop this foundation in recent years will succeed in broadening access and improving quality remains to be seen, but certainly they affirm meaningful progress in this regard.

Supportive Services to Address the Social Determinants of Health

Community health workers improve the cultural competence of the health care structure and support participants in addressing their priority needs. The growing professionalization of this role within the health care system acknowledges the specific, invaluable expertise of the care provider with lived experience similar to that of the person being helped, something that is especially relevant to the experiences of former prisoners with community reentry. These roles extend the practical influence of community health care beyond the clinic walls, recognizing and responding to the influence of social factors on health outcomes. In other words, they can address and reduce the risk of reincarceration head-on. For the formerly incarcerated, the creation of the community health worker role also offers an employment opportunity, important because extended unemployment in the period after incarceration is a significant risk factor for reincarceration.[25]

The involvement of reentry community health workers in health care delivery for justice-involved individuals, such as with the transitions clinic model, can dramatically reduce recidivism among patients. At a program site of the Michigan Prisoner Reentry Initiative, a community health worker program that focuses on recent parolees with serious medical needs, the recidivism rate declined by half in the five years after the program began.[26] Outcomes such as this affirm the intrinsic value of provider lived experience for attending to the social determinants of health. In the community health center model, community health workers could help to reverse the local effects of hyperincarceration and prove invaluable for shrinking the criminal justice system.

Since the 1990s, states have had the opportunity to allocate Medicaid funding for case management services to particular populations, such as the seriously mentally ill. With the Affordable Care Act, eligible populations for this care coordination model, called Medicaid health homes, were expanded to include people with any one of a number of chronic health conditions, including diabetes, hypertension, and asthma, and also including substance use disorders. By allocating health care dollars to fund supportive services for low-income individuals, this arrangement introduced a pathway for strengthening the social safety net. Justice-involved individuals with one of the targeted chronic health conditions could gain invaluable case management assistance from this model.

In another model, supportive services can operate as the connective tissue in a structural network of health care providers, to promote care coordination and facilitate engagement and retention in care. The Affordable Care Act offered several mechanisms for structuring such a network, one example being the accountable care organization (ACO). This approach allowed the network to accrue and reinvest the cost savings it realized in patient care, such as through patient-level reductions in emergency department visits. An ACO serving a community characterized by hyperincarceration could choose to invest cost savings into reentry case management as a supportive service of the network, for example, or into hiring community health workers as network staff. Evidence suggests this approach would reduce both recidivism and emergency department visits by the justice-involved individuals it served, while improving their engagement in health care.

In short, supportive services could improve reentry, reduce recidivism, and facilitate diversion away from the criminal justice system entirely. With a community-oriented approach in their design and implementation, these features can be leveraged to reduce hyperincarceration in communities and prevent individual-level justice involvement. Coverage will ensure access to services, treatment, and care. And services, treatment, and care—especially for mental health and substance use disorders—could reduce recidivism, bolster reentry services, and provide options for diversion and deflection away from the criminal justice system.

Contexts and Futures

Much of the content described here emerged in part from the 2010 Affordable Care Act, a watershed moment for U.S. health care. Although the act captured some of the best among the accumulated policies and initiatives from the past thirty years for strengthening the U.S. health care structure, it did not go far enough. It did not achieve universal coverage, although it made a significant dent in the problem of the uninsured. And while the act offered innovative models for building supportive services, these were not widely nor uniformly adopted by states. Behavioral health care in the United States remains woefully sparse and still suffers from a lack of integration with general health care. The evidence base for substance use disorder treatment remains thin. While the gains made by the act were tremendously important for strengthening and improving the U.S. health care system, there is still considerable distance to travel if we are to reach a public health vision.

At the time of this writing in 2017, the future of the 2010 Affordable Care Act is deeply uncertain. Whether and how the act will be repealed and replaced remains unknown. Even worse are the threats to convert the federal Medicaid program to a block grant for states, effectively undoing the federal standards currently set for services and care delivered with these funds, and restricting the dollars supporting them in what will most certainly result in cuts to care. In spite of this political jousting, optimism about improvements and developments in the future might be found in the positive experiences of Americans with the recent health care reforms. The effectiveness of the explicit public health vision adopted by the Affordable Care Act's version of health care reform has not been lost on the many millions who have gained coverage and on the many thousands who accessed behavioral health care or benefited from care coordination services. If the stories of constituents mean anything in federal policy making, these experiences could help to generate an even better health care approach for coverage, behavioral health care, and services in the future. It is possible that, in the contested political landscape of U.S. health care, we may finally land on a national single-payer plan quite soon.

The case for health care as a vehicle for decarceration is located in the structural context of public systems and in the sociohistorical context of class and race in the United States. Making this case a reality demands an cross-sectoral perspective on public systems and a belief that this type of vision can be realized with coordinated leadership. In the mirrored worlds of policy making and policy advocacy, where actors prefer to "stay in their lane" and operate within their system silos, meaningful work across the divides can be difficult to accomplish. Finding the best mix of stakeholder involvement, telling compelling stories to the audiences that will have the most impact, and assuring all sides that they will benefit from working together to achieve this kind of change—these elements represent important challenges to making the cross-sectoral vision a reality. At its best, this vision is still a threat to the structural status quo.

The inequities characterizing both the health care system and the criminal justice system in the United States emerge from the nation's sociohistorical conflict with race and class—its categorical allegiance to the former, and its cultural denial of the latter. The case for health care as a mechanism for decarceration rests principally on these issues of civil rights and status. This vision expresses hopeful potential for the impact of focused and sustained public-health-oriented health care investments directed to hyperincarcerated communities, which are low-income and predominantly Black and Latino.

But could this same framework also protect other groups from vulnerability to criminalization in the future? At the time of this writing, the federal government is launching a massive national campaign to deport thousands, perhaps millions, of undocumented immigrants from the country. Even in self-proclaimed sanctuary cities, where safety net providers are strictly prohibited from requesting immigration documents from patients, health care utilization has already dropped off. Despite assurances from local authorities, people are understandably fearful that public health care providers will be legally obliged to cooperate with immigration law enforcement. If these fears do not come true, then the health care decarceration vehicle could offer some relief. This group would benefit from inclusion in universal coverage and the availability of relevant supportive services, such as the medical-legal partnership model at community health centers. While this arrangement could help to prevent detentions and deportations, it is still too early to predict how the current situation will evolve.

Over the past decade, the term "mass incarceration" joined popular discourse in the United States, and some intimations of a public reckoning with our practice as the world's leading jailer occurred. It remains to be seen whether the political will is strong enough to pursue meaningful action for reversing this practice and for repairing the damage it has done. What is certain, however, is that the construction of a health care system truly grounded in a public health vision could play a central part in this shift. The combined effect of the three features presented here could actually generate a lot of the systemic change necessary to accomplish decarceration. Taken together, and designed and implemented to achieve health and social equity, they could produce a health care system that advances and secures the social safety net and reduces the now-habituated overreach and reliance on the criminal justice system to address health and social problems.

None of this will happen without intent. An engaged citizenry must voice their demands and expectations for an improved and expanded national health care system, and their commitment to considerable public investments ensuring its sustainability. Advocates and scholars can produce imaginative and thoughtful ideas for leveraging the health care system to promote decarceration, and policy makers and public officials have to orchestrate the pathways and structures for getting there. The commitment to decarceration must become rooted deep in U.S. policy, business, and culture. We have seen a vision for how health care could be a vehicle for building some of this foundation now, and we have an obligation to ensure it remains strong and grows.

Notes

1. Throughout this chapter, the terms mental illness and addiction are used for ease of understanding, instead of the standard clinical terminology, mental health condition and substance use disorder, respectively. These terms, in the general vernacular, are sometimes used pejoratively; such meaning is not intended in any part of this text.

2. L. Wacquant, "The Body, the Ghetto and the Penal State," *Qualitative Sociology* 32 (2009): 101–29.

3. P. Farmer, *Pathologies of Power: Health, Human Rights, and the New War on the Poor* (Berkeley: University of California Press, 2003).

4. L. Wacquant, "The New 'Peculiar Institution': On the Prison as Surrogate Ghetto," *Theoretical Criminology* 4, no. 3 (2000): 377–89.

5. T. Skocpol, *Health Care Reform and the Turn Against Government* (New York: Norton, 1996).

6. E.A. Wang, M.C. White, R. Jamison, J. Goldenson, M. Estes, and J.P. Tulsky, "Discharge Planning and Continuity of Health Care: Findings from the San Francisco County Jail," *American Journal of Public Health* 98, no. 12 (2008): 2182–4.

7. K. Patel, A. Boutwell, B.W. Brockmann, and J.D. Rich, "Integrating Correctional and Community Health Care for Formerly Incarcerated People Who Are Eligible for Medicaid," *Health Affairs* 33, no. 3 (2014): 468–73; J.D. Rich, R. Chandler, B.A. Williams, D. Dumont, E.A. Wang, F.S. Taxman, S.A. Allen, J.G. Clarke, R.B. Greifinger, C. Wildeman, F.C. Osher, S. Rosenberg, C. Haney, M. Mauer, and B. Western, "How Health Care Reform Can Transform the Health of Criminal Justice–Involved Individuals," *Health Affairs* 33, no. 3 (2014): 462–67.

8. National Research Council, *The Growth of Incarceration in the United States: Exploring Causes and Consequences* (Washington, DC: National Academies Press, 2014).

9. B. Western and B. Petit, "Incarceration and Social Inequality," *Daedalus*, Summer 2010, 8–19.

10. A.E. Cuellar and J. Cheema, "Health Care Reform, Behavioral Health, and the Criminal Justice Population," *Journal of Behavioral Health Services and Research* 41, no. 4 (2014): 447–59; Patel et al., "Integrating Correctional and Community Health Care."

11. S.N. Bandara, H.A. Huskamp, L.E. Riedel, E.E. McGinty, D. Webster, R.E. Toone, and C.L. Barry, "Leveraging the Affordable Care Act to Enroll Justice-Involved Populations in Medicaid: State and Local Efforts," *Health Affairs* 34, no. 12 (2015): 2044–51.

12. S.A. Somers, E. Nicolella, A. Hamblin, S.M. McMahon, C. Heiss, and B.W. Brockmann, "Medicaid Expansion: Considerations for States Regarding Newly Eligible Jail-Involved Individuals," *Health Affairs* 33, no. 3 (2014): 455–61.

13. J. Guyer, D. Bachrach, and N. Shine, "Medicaid Expansion and Criminal Justice Costs: Pre-expansion Studies and Emerging Practices Point Toward Opportunities for States," State Health Reform Assistance Network, November 2015, 1–8.

14. K.A. Chari, A.E. Simon, C.J. DeFrances, and L. Maruschak, "National Survey of Prison Health Care: Selected Findings," National Health Statistics Reports no. 96, National Center for Health Statistics, 2016.

15. R.L. Trestman and R.H. Aseltine Jr., "Justice-Involved Health Information: Policy and Practice Advances in Connecticut," *Perspectives in Health Information Management*, Winter 2014, 1–11.

16. D. Cloud, M. Dougherty, R.L. May II, J. Parsons, P. Wormeli, and W.J. Rudman, "At the Intersection of Health and Justice," *Perspectives in Health Information Management*, Winter 2014, 1–4.

17. B. Butler and J. Murphy, "The Impact of Policies Promoting Health Information Technology on Health Care Delivery in Jails and Local Communities," *Health Affairs* 33, no. 3 (2014): 487–92.

18. E.A. Wang, C.S. Hong, L. Samuels, S. Shavit, R. Sanders, and M. Kushel, "Transitions Clinic: Creating a Community-Based Model of Health Care for Recently Released California Prisoners," *Public Health Reports* 125, no. 2 (2010): 171–77.

19. E.A. Wang, C.S. Hong, S. Shavit, R. Sanders, E. Kessell, and M.B. Kushel, "Engaging Individuals Recently Released from Prison into Primary Care: A Randomized Trial," *American Journal of Public Health* 102, no. 9 (2012): e22–e29.

20. M.E. Domino, E.C. Norton, J.P. Morrissey, and N. Thakur, "Cost Shifting to Jails After a Change to Managed Mental Health Care," *Health Services Research* 39, no. 5 (2004): 1379–401.

21. U. Aviram, "Community Care of the Seriously Mentally Ill: Continuing Problems and Current Issues," *Community Mental Health Journal* 26, no. 1 (1990): 69–88.

22. A. Searing and J. Hoadley, "Medicaid Expansion: Driving Innovation in Behavioral Health Integration," *Health Affairs Blog*, July 5, 2016, http://healthaffairs.org/blog/2016/07/05/medicaid-expansion-driving-innovation-in-behavioral-health-integration.

23. J.P. Morrissey, H.J. Steadman, K.M. Dalton, A. Cuellar, P. Stiles, and G.S. Cuddeback, "Medicaid Enrollment and Mental Health Service Use Following Release of Jail Detainees with Severe Mental Illness," *Psychiatric Services* 57, no. 6 (2006): 809–15; J.P. Morrissey, G.S. Cuddeback, A.E. Cuellar, and H.J. Steadman, "The Role of Medicaid Enrollment and Outpatient Service Use in Jail Recidivism Among Persons with Severe Mental Illness," *Psychiatric Services* 58, no. 6 (2007): 795–801.

24. D. Mancuso and B.E.M. Felver, "Chemical Dependency, Public Safety: Implications for Arrest Rates, Victims, and Community Protection," Washington State Department of Social and Health Services Research and Data Analysis Division, February 2009, www.dshs.wa.gov/sites/default/files/SESA/rda/documents/research-11-140.pdf.

25. J.D. Morenoff and D.J. Harding, "Incarceration, Prisoner Reentry, and Communities," *Annual Review of Sociology* 40 (2014): 411–29.

26. Patel et al., "Integrating Correctional and Community Health Care."

12

Come Close In
Voices of Survivors
of Mass Incarceration

KATHY BOUDIN

In September 2016 I attended the first national conference of the Formerly Incarcerated and Convicted People and Families Movement in Oakland.[1] We were more than six hundred people from thirty-six states. Some walked with limps, used canes, and had spent more than forty years inside. Others were mothers, sisters, and brothers—lifelines who had supported family members in prison and returning home. Old friends hugged, tears flowed. We were home, together, celebrating a new life, and organizing for change. People crowded into the large meeting room, women and men, and listened to one another on panels; they sat on the benches at tables outside the meeting room sharing their lives and their work: getting the vote, banning the box on employment forms and college applications, securing housing for people returning from prison, and challenging the mass incarceration and mass criminalization system. They spoke of their efforts to run organizations to develop housing, their attempts to make health care accessible for people returning home, and their policy work to bring higher education back into prisons. Chants resounded: "All of us or none"; "Those closest to the ground are closest to the solution"; "Nothing about us without us."[2]

For years, lawyers, advocates, activists, policy makers, service providers, health workers, and others have devoted themselves to improving the lives of people impacted by incarceration. And substantial numbers of people in prison and those who have returned home have worked at advocacy and change even as they struggle to survive. However, this is the first time that people who were in prison, together with those who are supporting loved ones inside, are becoming a national organized voice. More than two million people are currently incarcerated, and between seventy million and a hundred million people—one out of three Americans—have criminal records.[3] It is estimated that six hundred thousand people will return from prison each year. And tens of millions of people are enduring the consequences of felony convictions. There is a growing willingness to come out of the shadow of stigma and the shame to proclaim our humanity and be actively engaged in change. These new voices turn out to be those of your neighbors, co-workers, parents, elders, students, and friends. As with the AIDS epidemic, when the very people who are dehumanized and stigmatized struggle against dehumanization and stigma, they can change social attitudes and culture, policies and laws.

Who Are the Change-Makers?

Some years ago, I attended a conference on prison reform where I realized that almost none of the speakers spoke about the role of those inside prison in contributing to change. From my seat in the audience, I asked: "Does anyone here think that people in prison or home from prison make a contribution to changing the system?" There was a dead silence. Finally one panelist said from the podium, "I think they do. They help humanize the situation."

I was grateful for his comment because the humanizing is critical. But the answer missed what I knew from my own experience in prison about how people inside and those who have returned play major roles in creating change. The Oakland conference revealed how they have become a significant force against mass incarceration and all its devastating human consequences. It is important to recognize this, not only because the formerly incarcerated show the human face of mass incarceration but also because they bring practical solutions based upon their own experiences, as well as a commitment to a better society because of what they have endured.

The fundamental premise of this chapter is that the experience of incarceration and the struggle to reintegrate create a particular knowledge that often combines with a passion for change. Of course it does not assume that just because people have been incarcerated they are clear about causes or solutions, or that they are skilled advocates or policy makers. But when a person's experience combines with reflection, contributions to their communities, work with peers, knowledge, and self-transformation, change-makers develop among the formerly incarcerated, and they occupy diverse roles in the movement to end mass incarceration and criminalization of their communities.

This chapter begins inside prison because it is during incarceration, despite the brutal conditions, that significant numbers of people emerge as change-makers. It describes the role of formerly incarcerated people when they return back to society. It looks at the role of women, who are often left out of discussions about prison. The final section focuses on long-termers, those convicted of violent crimes, who are usually demonized and removed from criminal justice reform. It advocates for recognition of the complex humanity of those who struggle against being frozen forever into their single worst moment by labels like "offender" and "ex-offender." And it addresses both the objective conditions and the social narratives responsible for mass incarceration.

Collective Challenges to Prison Conditions: Uprisings, Strikes, Class-Action Lawsuits

The most widely known ways that people in prison have contributed to changes have come through uprisings, protests, and class-action lawsuits. The historic Attica uprising took place in September 1971. The men were driven by the desperation of unbearable conditions inside—constant abuse by guards, medical neglect, lack of showers—as well as inspired by liberation movements outside of prison walls. Most basically, they were asking for an acknowledgment of their humanity: "We are men, not beasts, and we do not intend to be driven as such. The entire prison populace—that means each and every one of us here—has set forth to change forever the ruthless brutalization and disregard for the lives of the prisoners here." These words were spoken on September 9, 1971, by L. D. Barkley, who served as a spokesperson during the Attica uprising and who was killed at the age of twenty-one on September 13, 1971.[4] The men tried to gain control of the prison and took a number of hostages. Once this occurred, they tried to negotiate a peaceful settlement, including amnesty for those involved in the takeover, educational classes, religious freedom, and fairer disciplinary practices. But Governor Nelson Rockefeller ordered state troopers to storm the prison. By the end of the assault, thirty-nine people—twenty-nine people who were incarcerated and ten hostages—had been killed by the state police. This insurrection changed the entire dynamic within prisons and initiated a national discussion about prison policy and practices. This uprising, brought about by the denial of the humanity of incarcerated people, echoes today. The assertion of their humanity and the fight for that humanity are the most lasting legacy of Attica.

More recently, the incarcerated men at the Pelican Bay facility in California went on hunger strikes to protest the use of solitary confinement. Three hunger strikes—the last one in 2013—involved thirty thousand people in California prisons, supported by the movement among their family members on the outside. This organizing and solidarity achieved a settlement relating to serious abuse of solitary confinement. Unprecedented was the fact that the incarcerated men were part of the team negotiating with the state. They worked in a unified committee across lines of race and ethnicity, traditionally used by corrections personnel to keep people in prison divided.[5]

And in the summer of 2016, what may be the first nationally coordinated prison labor strike took place, protesting prison labor conditions. The Thirteenth Amendment to the Constitution abolished slavery but left an exception for people who have been convicted of crimes. This means that incarcerated people can legally be put to work for little or no pay. The labor strike, involving more than twenty thousand incarcerated people in at least twelve states, contributes to the growing awareness about the clause in the Thirteenth Amendment that continues to permit slavery in prison.[6]

Individual and class-action lawsuits have been another form of the struggle for change, relying on the people inside in collaboration with their lawyers, and often family members and community advocates. Class-action lawsuits include but are not limited to medical conditions, parole, solitary confinement, lack of education programs, and violence by correctional staff; in women's prisons there have been many lawsuits about sexual abuse by the staff.[7]

Building Programs and Projects Inside the Prison: Collectively and Individually

In less well-known and less likely situations, people in prison have developed programs and projects that touch and change those inside and often reach beyond the prison. Being separated from society requires learning to survive and transform oneself under the most difficult conditions. For many, this means making a contribution to others, in conditions that also include daily humiliations, degradation, and often actual violence.

The following examples profile significant contributions men and women in prison have made to solving problems within prison as well as addressing national problems. They illustrate the talent and lessons available if only we see them for what they are: critical resources in the struggle against over-criminalization and mass incarceration.

Incarcerated Women as Engines of Change

Most people don't think about women when discussing people in prison. Yet women now account for a larger proportion of the prison population than ever before, with the female prison population today nearly eight times higher than it was in 1980. Though many more men are in prison than women—women are approximately 7 percent of the total prison population—the rate of growth for female imprisonment has outpaced men by more than 50 percent between 1980 and 2014.[8]

During the twenty-two years I was incarcerated at Bedford Hills Correctional Facility, a maximum-security facility for women, we saw ourselves as agents of transformation—always in collaboration with people outside the prison, some extraordinary staff in the prison, and the required permission of the prison administration. But we imprisoned women were key engines of change.

The AIDS Counseling and Education organization was an early example. At the height of the AIDS epidemic, in 1988, almost 20 percent of the women entering the state system were HIV-positive.[9] The prison atmosphere was defined by fear, ignorance, and stigma. "Don't sit next to her," they whispered, "she's been to see the nurse a lot." "Don't use her tray," they said, loud enough for people to hear in the mess hall. Corrections personnel knew that both management and public health required change. In most prisons, this meant isolating those infected with HIV.

We knew that in order to foster stability, create humane conditions for those who were infected, and reduce transmission, we needed to transform the culture of fear and stigma to one of caring, support, and knowledge. We became educated, held the dying in our arms, and, when they died, held memorials. We taught workshops about the disease and its prevention. We joined a national movement to raise awareness and support, making quilts and doing our own walkathons around the prison yard. And we supported those with the virus who now spoke out and gave others courage. We changed the face of AIDS sufferers from that of monster to neighbor, friend, even best friend. And in six months we managed to get our program funded by the AIDS Institute.

Within two years, the head of correctional health care came to see our program as a model for all the New York State prisons, and within four years, it had become an inspiration for people in other states and a model adapted by some other prison administrations. In order to share the experience, and the model, we wrote *Breaking the Walls of Silence: AIDS and Women in a New York State Maximum Security Prison*.[10] It made the program's history, activities, and curriculum widely available, and was distributed to prison libraries around the country. The women who founded the program, sat with the dying, and acted as peer educators and counselors, changed, grew, and went home to real jobs, becoming much-needed HIV/AIDS counselors and educators in their own communities.

On another front, in 1986, some women who had been convicted of murder after being subjected to domestic violence participated in public hearings, held in the gym, that were attended by media, judges, and state legislators. They broke a different barrier of silence, fear, and shame by testifying about how the violence in their lives had affected them, raising consciousness about the relation between domestic violence and crime. The issue of "battered women" was also a focus in California, where twenty-five women at California Institution for Women who had killed their abusers mobilized and built a coalition to free women who had been abused, signing a joint habeas corpus petition. The initiative came from the inside and led to an outside coalition that became a significant movement challenging hundreds of convictions of women who had been abused and building consciousness about abuse of women and the need for criminal justice reform.

Parenting was another area where women imprisoned at Bedford took the initiative. With the support of exceptional staff and a model children's center in the visiting room, women learned to move beyond the guilt and paralysis of the "bad mother" label to support and understand their children. They also went on to teach parenting classes, including prenatal classes, classes about parenting from a distance, and classes about being mothers of adolescents; they became caregivers in the nursery and in the children's center in the visiting room, and became children's advocates who worked with mothers, children, and guardians.

Education was a major theme of the work to improve our lives and those of others. In 1995, when Congress ended Pell grants for people who were incarcerated, women at Bedford initiated a process that ultimately brought privately funded college courses to the prison. College presidents began visiting and learned from the women at Bedford about the importance of higher education in helping to redirect their lives. With local community support, one by one the college presidents agreed to donate a professor a semester to a newly established degree-granting consortium led by Marymount Manhattan. In part as a result of this success, privately funded colleges throughout New York State now offer programs to incarcerated people. Veterans of that experience are leading organizations to support men and women returning from prison who want to pursue higher education, and they are advocates for public support for college inside prisons.

And women in prison have tackled problems no one else would even know about. In 1985, women in Central California Women's Facility, Valley State, and California Institute for Women mobilized to end the barbaric practice of shackling women during childbirth. Their example inspired a movement of women inside and outside prison in New York State that took thirty years to get legislation passed outlawing the practice.[11]

Men in Prison as Movers

It is often harder to initiate and carry out collaborative work among men in prison because such efforts are more often seen as threats to discipline and order. Despite this, men too have been active and created programs. Men in prison created PACE to meet the challenge of the AIDS epidemic throughout New York State prisons. After the Omnibus Crime Control Act ended Pell grants for higher education for incarcerated people, the men at Sing Sing initiated a program to reestablish college. Soon the community in Westchester joined with the men inside to establish a robust college program carried out by Mercy College.

One of the better-known projects was organized by a small group of men calling themselves the Think Tank at Green Haven prison in 1968. In research that has had a national impact, the men found that more than 85 percent of incarcerated people in the state are black or Latino and—most phenomenal of all—that 75 percent of the state's entire prison population came from just seven neighborhoods in New York City.

Their work made concrete the connection between poverty and race and prison. There should be investment in housing, schools, health care, and jobs in these communities.[12] The work done by the men in Green Haven ultimately laid the foundation for the establishment of the Justice Mapping Center at

Columbia University's School of Architecture, which helps urban centers analyze their cities with the idea of justice reinvestment.[13]

Even when conditions make organizing impossible, and they often do, men have found ways to make enormous contributions, for both those inside and those outside. Wilbert Rideau not only fought his way off death row at the infamous Louisiana State Penitentiary, known as Angola, but in the forty-four years before his release founded and edited a prize-winning newspaper, *The Angolite*, which became a national model. He has gone on to speak and write, contributing to and editing books and documentaries about prisons, justice, and peace education.

Thousands of often self-educated law librarians and jailhouse lawyers dedicate all the time allowed by their obligatory prison work schedules to researching, counseling, and fighting to uncover and reverse wrongful convictions—their own and those of others in prison with them. It is, after all, thanks to people such as the prison-educated Earl Gideon, who insisted that poor people should have the right to representation by a lawyer, that this right exists today.[14]

Why, Then, Are These Programs the Exception Instead of the Rule?

First, we have to recognize that this heartening work could happen only because some women and men had the courage to challenge the prevailing narrative. Punitive criminal justice models reinforce and are reinforced by racism, unequal distribution of social and economic goods, and political power. Together, these lead prison officials to view people in prison as less rational and less capable than others, as people to be "corrected"—in short, as the problem itself. The notion that incarcerated people could be part of the solution, that they could make a positive difference in a worldwide crisis such as AIDS, is inconceivable to most correctional authorities, as well as to the broader society.

Prison life is predicated on most administrators' views that society has given them a mandate to maintain absolute security, which they take to mean absolute control. Initiatives by and empowerment of incarcerated people are seen as threats to that mandate. Although prisons are theoretically designed to carry out the mission of incapacitation, deterrence, punishment, and rehabilitation, the emphasis is always on punishment. In the age of mass incarceration, the goal of supporting personal growth, referred to as "rehabilitation," has largely disappeared.

The conditions that people live in, even in prisons where more initiative is allowed, create obstacles and disincentives. They are filled with constant humiliations, disrespect, and the ever-present threat and reality of violence: beatings, fights, and rapes by prison guards, all of which create an atmosphere engendering violence among those who are incarcerated. Occasional news stories provide a glimpse: beatings by guards, overcrowding leading to people sleeping three to a cell with one on the floor, the elimination of programs.[15] Things that happen every day lead to enormous stress, frustration, hopelessness, and violence among the people in prison, directed at themselves.

But these news items can't capture the routine humiliations. You are a number. You are counted several times a day. Told when to be where. Subject to cell searches in which the guard throws your sheets, your toothbrush, your legal papers, and a photo of your son together on the floor as you stand outside and watch, and then announces: "No contraband found. Clean up your cell." Had a privilege—say, education—threatened by a misbehavior report for having an extra piece of underwear.

And then there is the large number of mentally ill people, who receive little or no help in prison but instead, when they are in crisis, are sent to solitary confinement, which challenges the stability of the most level-headed. Plus the impunity of corrections officers—just another fact of life in prison. The reality is hard to communicate, perhaps best done by stories or poetry.[16]

Mass incarceration, brutalization, solitary confinement—it doesn't have to be this way. Germany, the Netherlands, and Norway, among other countries, do not increase the punishment beyond that of separation from society.[17] Their goal is to treat people as human beings with dignity and respect so that when they return to society they can build successful lives.

Change the Narrative

The narrative about people in prison is not just developed by the prison administrations and personnel. It is based on a narrative from the broader society. To move beyond defining people as "offenders" and "ex-offenders" requires dealing with racism, the history of white supremacy, and the legacy of slavery, all of which has been a key factor in dehumanizing people throughout our history—one result being mass incarceration. A history of toxic racism reinforces media images, academic theories, and policies that contribute to stereotypes of black boys and men (and, increasingly, black girls and women) as somehow threatening or dangerous to white people. When instead of shared humanity and empathy there is merely the chasm of race, punishment is the easy answer. We must increase awareness that we live in the grip of a racialized punishment paradigm and not just in the criminal justice system. Look at the punitive and disciplinary approach in schools in low-resourced neighborhoods, resulting in the school-to-prison pipeline and in a zero-tolerance approach instead of a problem-solving one.

In addition to the general view of people in prison, different narratives are used to justify the treatment of women and men. Women are frequently defined as victims of abuse or by deficits such as low education or drug addiction. They are often reduced to a label flowing from the act that brought them to prison: "ho," "monster," "man-hater," "mule," or "baby-killer." A narrative about women is often based on the judgment of the "immoral" or "fallen" woman who has betrayed the ideals of the "good woman" or the "good mother."

These paradigms tend to render women passive; they focus on a woman's weaknesses or limitations rather than on her strengths. This ignores a greater truth about women in prison. Women in prison are filled with ideas, energy, dreams, and possibilities. Women in prison can be critical agents of their own change, including facing responsibility for our acts and the damage caused. They can inspire and help other women to change; they can tackle the social problems that they confront inside the prison, and upon going home, they can help change the social conditions that plague society.

Men in prison are more often categorized as dangerous. In New York State, when the three men initiated the idea of an AIDS peer education and counseling program, the first in the state, one was quickly transferred. The program began anyway, but with real limitations. A former corrections official said that when women got together to initiate a new privately funded college program in prison, the organizing process was more acceptable because they were women; once that program was up and running, it was less threatening when men did the same. The racism that was used by politicians, the academy, and the press to fuel public opinion and the growth of mass incarceration follows men into prison. Demagogic language of fear, such as "super-predator," reinforced the police war on youth of color, resulting in gross increases of extreme sentencing and in extreme racial disparities in the criminal justice system. Hysteria about crack cocaine and the rhetoric of war contributed to racial disparities in arrests, passage of laws mandating life sentences without parole, and the increased use of solitary confinement. Men of color are defined as "perpetrators," presented as a permanent unchanging and unchangeable object of fear and hatred. Yet these very same men convicted of crimes of violence have so often themselves been victims of violence. The divide between "perpetrator" and "victim" is a destructive binary. Just as with women, such stereotypes must be thoroughly challenged and overturned.

Returning Citizens

People returning home face continuing punishments, stigma, and exclusion. Almost all will have stories about being turned down for jobs and apartments, having to check boxes and explain their past, paying money for parole supervision and required programs when they have a minimum-wage salary, not being allowed to vote, and the general stigma of having been in prison. Defining people as "ex-offenders," "ex-felons," or "ex-cons" results in a continuing collapse of individuality into the crime. And they return to the same community conditions that they lived in before going to prison. It is not surprising that the return to prison is as common as it is: within three years approximately two-thirds of the people returning from prison are rearrested.[18]

And yet, in spite of these conditions, those who are able to survive the challenging conditions often contribute in many ways. People figured out during their years inside how to get things done and that they want their lives to be part of making change.

Continuing the Work from Inside on the Outside

Often people continue the work they did inside, but in new forms. When a number of men sentenced to the death penalty or to life without parole as juveniles finally were released in Illinois after decades in prison, they helped others by exposing the torture that had led to their coerced and false confessions; they continued their struggle to expose Police Commander Jon Burge and the other police officers under his command in Area 2 and 3 police stations. They spoke to the media, organized rallies, and went to court, now as free men. Ultimately, not only did Burge end up convicted and sentenced to federal prison for perjury, but the City of Chicago, thanks to a campaign for reparations, finally agreed to a historic reparations settlement. The city apologized to the one hundred African American torture survivors, paid each of the men $100,000, committed to providing a free community college education to the survivors and their children and grandchildren, committed to having this history taught in the Chicago public school curriculum, financed a Center for the Victims of Torture in the Southside neighborhood of Burge's Area 2 police station, and commissioned a sculpture or monument to remember the history of Chicago police torture.[19]

When women who had been part of the HIV/AIDS program at Bedford Hills came home, they founded and staffed the Coming Home Program in a New York City hospital to support men and women returning from prison in need of health care. The men involved in the Think Tank at Greenhaven Correctional Facility went on to create NuLeadership, an organization founded by formerly incarcerated men who initially built a base in a college, developing curriculum and educating the public, and went on to be a community-based organization in Brooklyn.[20] Former director Eddie Ellis, in a now well-known "letter to friends," publicly initiated a campaign about the power of language, arguing that those in prison should be referred to as "people," not "felons," "cons," "ex-felons," or "offenders."[21] Recently, fifteen years after this initiative began, the *New York Times* ran a supportive editorial.[22] Some of the men involved in creating the college program at Sing Sing went on to create Hudson Link for Higher Education in Prison, which developed college programs in additional prisons and became a national advocate for higher education in prison.[23]

Meeting the Survival Needs of Those Coming Home and Contributing to the Broader Community

An entire "reentry"/"reintegration" set of services and organizations, both private and governmental, has grown up to meet the needs of the 650,000 people who return home every year from prisons and jails.[24] Many of those working in organizations providing housing, counseling, health care, mentoring, and job searches are themselves "returned citizens." In the experiences of people who staff organizations such as the Fortune Society, the Osborne Association, or the Coming Home Program, it is the connection to a trusted peer that helps people make the transition, start building a new life, cope with the stigma they face, and not give up. Many of those participating in the Oakland conference were directors or creators of organizations that fit this pattern. People returning from prison could be employed on a massive level to support each other to return to society. This would provide employment, draw on the strengths of people who want to help their peers, and reduce recidivism by providing jobs, meaningful work, and the self-esteem and emotional rewards that come from peers helping peers. Still, in some states, parole regulations prohibit people on parole from having contact with each other, aggravating the isolation, stigma, and lack of resources to cope with everyday living.

People returning from prison contribute to the broader community in many other ways as well: as educators in universities, writers, health professionals, social workers, artists, youth workers, executive directors of housing development organizations, government officials, and family and community members.

Changing Policies and Strengthening the Role of the People Impacted by Mass Incarceration

People who have come home from prison have initiated national and local campaigns to change a range of criminal justice policies and to challenge the basic premises of mass incarceration and criminalization of communities.

- Education Inside and Out spearheaded a nationwide campaign to reinstate government support for higher education inside prisons, cut off as part of the 1994 Omnibus Crime Bill.[25]
- All of Us or None began a national campaign to remove the box on employment applications requiring a person to check it if they have a felony conviction, because it stigmatizes and creates an obstacle to employment. Campaigns are now being carried out in cities around the country and extended to college applications.[26]
- JustLeadershipUSA is training formerly incarcerated people throughout the United States to be advocates and to develop a national network to be a force for change. JustLeadershipUSA is leading a campaign to close Rikers Island and advocating to cut incarceration by half by 2030.[27]
- A group of formerly incarcerated people have worked with the Federal Reentry Council setting up meetings between federal officials and formerly incarcerated people to develop and implement change in housing, education, and employment policies.
- In New Orleans, formerly incarcerated people have initiated voting rights campaigns, including Voices of the Experienced (VOTE), to end felony disenfranchisement.[28]

The women's voices increasingly involved in the struggle to end mass incarceration go beyond women who are incarcerated; they include women in communities who must hold together families and community life while the men are in prison. Today, the National Council for Incarcerated and Formerly Incarcerated Women and Girls, an organization that stands on the shoulders of many previous efforts to build and express the voices of women, is developing a national network.[29] In New York, formerly incarcerated women are part of the Women's Building project, transforming the former Bayview prison for women into an international women's center.[30] In Los Angeles, A New Way of Life, created by a formerly incarcerated woman, operates five safe homes that provide a lifeline to hundreds of formerly incarcerated women and children.[31]

Although these organizations and many others raise specific women's issues, they also contribute to a culture of community, family, and relationships for the movement as a whole.

Legitimate Hope: The Long-Termers and Their Unique Role

Long-termers, people with long sentences, are a particular and growing group within the larger population of people in prison. Inside, everyone— incarcerated people and administrators alike—knows that long-termers serve a vital function.[32] Wardens throughout the country have confirmed that they count on them because when long-termers settle and mature, they invest in the prison community to create a life with meaning in spite of facing brutal and humiliating conditions. Long-termers created and led many of the programs described in this article both inside and outside prison: the AIDS programs, the Think Tank, the college programs at Sing Sing and Bedford Hills, the organization of women in California prisons for domestic violence reform, the Pelican Bay hunger strikes. And when long-termers come home they often play key roles in changing policies: NuLeadership, All of Us or None, Ban the Box, and Release Aging People in Prison (RAPP).[33]

Long-termers are usually people convicted of a violent crime. And, as a result of the "tough on crime" decades and the ongoing punishment paradigm that defines the criminal justice system, they are held in prison beyond the minimum of their already lengthy sentences by laws, regulations, and policies that result in denials of parole, compassionate release, clemencies, and work release, as well as exclusion from sentencing reforms.

There is a lack of investment in long-termers on the inside. Scarce resources—programs, education, opportunities for work—are limited either to those without violent offenses or to those with proximate release or potential release dates. Waiting lists for programs often give priority to those with earlier release dates.[34] For example, the recent amendment to the new Pell grant proposal excludes people with more than five years before their next parole date. Given the role that long-termers played in developing college programs when government support was withdrawn, and their general role of leadership and stabilizing the community, this is cruel and shortsighted.

A narrative exists among policy makers, the general public, and many in the prison reform movement, reinforced by media, that divides people in prison into the good (nonviolent) and the bad (the violent). When President Obama spoke at the NAACP convention in 2015 about the need to end mass incarceration, he assured his audience that his modest reforms, such as sentencing reductions and clemency for nonviolent first-time drug offenders, would not lead to the release of the "murderers, the thugs." When people hear "murderer" or "convicted for a violent crime," they see a person who is defined by that one act, frozen into that act. They don't see a person with a story, someone whose life was impacted by social and economic conditions of disadvantage, a person who can change and does change—a person who often becomes a leader in prison and frequently a leader for change when she or he comes home. This narrative reinforces people's fears and supports inhumane treatment inside prison as well as the determination to hold people in prison for as long as possible.

Since coming home after I served twenty-two years for felony murder, I have spoken with many people who fully support criminal justice reform yet can't imagine that this applies to those convicted of violent crimes, including murder. They don't know that long-termers are a special group within the incarcerated and formerly incarcerated in their role as change agents. They never heard of Mujahid Farid, who at the age of forty-five completed the first fifteen years of his fifteen-to-life sentence for attempted murder—and by that time had also completed two bachelor's degrees and two master's degrees, initiated a peer HIV/AIDS program, and worked as a brilliant law paralegal in the law library. For the next eighteen years, he was denied parole over and over, until he finally went home at the age of sixty-three. When he was released, Farid created RAPP, supported by a Soros Foundation Justice Fellowship. RAPP advocates for the release of elderly people in prison who face parole denials because of a crime committed twenty, thirty, or even forty-five years ago.[35] These supporters of criminal justice reform do not know about Sharon, sentenced to eight and a half to eighteen years for the death of a man who raped her, and who came home and earned her master's degree in social work and now is the director of a homeless shelter for the Women's Prison Association. They don't know about Malachi, given a life sentence at fifteen, who helped create an organization for other juveniles sentenced to life in California. They don't know how he and others supported one another, mentored new young people coming into prison, and created projects such as the annual fund-raiser to put together one thousand backpacks filled with health-related products for homeless youth, nor that after coming home Malachi has worked to build restorative justice among Oakland youth.

These are all long-termers who made it home in spite of the policies, rules, and regulations, and they are now contributing to their communities and to the struggle to end mass incarceration. But many do not make it and spend endless years growing older in prison. One was John MacKenzie, sentenced to twenty-five to life. A respected and beloved long-termer, he made many contributions, including the creation of a program to help others face the suffering their acts had caused others. At age seventy, after forty years in prison and having been denied parole ten times, he learned that the parole board had again denied his release, despite a judge having held the parole board in contempt for continuing to do so. Upon learning the news, he went to his cell and hung himself. John MacKenzie had written in an essay: "If society wishes to rehabilitate as well as punish wrongdoers through imprisonment, society—through its lawmakers—must bear the responsibility of tempering justice with mercy. Giving a man legitimate hope is a laudable goal. Giving him false hope is utterly inhuman."[36]

BOUDIN

Legitimate hope is a powerful force for transformation. Seeing those hopes extinguished generates cynicism and despair among an entire population in prison. Refusing to accept the rehabilitation of long-termers also robs society of the unique contributions they can make, and devastates their families.

Long-termers are not a tiny segment of the prison population. Over half of those incarcerated in state prisons have been sentenced for a violent crime. One of every seven people in prison in the United States is now serving a life sentence or a virtual life sentence of more than fifty years. About a third have been sentenced to life without parole. Nearly half of lifers are African Americans, and one out of six is Latino.[37] The United States is far out of step with other countries in its use of life without parole and in the length of time parole-eligible lifers continue to be imprisoned.[38]

Some people say, "We have to go step by step. Let's first get out those who have committed non-violent crimes. It's a tactical question. Later we will get to those convicted of violent crimes." But there is a consequence to separating incarcerated men and women into the "good ones" and the "bad ones." This deepens the dehumanization of a large proportion of the prison population and continues to devalue or ignore the potential for human transformation. It ignores the reality that many in prison convicted of violent crimes have themselves suffered from violence. The dichotomy that divides "victims" from "perpetrators" misses the connection in individuals' lives. It does not actually relate to protecting public safety, nor does it adequately address transforming a bloated and failing system of mass incarceration.

When harm is done, when people are hurt or killed, there is often grief, rage, and endless loss, and accountability is critical. During the past decades, some "victims" or "survivors" of violent crimes have created organizations that advocate incarcerating long-termers for as long as possible. However, a growing number of victims or survivors are saying that the lengthy punishments do not meet their needs. They are asking what a system of accountability would look like if it didn't rely solely on punitive, lengthy sentences.[39] They are part of the larger conversation that is questioning the role of lengthy incarceration and asking how much punishment is enough. Restorative justice projects, some before incarceration and others inside prisons, are one way of addressing this issue.[40] And individual accountability is only one part of the picture. *Social* responsibility is needed to address the impact of harm resulting from the social conditions and structure.

The memory of a few, exceptional, sensationalized cases in which people released after conviction for violent offenses committed a new act of violence has frozen politicians and others in fear. The reality is that people released following murder convictions have the lowest rate of return, both for technical violations while under supervision and for new offenses. In New York State, the recidivism rate for long-termers convicted of murder is 15.5 percent, with only 2.1 percent for new offenses and 13.4 percent for parole violations. And for people over fifty-six, the recidivism rate is 6.6 percent, with a 1.3 percent rate for new offenses. This low rate of recidivism is in comparison to a rate of around 40 percent for the general population of people released from prison.[41] Denial of parole for these long-termers is not based upon any objective criterion related to public safety and recidivism.

The focus on perpetual punishment of long-termers is tied to the "tough on crime" policies that emphasize the retributive goal of corrections. Parole boards continually look backward, extending sentences because of the "nature of the crime"—something for which the judge already gave a minimum sentence—instead of looking forward to whether or not there is a risk to public safety. It is well documented that the maturing of young adults leads to a sharp reduction in involvement in crime by their late thirties; holding people in prison beyond fifteen or twenty years produces diminishing returns for public safety. In particular, such parole policies ignore the existence of risk and needs assessments that can contribute to evaluations of people as a basis for a decision for release. Fear among politicians focusing on reelection, fear among the public, and ignorance of the facts, fueled by racism, continue to dehumanize and punish long-termers.

If we want to reduce mass incarceration and change the conditions that create it, prison reform has to include in policy change those convicted of violent crime. Moreover, we can't afford to ignore the experience of people in prison for long terms. Collectively, they have more experience and knowledge than anyone—inside or out—about what sends people to jail, what happens to them there, how they endure and transform themselves, and what needs to change, both inside and out of prison.

Did you see no potential in me? You noted my high IQ, how "articulate" I was, how "mature." I'd run away from home because I refused to let my mother keep hurting me. You put me in a home for bad kids; my roommate wasn't even sane. I left there, too, so you put me in a group home. You call that help? No matter who I tried to tell, no one got it. So then you sentenced me, said no hope for rehabilitation, said I'm as good as dead. Just like my mother: kicks, flights of stairs, words that made me flinch. Well, you were both wrong. I have a life. I have a beautiful daughter, a college education. I teach parenting skills. I made a difference in people's lives. You never gave me a chance, so I made my own. My poverty, skin color, background, past—who at age 17 can't change, won't grow? You robbed me of my youth, of my belief in justice. But from the graveyard, the barbed wire and the cinderblock, I'm resurrected. *I'm somebody.*

　　　　　—Roslyn D. Smith, arrested at seventeen, sentenced
　　　　　　　to fifty to life, and now in her thirty-eighth
　　　　　　　　　　year in prison[42]

More than seventy million people in our society have a criminal record; in the stories of these people is a reflection of our society. In these stories, being a person of color or from a community with few resources reveals a society that does not value those lives, does not put resources into their communities, and is unwilling to understand that drug use, violence in the community, and underground economic systems that constitute survival are all part of a society that excludes them. The narratives of each of their lives add up to the story of a society that needs to change. The narratives start by putting a human face on the people involved, by humanizing each one, so that many can identify with them. Collectively the stories add up to reveal what changes are needed. From there, the force of incarcerated and formerly incarcerated voices becomes one of demanding change, of pointing toward solutions. The voices have always been there, but now they are getting louder; now they can be heard. Let's listen.[43]

Notes

1. The title of this chapter is inspired by Bryan Stevenson's first piece of advice to people wanting to do something about mass incarceration: "Get close."

2. The mantra "All of us or none" is from the organization All of Us or None; "Those closest to the ground are closest to the solution" is from JustLeadershipUSA; and "Nothing about us without us" is from the National Council of Incarcerated and Formerly Incarcerated Women and Girls.

3. "Americans with Criminal Records," Sentencing Project, November 2015, www.sentencingproject.org/wp-content/uploads/2015/11/Americans-with-Criminal-Records-Poverty-and-Opportunity-Profile.pdf.

4. H. Zinn and A. Arnove, *Voices of a People's History of the United States* (New York: Seven Stories Press, 2004), 498.

5. The Pelican Bay settlement included limits on the length of time a person could spend in solitary confinement; an end to placing gang members in solitary confinement based solely on their gang affiliation; and an agreement to place in solitary confinement only people found guilty of serious prison infractions such as escape, violence, narcotics involvement, and weapon possession.

6. A. Speri, "The Largest Prison Strike in U.S. History Enters Its Second Week," *The Intercept,* September 16, 2016. The Thirteenth Amendment to the Constitution declares that "neither slavery nor involuntary servitude, except as a punishment for crime whereof the party shall have been duly convicted, shall exist within the United States, or any place subject to their jurisdiction." F. Forbes, *Invisible Men: A Contemporary Slave Narrative in the Era of Mass Incarceration* (New York: Skyhorse, 2016).

7. M. Schlanger, "Inmate Litigation: Results of a National Survey," *LJN Exchange* (Colorado: National Institute of Corrections, 2003), 3–12, https://www.law.umich.edu/facultyhome/margoschlanger/Documents/Publications/Inmate_Litigation_Results_National_Survey.pdf.

8. E. Ann Carson, "Prisoners in 2014," Bureau of Justice Statistics, Department of Justice, NCJ 248955, September 2015.

9. New York State Department of Health, AIDS Institute, *AIDS in Prison Fact Sheet* [newsletter], April 1994, edited by Miki Conn, 3.

10. ACE, *Breaking the Walls of Silence: AIDS and Women in a New York State Maximum Security Prison* (New York: Overlook Press, 1998).

11. "Governor Cuomo Signs Legislation to Prohibit Shackling of Pregnant Inmates During Transportation," press release, Office of the Governor, New York State, December 22, 2015.

12. F. X. Clines, "Ex-Inmates Urge Return to Areas of Crime to Help," *New York Times*, December 23, 1992.

13. See the website of the Justice Mapping center, www.justicemapping.org

14. K. Houppert, *Chasing Gideon: The Elusive Quest for Poor People's Justice* (New York: The New Press, 2013).

15. T. Robins, "'I Was Terrified': Inmates Say They Paid a Brutal Price for a Guard's Injury," *New York Times*, November 15, 2016; Michael Winerip and Michael Schwirtz, "Five New York Prison Guards Charged in '13 Beating of Inmate," *New York Times*, September 21, 2016.

16. Reality is captured in poems, stories, and film. Examples include Bell Gale Chevigny, ed., *Doing Time: 25 Years of Prison Writing* (New York: Arcade, 1999); H. Bruce Franklin, ed., *Prison Writing in 20th-Century America* (New York: Penguin Books, 1998), and *Rikers Island: An American Jail,* a documentary film by Bill Moyers.

17. R. Subramanian and A. Shames, "Sentencing and Prison Practices in Germany and the Netherlands: Implications for the United States," Vera Institute of Justice, Center on Sentencing and Corrections, 2013; J. Benko, "The Radical Humaneness of Norway's Halden Prison," *New York Times*, March 26, 2015.

18. National Institute of Justice, "Recidivism," last modified June 17, 2014, www.nij .gov/topics/corrections/recidivism/pages/welcome.aspx.

19. F. Taylor, "How Activists Won Reparations for the Survivors of Chicago Police Department Torture: A History of the Movement to Make Chicago Pay for the Crimes of Former Police Commander Jon Burge," *In These Times*, June 26, 2015.

20. Center for NuLeadership on Urban Solutions, http://centerfornuleadership .org.

21. Center for NuLeadership, "The Language Letter Campaign," https://www.nuleader ship.org/language-letter-campaign.

22. "Labels Like 'Felon' Are an Unfair Life Sentence," editorial, *New York Times*, May 7, 2016.

23. Hudson Link website: www.hudsonlink.org.

24. Department of Justice, "Prisoners and Prisoner Re-entry," www.justice.gov/archive /fbci/progmenu_reentry.html.

25. Education from the Inside Out Coalition website: www.eiocoalition.org/#home.

26. Ban the Box campaign website: http://bantheboxcampaign.org.

27. JustLeadershipUSA website: www.justleadershipusa.org.

28. "About Us," Voice of the Experienced website: www.vote-nola.org/about-us .html.

29. National Council website: http://thecouncil.us.

30. The Women's Building website: http://womensbuildingnyc.org.

31. S. Burton and C. Lynn, *Becoming Ms. Burton: From Prison to Recovery to Leading the Fight for Incarcerated Women* (New York: The New Press, 2017).

32. L. Kazemian and J. Travis, "Forgotten Prisoners: Imperative for Inclusion of Long Termers and Lifers in Research and Policy," *Criminology and Public Policy* 14, no. 2 (2015): 355–95.

33. Political prisoners are often long-termers, and they play a particular role around education and organizing. Political prisoners are often defined as those people who were arrested for self-conscious political activity directed at transforming society. Examples from different decades include people from the black liberation movement, the Puerto Rican nationalist movement, the Native American movement, the white anti-imperialist movement, the anti–Vietnam War movement, the Catholic left, and the environmental movement.

34. Ibid.

35. RAPP website: rappcampaign.org.

36. J. Wegman, "False Hope and a Needless Death Behind Bars," *New York Times*, September 6, 2016.

37. A. Nellis, "Still Life: America's Increasing Use of Life and Long-Term Sentences," The Sentencing Project, 2017, 5.

38. Ibid.

39. Some of these organizations and projects include Californians for Safety and Justice, and Common Justice (www.vera.org/centers/common-justice). See D. Sered, "Accounting for Violence: How to Increase Safety and Break Our Failed Reliance on Mass Incarceration," Vera Institute, February 2017.

40. Bridges to Life: www.bridgestolife.org. Coming to Terms: The Longtermers Responsibility Project: www.osborneny.org/programs.cfm?programID=19. Insight Prison Project: www.insightprisonproject.org. Common Justice: www.vera.org/centers/common -justice.

41. New York State Corrections and Community Supervision, *2011 Inmate Releases: Three Year Post Release Follow-up.*

42. K. Boudin and R. D. Smith, "Alive Behind the Labels: Women in Prison," in *Sisterhood Is Forever: The Women's Anthology for a New Millennium*, ed. Robin Morgan (New York: Simon and Schuster, 2003), 244–45.

43. S. Sturm and H. Tae, "Leading with Conviction: The Transformative Role of Formerly Incarcerated Leaders in Reducing Mass Incarceration," JLUSA, Center for Institutional and Social Change, Columbia Law School, 2017.

13

Dealing with Drug Use After Prison
Harm Reduction Therapy

JEANNIE LITTLE, JENIFER TALLEY, SCOTT KELLOGG,

MAURICE BYRD, AND SHEILA VAKHARIA

Steve is a thirty-year-old mixed-race gay man born and raised in the South. He is the youngest of four children; his parents split up when he was in elementary school. Steve grew up primarily with his mother but occasionally stayed with his father. Both parents smoked pot and drank alcohol, sometimes heavily. His mother was alternately affectionate and neglectful. His father was emotionally and physically abusive when he drank. By the age of nine, Steve was drinking and smoking pot regularly, and by fourteen he was experimenting with pills. He spent short periods in juvenile detention. He sold pot to support his drug habit. At fourteen he was shot in the back and became partially paralyzed. After a year of rehab he began running away from home and stealing for a living.

Over the next several years, Steve developed a dependence on alcohol and opiates. By nineteen he was shooting heroin daily, drinking large amounts of alcohol, and often using cocaine and speed. Violence became a part of his daily life—he was either involved with or witnessed fights and stabbings. He was often arrested and spent weeks or months in county jails. Eventually he was arrested on a drug charge and sent to state prison in Texas where he was raped. Once released and on parole, he moved to San Francisco—which violated the conditions of his parole—and joined a community of young people living in and around the downtown area of the city. It was in this community that he affirmed his identity as a gay man. When Steve met the staff of the Harm Reduction Therapy Center, he had been homeless for almost ten years. He was suffering severe symptoms of post-traumatic stress and depression, and he was in a great deal of pain related to his physical injuries. He was physically dependent on heroin and alcohol, and was a regular speed user. Steve was often violent. He had barely survived another recent shooting, and always seemed to be in the thick of trouble. The lifestyle that he had developed was an effort to escape and/ or medicate his reality. To achieve a less trouble-ridden life, Steve desperately needed sensitive trauma-informed treatment with the opportunity to set small, achievable goals and take gradual steps.

Steve's story is not unique. His life typifies those of hundreds of thousands of people who are in jails and prisons today. For many, difficult childhoods led to drug use or misuse and a whole host of other emotional and behavioral problems. A large study conducted by the Centers for Disease Control and Kaiser Permanente examined the association between drug use and eight types of childhood trauma (emotional abuse, sexual abuse, physical abuse, neglect, violence between parents, absent parents, parental substance use, and a parent in prison) in a large sample of adults and found that the presence of adverse childhood experiences contributed to earlier initiation of drug use and increased the probability of lifetime drug use. People with four or more adverse childhood experiences are five times more likely to have an alcohol use disorder, and those with six or more are forty-six times more likely to be an injection drug user. When the data are analyzed another way, 67 percent of all intravenous drug misuse is related to trauma, with the figure rising to 78 percent for women.[1]

Researchers estimate that 50–60 percent of women in the criminal justice system have a history of physical and sexual abuse in childhood and/or adulthood; some studies estimate that the rate is as high as 90 percent.[2] Men with a history of incarceration also have experienced multiple traumas (e.g., emotional and physical abuse) and experience more traumatic events while in prison. Additionally, incarceration can result in being abandoned and rejected by family members, increasing the risk of anxiety, depression, and substance use issues.[3]

People with substance use disorders also have very high rates of other mental health disorders—approximately 50 percent of respondents with a substance use disorder also met criteria for at least one mental health disorder in their lifetime, according to a major national survey.[4] Individuals with co-occurring disorders tend to have more severe and enduring symptoms. They are less likely to engage in treatment, more likely to be homeless, and at greater risk for being victimized.[5] A 2006 Bureau of Justice Statistics report on mental health problems in prisons found high rates of mental health problems: "state prisons: 73% of females and 55% of males; federal prisons: 61% of females and 44% of males; local jails: 75% of females and 63% of males. Nearly a quarter of both state prisoners and jail inmates who had a mental health problem, compared to a fifth of those without, had served 3 or more prior incarcerations."[6]

People who use and misuse drugs are extremely complex, and the challenges facing incarcerated people make matters worse. Focusing only upon whether or not a person is using or misusing drugs does not allow providers to adequately explore underlying causes of drug misuse or to discover and facilitate the development of motivation to change. Instead of turning to prisons and jails as a first line of defense against drug use, we must utilize a treatment approach that focuses more on underlying causes of substance use than on substance use alone.

Harm reduction therapy was developed to treat substance misuse as a health concern—not as a legal matter. It simultaneously addresses all of the complex issues facing people who use drugs. While abstinence is one possible goal of harm reduction therapy, it is not the only way to resolve drug problems. As a client-centered and motivational treatment approach, harm reduction therapy encourages people to identify their own needs and goals and the strategies they feel will best help them reach those goals. Harm reduction prioritizes safety first and employs strategies to keep people alive and healthy. Once people have reduced their risk-taking behaviors, they are in a better position to stabilize mental, emotional, and socioeconomic conditions. Only then are they likely to be ready to consider changing their relationship with drugs in more profound ways.

Limitations of Existing Substance Use Treatment Models

At present, drug addiction is conceptualized by the National Institute on Drug Abuse as a "chronic relapsing brain disease" requiring formalized treatment.[7] While the paradigm of care is changing, most treatment is dominated by the Twelve Steps of Alcoholics Anonymous, which promotes lifelong abstinence as the only way to "recover." It is estimated that 86 percent of treatment facilities utilize drug testing and 74 percent use Twelve-Step facilitation.[8] This one-size-fits-all approach is too narrowly focused on elimination of substance use rather than on treating the many co-occurring problems that substance users suffer. Only 10 percent of people who need treatment even go, and most of those who need treatment state that committing to abstinence as a precondition for treatment is a major deterrent.[9] Outcomes of abstinence-based treatments and of twelve-step groups are mixed at best—most people do not succeed at maintaining abstinence upon completing treatment.[10]

It is estimated that 46 percent of people in substance abuse treatment are mandated to be there, many by the criminal justice system (33.6 percent) or as a condition of other community agencies or services (12.1 percent).[11] Because of this, substance use treatment and coercion are inextricably linked. With the proliferation of drug courts and alternatives to incarceration, in which a person who is convicted of a drug offense may choose or be remanded to treatment rather than jail, we have only replaced one coercive situation with another. Externally imposed mandates and punishments actually reduce individual motivation, and confrontational approaches are more likely to create resistance and drive people out of treatment.[12] For people with multiple challenges and interlocking problems, we need client-centered treatment that offers a variety of interventions and a menu of options for change, based on an extensive assessment of each client's needs. Our job as treatment professionals is to facilitate healthier choices and change by offering treatment options that respect autonomy, show empathy, and invite collaboration.

Harm Reduction Therapy: An Alternative Treatment for Substance Misuse

Harm reduction therapy is a very different paradigm for the treatment of substance use disorders. It offers a significant alternative to the various "disease" models of addiction and abstinence-only treatment. It was developed by mental health professionals who were working with people with co-occurring substance use, medical issues, and mental health disorders. They were frustrated by fragmented treatment systems, concerned about the high threshold imposed by abstinence-only treatment, and alarmed by confrontational approaches that caused harm to fragile clients.[13]

Grounded initially in the public health approach to the HIV and hepatitis epidemics in the 1980s, harm reduction therapy emphasizes reducing the harms associated with substance misuse, both for the individual and for society, without necessarily eliminating the consumption of drugs.[14] The goals of harm reduction are pragmatic: address the immediate threats of drug use to life and health, engage people in a compassionate and supportive relationship, and then build motivation to make larger changes. The most well-known of all harm reduction interventions, needle exchange, has been very effective in reducing the transmission of HIV and hepatitis without increasing the use of drugs.[15] Other important harm reduction interventions include distribution of naloxone to reverse opiate overdose; supervised injection facilities that reduce overdose and have shown success at increasing access to drug treatment;[16] Good Samaritan laws that protect drug users from arrest when they call emergency medical services; and the ending of discrimination in employment and housing for people with drug convictions.

Harm reduction therapy is a welcoming and low-threshold approach that simultaneously addresses substance use, mental health disorders, unhealthy relationships, and socioeconomic problems. It facilitates the transformation of identity from someone whose life has been dominated by the criminal justice system to someone who has real choices—personally, socially, and economically. Harm reduction therapy does not require abstinence as a condition or goal of treatment. The selection of interventions, the goals, and the intensity of treatment are determined by each client in collaboration with his or her therapist. Goals might include complying with the terms of the criminal justice system. Harm reduction therapy integrates a wide array of evidence-based models and interventions from motivational interviewing;[17] cognitive-behavioral, psychodynamic, experiential, and mindfulness therapies; self-help models; case management; and psychiatry and addiction medicine. It is practiced in many community-based and private settings and has been adapted to work with families and groups.[18]

"Come as you are" is one of harm reduction therapy's core values. By starting where the client is, not requiring change as a condition of treatment, and moving at the client's pace of change, harm reduction therapy engages people who avoid or are excluded from traditional abstinence-only programs. Harm reduction practitioners accept that we live in a society where people will use drugs; our focus is on reducing the harmful effects of substance use rather than on coercing people to stop using drugs.

Any positive change is another guiding principle of harm reduction therapy. This means that many outcomes—ranging from controlled use to moderation to abstinence (which can mean abstinence from some substances but not from others)—are considered to be forms of success in harm reduction therapy. For some people, using sterile syringes and adopting safe injection practices can be the initial stages in a process that leads to reduction in intravenous heroin use. Other clients may benefit from alleviating PTSD symptoms and increasing their ability to form relationships in order to become less isolated. Gradually, the need to use substances to cope with anxiety, hyperarousal, and other symptoms or with trauma, depression, and loneliness decreases.[19]

While it is true that harm reduction therapy, with its embrace of active drug users and its broad array of options for change, is philosophically at odds with the top-down mandates of the criminal justice system, including its requirement for total abstinence from all drugs, in practice the two can work in tandem. Harm reduction therapy is pragmatic and flexible enough to help people comply with the conditions of early release at the same time as it helps people develop the motivation and skills to change their relationship with drugs and transform their lives. The result of this delicate balance is that people are more likely to feel understood and respected, and they are more likely to engage in and stay in treatment. With its flexibility and sophisticated understanding of interlocking issues, harm reduction is an ideal treatment model for reentering individuals.

Understanding Why People Use Drugs

People use drugs for many reasons—relaxing, increasing feelings of pleasure, reducing feelings of physical or emotional pain, connecting with other people, and coping with social oppression.[20] As one user put it: "After a lifetime of depression and long bouts of self medication with alcohol, cocaine, and whatever else was available, heroin was a godsend. In fact I can truly say that junk is one of the best things that's ever happened to me."[21] There are many drivers of substance misuse, and it is important to understand them, rather than judge, if one is to truly help someone to change his or her behavior. Edward Khantzian's self-medication hypothesis helps to explain why many people use substances.[22] The use of alcohol and other drugs may also serve as a vehicle for identity and group membership. It may be culturally sanctioned or a response to one's environment. In addition, problematic substance use may serve as a way of coping with social oppression. As Carol Draizen put it: "The vast majority of the addicted poor living on the streets have life histories of severe, cumulative trauma, made worse by the inhuman conditions homeless people face. Getting high is also one way to have a little privacy—at least in your own mind."[23]

Not all substance use is misuse. Most people use drugs with no problem, and this is true both of alcohol and of other drugs. For example, only 23 percent of people who try heroin go on to develop an opiate use disorder.[24] All substance use (not just alcohol use) occurs on a continuum from experimentation to occasional, regular, or heavy. Only some use spirals out of control, which harm reduction practitioners call chaotic use. While most people's alcohol and other drug use does not rise to the level of misuse, harms can and do occur at any level. For example, most people who drink and drive, most college students who participate in drinking games, and some people who contract HIV when they first experiment with injecting drugs do not have a substance use disorder, yet they can suffer and cause great harm. Harm reduction focuses on the actual harm each person's substance use causes to him or her and to others, not on whether or how much a person is using.

Harm reduction practitioners believe that people have a relationship with drugs. As with all relationships, an individual's relationship with drugs might be more or less harmful at different points throughout the life span. Problems with drugs develop out of a unique interaction between an individual (including his or her state of mind, health, and motivations), the physiological effects of the drug as well as the method of use (swallowing, smoking, or injecting, for example), and the sociocultural environment in which substance use occurs (including whether a drug is legal or illegal, which affects quality and dangerousness as well as the risk of arrest and incarceration). This evidence-based model, developed by Norman Zinberg in the 1970s, involves three components: drug, set (that is, a person's mind-set), and setting.[25] Based on his research, Zinberg came to understand that the use of legal drugs is governed by a set of cultural norms, whereas illegal drugs live underground. While drug-using subcultures have their own rules and customs, stigma and fear keep many people using in secrecy, which drastically increases the risk of harmful consequences. Imprisonment only complicates matters further.

We might expect that many who are coming out of prison and who also have histories of substance misuse, poverty, trauma, and social deprivation will emerge demoralized. Assessing past and current use within this framework helps to understand the complexity of drug misuse rather than simply pathologize it. By paying very close attention to the reasons, manner, and circumstances of each individual's use, we can understand each person's relationship with drugs, accurately assess harm, and find solutions that fit both the circumstances and the individual.

Motivation and Change

Harm reduction therapy is a client-specific and client-directed treatment approach grounded in the values of self-determination and the facilitation of client motivation.[26] The therapist works with a client according to the client's readiness and willingness for change, based on the client's definition of the problem and the client's perception of what is needed. The client's motivation for change is the primary focus unless there are urgent safety issues requiring immediate attention. But harm reduction understands that motivation is not a simple matter. When challenged to change important relationships or long-held habits, people are often ambivalent. Broadly speaking, the forces that favor ongoing drug use are centered on ways that substances bring pleasure and life enhancement as well as the ways that drugs and alcohol reduce pain and suffering. The forces within the person that seek change are two-fold. The first is the fear of loss; the other is a desire for a better life. Given the reality of these forces, the job of the harm reduction practitioner is to help people discover and enhance their motivation for healthy change and mourn the loss of a loved object or habit.

Motivation that is driven by internal desire is enhanced in contexts that foster competence, relatedness, and autonomy.[27] Encouraging clients to select their own treatment goals leads to improved substance use outcomes regardless of severity of symptoms at the onset of treatment.[28] This is a contrast to the traditional substance use treatment system, which emphasizes abstinence as the primary goal and has historically been more directive and authoritarian rather than collaborative and client-centered.[29]

Harm reduction therapy is an integration of four core components. The most important element is a strong therapeutic alliance, one that meets people where they are and accepts and honors their choices.[30] The good therapist also holds the future and the sense of possibility for those having difficulty doing so.[31] As Goethe said, "If I treat you as though you are what you are capable of becoming, I help you become that."[32] Second, harm reduction therapy is trauma-informed—it recognizes that the client's history and other issues are often more critical than substance use. Third, it utilizes a three-dimensional assessment approach, based on Zinberg's drug/set/setting model, that helps the client and therapist to work simultaneously with multiple issues.[33] Finally, harm reduction offers people a menu of options to change their substance use. Substance use management is the technique of helping people change in the direction of safety, moderation, or abstinence.[34]

From a harm reduction perspective, the term "recovery" does not mean abstinence from psychoactive substances. Rather, it means those steps that enable drug users to develop, often for the first time, a meaningful and satisfying life. Recovery should include the autonomy to guide one's own choices; positive relationships that support those choices; feelings of well-being, competence, and confidence; optimal health; and a sense of purpose in life. Recovery also means having a non-problematic relationship with drugs: the ability to use in a responsible manner with a minimum of risk. For some, recovery occurs most easily in the absence of alcohol and other drugs. For others, safer or moderate use is sufficient (even helpful) to live healthily and well. There is no single path to achieving a sense of well-being and optimal health. There is no such thing as "the program." Each person's journey is unique, and harm reduction therapy is designed with enough flexibility to help each person discover and develop his or her unique way of changing.

Success Is Any Positive Change

Steve's therapist began working with him while he was homeless, treating his mental health and substance use problems concurrently. A nonjudgmental attitude toward his drug use enabled him to explore personal issues and to access other services without fear that he would be mandated or pressured to quit using as a condition of getting help. During the first year a strong therapeutic alliance developed, and Steve became open to the idea of housing. Because he was in treatment when a housing opportunity became available, he was able to take advantage of it, and his aggressive behavior diminished somewhat.

Soon after moving into an apartment, Steve began exploring the idea of not using heroin. He and his therapist discussed heroin as his medicine. He met with a psychiatrist and was prescribed antianxiety and antidepressant medications. Eventually he quit using heroin and speed. He did continue using pot and alcohol, however, and he and his therapist focused on a substance use management plan.

As treatment continued, the focus turned to treatment of his PTSD symptoms. He decided that he wanted to try somatic treatment; he learned grounding techniques and started practicing meditation. Although he greatly reduced his alcohol intake, he was still struggling with it and had occasional relapses with meth. Eventually he came around to a moderation approach to drinking that involved a lot of education and the development of a detailed drinking plan. He dedicated himself to moderation, and significantly reduced his alcohol use. When episodes of overdrinking occurred, the events and the emotional states leading up to the episode were explored and plans made to anticipate future episodes.

Now, six years later, Steve does not use heroin or speed. He smokes a small amount of pot daily which helps him with pain management. He drinks moderately two to three times a week, with an occasional (every few weeks) episode of heavy drinking. His PTSD symptoms are significantly reduced and well managed through somatic therapy and psychiatric medications. He recently moved to a supportive housing apartment that is more appropriately suited to his physical needs. He volunteers at an LGBTQ youth drop-in center, has connected with state vocational rehabilitation, and is taking computer programming classes. Steve has achieved far more than "any positive change." He has become a changed person.

Challenges to Harm Reduction

Many concerns have been expressed both about harm reduction as a philosophy and about its implementation. Concerns fall into several categories, but typically they are driven by the belief in the United States that addiction is a disease, that drugs' sole property is that they are dangerous, and that life-long abstinence from psychoactive substances is the best (and only) way to live. Here are a few categories of concern and our responses to them.

People fear that we are "enabling" continued substance use. When people say this, they mean that harm reduction enables people to keep using. First of all, none of us has the power to enable or prevent others to do anything. We can only do our best to influence healthy decision-making. Harm reduction recognizes that many people are going to use drugs, and it enables people to do so more safely.

What if someone keeps using, having risky binges or relapsing? This is typically a signal that the deeper conflicts and underlying pain that are driving the use have either not been identified correctly or they have not been adequately addressed. Instead of kicking people out of treatment for relapsing, or refusing to work with them if they are using, treatment should continue to engage clients in discussions of safety and motivation. As long as people are showing up, they are working on their problems. To kick people out for exhibiting the very behavior that got them to treatment in the first place makes no sense and only leaves families and communities on their own with the problem.

People believe that abstinence is the only way in part because it's what we've been taught. It's scary to see a person who has serious problems keep on using, even if he or she is making progress. But abstinence is not the only way. Many people pull themselves back from problematic use to a healthier pattern.

Second, people believe that harm reduction is opposed to abstinence. This is not true. Abstinence is a part of the harm reduction continuum. It is a very effective harm-reducing option, and many people end up choosing it for one or more of their drugs. It just is not the *only* option. And in many cases abstinence is not necessary, since many people successfully resolve their issues with substances without quitting.

Drug Use After Prison

Adopting harm reduction as its guiding philosophy and strategy for reentry would enable the criminal justice system to remove abstinence as a condition of probation and parole and instead focus its attention on activities that harm other people or property. If the criminal justice system required its contracted treatment providers to accept people as they are, omit the abstinence-only requirement, work with all underlying conditions, and offer a menu of options for change, this would lead to much more effective treatment and better lives. We would have a system that practices client-centered care, honors self-determination, removes barriers, encourages trust, and thereby enjoys cooperative relationships, rather than enduring resistant ones, with people under its supervision and in its care.

Harm reduction is the most compassionate and realistic drug treatment model developed to date. Embracing harm reduction models and objectives would allow the entire treatment and legal system to help people who use drugs to make lasting and sustainable change and to exit the criminal justice system. As a system, either we can choose to maintain the status quo, so that only those willing and able to be abstinent can stay out of jail, or we can choose to meet these individuals "where they're at," facilitating healthier decisions and living better lives.

Notes

1. V.J. Felitti, "The Origins of Addiction: Evidence from the Adverse Childhood Experiences Study," *Praxis der Kinderpsychologie und Kinderpsychiatrie* 52 (2003): 547–59.

2. N.A. Miller and L.M. Najavits, "Creating Trauma-Informed Correctional Care: Balance of Goals and Environment," *European Journal of Psychotraumatology* 3 (2012).

3. N. Wolff and J. Shi, "Childhood and Adult Trauma Experiences of Incarcerated Persons and Their Relationship to Adult Behavioral Health Problems and Treatment," *International Journal of Environmental Research and Public Health* 9, no. 5 (2012): 1908–26.

4. R.C. Kessler, "The Epidemiology of Dual Diagnosis," *Biological Psychiatry* 56 (2004): 730–37.

5. Ibid.

6. D.J. James and L.E. Glaze, "Mental Health Problems of Prison and Jail Inmates," Bureau of Justice Statistics, Department of Justice, 2006, NCJ 213600.

7. National Institute on Drug Abuse, "Drugs, Brains and Behavior: The Science of Addiction," 2014, http://www.drugabuse.gov/sites/default/files/soa_2014.pdf.

8. Substance Abuse and Mental Health Services Administration, *National Survey of Substance Abuse Treatment Services (N-SSATS): 2013. Data on Substance Abuse Treatment Facilities* (Rockville, MD: Substance Abuse and Mental Health Services Administration, 2014).

9. Substance Abuse and Mental Health Services Administration, *Results from the 2013 National Survey on Drug Use and Health: Summary of National Findings* (Rockville, MD: Substance Abuse and Mental Health Services Administration, 2014).

10. R.H. Moos and B.S. Moos, "Rates and Predictors of Relapse After Natural and Treated Remission from Alcohol Use Disorders," *Addiction* 101 (2006): 212–22.

11. Substance Abuse and Mental Health Services Administration, Center for Behavioral Health Statistics and Quality, *Treatment Episode Data Set (TEDS): 2002–2012. National Admissions to Substance Abuse Treatment Services* (Rockville, MD: Substance Abuse and Mental Health Services Administration, 2014).

12. R. Ryan and E. Deci, "Self-Determination Theory and the Facilitation of Intrinsic Motivation, Social Development and Well-Being," *American Psychologist* 55 (2000): 68–78.

13. P. Denning, "Therapeutic Interventions for People with Substance Abuse, HIV, and Personality Disorders: Harm Reduction as a Unifying Approach," *In Session: Psychotherapy in Practice* 4, no. 1 (1998): 37–52; P. Denning, *Practicing Harm Reduction Psychotherapy: An Alternative Approach to Addictions* (New York: Guilford, 2000); J.R. Gordon, "Harm Reduction Psychotherapy Comes out of the Closet," *In Session: Psychotherapy in Practice* 4, no. 1 (1998): 69–77; J. Little, "Treatment of Dually Diagnosed Clients," *Journal of Psychoactive Drugs* 33, no. 1 (2001): 27–31; J. Little, "Harm Reduction Group Therapy: The Sobriety Support Group," in *Harm Reduction Psychotherapy: A New Treatment for Drug and Alcohol Problems*, ed. A. Tatarsky, 310–46 (Northvale, NJ: Jason Aronson, 2002); G.A. Marlatt and S.F. Tapert, "Harm Reduction: Reducing the Risks of Addictive Behaviors," in *Addictive Behaviors Across the Life Span: Prevention, Treatment and Policy Issues*, ed. J. Baer, A. Marlatt, and R.J. McMahon, 243–73 (Newbury Park, CA: Sage, 1993); G.A. Marlatt, *Harm Reduction: Pragmatic Strategies for Managing High Risk Behaviors* (New York: Guilford Press, 1998); D. Rothschild, "Treating the Resistant Substance Abuser: Harm Reduction (Re)emerges as Sound Clinical Practice," *In Session: Psychotherapy in Practice* 4, no. 1 (1998): 25–35; A. Tatarsky, "An Integrated Approach to Harm Reduction Psychotherapy: A Case of Problem Drinking Secondary to Depression," *In Session: Psychotherapy in Practice* 4, no. 1 (1998): 9–24; A. Tatarsky, ed., *Harm Reduction Psychotherapy: A New Treatment for Drug and Alcohol Problems* (Northvale, NJ: Jason Aronson, 2002).

14. S.E. Collins et al., "Current Status, Historical Highlights and Basic Principles of Harm Reduction," in *Harm Reduction: Pragmatic Strategies for Managing High-Risk Behaviors*, ed. G.A. Marlatt, M.E. Larimer, and K. Witkiewitz, 3–30 (New York: Guilford Press, 2012); E. Drucker et al., "Harm Reduction: New Drug Policies and Practices," in *Substance Abuse: A Comprehensive Textbook*, 5th ed., ed. P. Ruiz and E. Strain (New York: Williams and Wilkins, 2011); E. Drucker et al., "Treating Addictions: Harm Reduction in Clinical Care and Prevention," *Journal of Bioethical Inquiry* 13, no. 2 (2016): 239–49; P. O'Hare et al., *The Reduction of Drug Related Harm* (London: Routledge, 1992).

15. World Health Organization, *Effectiveness of Sterile Needle and Syringe Programming in Reducing HIV/AIDS Among Injecting Drug Users* (Geneva: World Health Organization, 2004).

16. E. Wood et al., "Attendance at Supervised Injecting Facilities and Use of Detoxification Services," *New England Journal of Medicine* 354, no. 23 (2006): 2512–4.

17. W. Miller and S. Rollnick, *Motivational Interviewing: Preparing People to Change*, 3rd ed. (New York: Guilford Press, 2013).

18. P. Denning and J. Little, *Practicing Harm Reduction Psychotherapy: An Alternative Approach to Addictions*, 2nd ed. (New York: Guilford Press, 2012).

19. Two excellent reviews of the research on successful controlled drinking and on harm reduction therapy demonstrate the vast potential for non-abstinence approaches to eliminate the harm of substance use. M.E. Saladin and E.J. Santa Ana, "Controlled Drinking: More than Just a Controversy," *Current Opinions in Psychiatry* 17, no. 3 (2004): 175–87; D.E. Logan and G.A. Marlatt, "Harm Reduction Therapy: A Practice-Friendly Review of Research," *Journal of Clinical Psychotherapy* 66, no. 2 (2010): 201–14.

20. Denning and Little, *Practicing Harm Reduction Psychotherapy*, 2nd ed.; S. Kellogg, "A Struggle for the Soul of Addiction Treatment," 2014, www.substance.com/a-struggle-for-the-soul-of-addiction-treatment/13798; A. Tatarsky and S. Kellogg, "Harm Reduction Psychotherapy," in *Harm Reduction: Pragmatic Strategies for Managing High-Risk Behaviors*, ed. G.A. Marlatt, M.E. Larimer, and K. Witkiewitz (New York: Guilford Press, 2012), 36–62.

21. I. Thaca, "One Junky's Odyssey," *Harm Reduction Communication* 5 (Fall 1997): 28–30.

22. E.J. Khantzian, "The Self-Medication Hypothesis of Addictive Disorders: Focus on Heroin and Cocaine Dependence," *American Journal of Psychiatry* 142 (1985): 1259–64; E.J. Khantzian, *Treating Addiction as a Human Process* (Northvale, NJ: Jason Aronson, 2007).

23. C.A. Draizen, "Your Letters [Letter to the Editor]," *Harm Reduction Communication* 5 (Fall 1997): 26–27.

24. National Institute on Drug Abuse, "Drug Facts: Heroin," 2014, www.drugabuse.gov/publications/drugfacts/heroin.

25. N.E. Zinberg, *Drug, Set, and Setting: The Basis for Controlled Intoxicant Use* (New Haven, CT: Yale University Press, 1984).

26. Ryan and Deci, "Self-Determination Theory"; Miller and Rollnick, *Motivational Interviewing.*

27. Ryan and Deci, "Self-Determination Theory."

28. B.E. Lozano and R.S. Stephens, "Comparison of Participatively Set and Assigned Goals in the Reduction of Alcohol Use," *Psychology of Addictive Behaviors* 24, no. 4 (2010): 581–91; B.E. Lozano, R.S. Stephens, and R.A. Roffman, "Abstinence and Moderate Use Goals in the Treatment of Marijuana Dependence," *Addiction* 101 (2006): 1589–1597; B.E. Lozano et al., "To Reduce or Abstain? Substance Use Goals in the Treatment of Veterans with Substance Use Disorders and Comorbid PTSD," *American Journal on Addictions* 24 (2015): 578–81; M.B. Sobell and L.C. Sobell, "Guided Self-Change Model of Treatment for Substance Use Disorders," *Journal of Cognitive Psychotherapy* 19, no. 3 (2005): 199–210.

29. W. White and W. Miller, "The Use of Confrontation in Addiction Treatment: History, Science and Time for Change," *Counselor* 8, no. 4 (2007): 12–30.

30. Tatarsky and Kellogg, "Harm Reduction Psychotherapy."

31. S.H. Kellogg, "On 'Gradualism' and the Building of the Harm Reduction-Abstinence Continuum," *Journal of Substance Abuse Treatment* 25 (2003): 241–47.

32. T.L. Mayo, *Words to Live By* (Sarasota, FL: Pinnacle Press, 1996).

33. Zinberg, *Drug, Set, and Setting.*

34. D. Bigg, "Substance Use Management: A Harm Reduction–Principled Approach to Assisting the Relief of Drug-Related Problems," *Journal of Psychoactive Drugs* 33 (2001): 33–38; Denning and Little, *Practicing Harm Reduction Psychotherapy*, 2nd ed.

14

Prisons to Ploughshares
New Economies for Prison Towns

ERIC LOTKE

"This is one of the largest employers in the North Country. We need
to fight this tooth and nail."

—New York State senator Betty Little, October 2013
New York, May 2013[1]

"We need the jobs."

—Lake County commissioner Dan Sloan, trying to reopen
the North Lake Correctional Facility in Baldwin,
Michigan, April 2013[2]

"We cannot replace those jobs with jobs that are already in the
community. . . . Jobs aren't there to fall back on. And the income's
not there to fall back on."

—President of AFSCME Local 2758, Toby Oliver, regarding
the closure of Tamms Correctional Center in 2012[3]

Mass incarceration seems to be crumbling under its own weight. Even as the
federal government reverts to blood and soil, states are exploring different solutions. "Tough on crime" is giving way to "right and smart." Former drug

warriors are promoting sentencing reform, and "treatment not jail" is popular at the polls. That's a good start. But a crucial element is missing.

Most of the attention is on what I call the push side. Too many people are being pushed into prison, for too many years. The push side is the heart of the agenda for justice reform: sentencing and parole reform, treatment not jail, supportive reentry, geriatric release, and so forth. Some reforms go beyond the justice system to matters of poverty, education, and mental health—problems that lead people to crime and drugs in the first place. Such reforms are vitally important, of course, but they affect only the push side of the system. They're about why people go to prison, who gets incarcerated, and for how long.

What's missing is the pull side. Too many rural communities rely on prisons for jobs. They want to pull people in, and more are better. "Prisons are viewed as the anchor for development in rural areas," explained New York State's corrections commissioner, Thomas Coughlin, in 1990.[4] Farms and factories have closed; prisons are the new economic centerpiece.[5] From the corrections staff to the local shopkeepers, most people in a prison town have an interest in keeping that prison open. The mayor and the state representative can be expected to take their side. Patrick Mulhern, mayor of Cresson, Pennsylvania, put it this way regarding the closure of Cambria State Prison near Pittsburgh in 2013: "It's going to hurt the restaurants, the hardware store, every business place here is going to be affected. Five hundred employees in one fell swoop—that's an awful lot."[6] And serious money is indeed at stake.

The Bureau of Justice Statistics estimates state and federal spending on corrections as $58 billion in 2012.[7] Annual operating costs for a single prison range from $20 million to $60 million, depending on its size and security level. Reformers often point to cost savings as an object for reform, surely a desirable goal.

But spending is only one way to look at that money. Money is not only spent, it is earned. The $20 million spent to operate a prison counts as income in the host community. It is paychecks for corrections officers as well as prison nurses, electricians, administrators, and food service providers. It is revenue for businesses where corrections personnel buy their food and get their hair cut. Removing that money may be a savings from the state's point of view, but it is a loss from the community's point of view. Typically it is a loss with nothing in line to replace it. Regarding closure of the Chateaugay state prison in New York, an *Adirondack Daily Enterprise* editorial titled "Say No to Closures" wrote, "While saving the state money is a good thing, it's not so good for the North Country. Jobs will be lost, the local economy will suffer, and abandoned real estate will deteriorate all while drug problems spread."[8]

The past thirty years have made it clear that prisons do not work for rural economic development.[9] State money comes in, but little more. Prisons are not investments that attract other investments, like an airport, college, hospital, or factory. To the contrary, other enterprises appear to avoid a prison town. Thus the loss of a prison leaves a hole in the local economy.

"Prisons as a conscious economic development strategy for depressed communities forge a fateful, symbiotic bond between depressed communities in urban and rural America," observed filmmaker Tracy Huling in 1999.[10] Her film *Yes, in My Backyard* tells the story of Greene County, New York, which starts as a thriving farm community with a small manufacturing base and ends with half the working population employed as corrections officers.[11] The natural economy disappeared and was replaced by state subsidy via the Department of Corrections.

As reform moves forward, entire towns and communities stand to lose their livelihoods. We can expect them to resist. The reform agenda needs to take this resistance seriously. As a political matter, we want the host communities to embrace the change, not to fight it. Justice reform is more likely to succeed if it reduces the demand for prisons as well as the supply of prisoners.

Just as programs are needed to help people returning from prison or addicted to drugs, programs are needed to help former prison communities make the transition. Reformers talk about closing prisons and moving the savings into drug treatment or community development in incarcerated neighborhoods. Those are good goals, of course, but it's equally important to pose different questions: Can some of the savings stay in the host community?

How? Who has ideas when the mayor wonders what will happen if the prison closes?

The new goal is, in epidemiological terms, to change the environment. The "plague of prisons" is spreading in an environment in which prison towns benefit from prison growth. A medical way to thwart a plague is to make the environment more "inhospitable to the agent's survival or spread."[12] Giving prison towns more economic alternatives would strengthen the prison prevention program.

Here I outline some steps and flirt with solutions. I suggest ways to think about the problems and steps toward solving them, at the level of both individual communities and national policies. I also provide examples of successful experiments. This is early and preliminary research, intended to provoke questions as much as provide answers.[13]

The first step for reform is to recognize that every place is different. Some prisons are near urban areas with diverse economies and expensive land; many prisons are in remote areas where land is cheap and work scarce. Some prison towns might have once been or could again become manufacturing centers, as they were before the factory left and the prison arrived. Other prison towns are naturally agricultural, with a climate for farming. Still other regions can attract tourists or could benefit from a hospital or community college. There are 1,821 individual state and federal prisons in America.[14] Each has its own strengths and faces its own unique challenges.

Every prison is different, too. Construction can be recent and modern or dilapidated and old. Prisons may have interesting architecture or historical designations. Prison sites can contain flowering fields or toxic contamination. Architect Raphael Sperry points out that "a large state prison isn't just a series of cellblocks—it typically has many other buildings that are easier to reuse, like central kitchens, vocational training buildings, and administration buildings."[15] Prison sites also contain unused acreage that was once the firing range or simply the exposed distance between the last building and the perimeter fence. Sperry is disappointed when jurisdictions simply put rural prison sites up for auction and act surprised when nobody bids. He compares those to a Canadian province that planned the reuse of a prison site by preparing a detailed study of the property conditions and by researching the market for prospective buyers.

Architect Michael McMillen adds that prison shops and warehouses can easily become industrial spaces, that school spaces can easily be converted to civilian classrooms or meeting rooms, and that former administrative offices can serve comparable professional functions.[16] Recreational facilities such as gyms or outdoor fields are often fit for new users, and even secure housing units can be used for residential purposes such as mental health care, drug treatment, or transitional housing for special populations.

Crises can bring people together. A prison closure creates an opportunity for local stakeholders to come together and collectively plan their response. The natural first step is to meet, discuss, and daydream about alternative uses for the prison site. Closure or downsizing is a time for communities to examine their natural gifts, histories, geographies, and interests. They can seek transitional funding sources and commercial partnerships. The community successes described below generally started with lengthy, wide-ranging discussions among diverse stakeholders, leading eventually to an agreed plan of action. Because no two places are the same, no two solutions are the same. Here I describe several examples to illustrate the breadth of possibility.

One option is to provide services to the same people who are (too often) incarcerated, but to serve them differently. When the Fulton Correctional Facility closed in New York City's Bronx in 2013, the nonprofit Osborne Association converted it into a reentry center for people being released, taking advantage of the metropolitan location to help people transition from prison to civilian life.[17] Osborne organized a combination of state and city grants to finance the capital restoration and transitional costs (more on such grant programs later).[18]

In Gainesville, Florida, the Alachua Coalition for the Homeless and Hungry converted the Gainesville Correctional Institution into a one stop center for services for homeless people—including meals, bus passes, job assistance, and housing benefits.[19] When the prison closed in 2012, the city purchased the land from the state for $900,000. In addition to the homeless center, the city set aside ninety-eight acres to expand the nearby Morningside Nature Center.

The Fort Lyon Correctional Facility in eastern Colorado started as an army fort in the late 1800s, then spent nearly seventy years as a Veterans Administration hospital, and finally became a prison. When the prison closed in 2011, a committee of local stakeholders convened in search of ways to mitigate the loss of two hundred jobs.[20] The winning idea was housing for the homeless, and county leaders fought for it in the state legislature. James Ginsburg of the Colorado Coalition for the Homeless described it as "an opportunity to sit down and sort of articulate what would be my ideal program."[21] The program will run on a combination of state funds, Medicaid funds, federal grants, and residents' payments.

In many cases, however, the new use is entirely different. The sampling below illustrates the diversity and potential.

The Arthur Kill Correctional Facility in Staten Island, New York, is being converted into a state-of-the-art film and television studio.[22]

The Brushy Mountain State Prison, a maximum-security facility in rural Tennessee, closed in 2009 after 113 years of operation. Private entrepreneurs are converting the site into a moonshine distillery tourist attraction, including an RV park, restaurant, gift shop, and riding stables.[23]

Camp Georgetown in central New York was a thirty-one-acre minimum security prison with 262 beds, three dormitories, and seventy-five bathrooms. A private investor bought it in 2013 for $241,000, planning to turn it into a summer camp for teenagers interested in science and technology—though he ultimately decided to turn it into a year-round yoga retreat center.[24]

Mid-Orange Correctional Facility in comparatively affluent southern New York closed in 2014. A private investor purchased it for $1.8 million to convert into an indoor and outdoor sports training facility and overnight summer camp.[25]

The Dwight Correctional Center in Illinois closed in 2012, at the same time as the notorious Tamms.[26] Tamms stayed closed, but the state repurposed Dwight into a facility for paper file storage for the Department of Human Services.

Michigan's Jackson State Prison was more than 150 years old when it closed, shuttering classic prison buildings and a striking twenty-five-foot-high turreted stone wall.[27] The Enterprise Group bought the decaying facility and turned it into an artists' community, where every apartment retains original architectural elements, ranging from window bars to cell numbers painted on exposed brick walls.

In other cases the land simply becomes available for traditional or mixed-use redevelopment. Michigan's Robert Scott Correctional Facility was located in Northville Township, midway between Detroit and Ann Arbor. The state of Michigan closed the prison in 2009 and sold the property to Northville for $1.27. A demolition company demolished it for free, earning only the value of materials it could salvage, estimated at $400,000 including the generator. Five years and many negotiations later, a developer bought the land and plans to spend $150 million on mixed-use retail, residential, and hotel space.[28]

The Tryon Youth Detention Facility in Perth, New York, an hour north of Albany, closed in 2011. The state transferred ownership of the 515 acres at no cost to the Fulton County Industrial Development Agency, which considered it "the centerpiece of Fulton County's economic development efforts."[29] Newly renamed the Tryon Technology Park and Incubator Center, the center itself is a complex of finished office and professional spaces, including parking lots, a gymnasium, and an auditorium, as well as separate "shovel-ready" plots of sixteen to seventy-two acres each.

In more interesting or visionary cases, prison closures can be conceived as regional transformation. When prisons started to close in upstate New York, the nonprofit Milk Not Jails started a cooperative with dairy farms to help market and distribute their products to consumers in New York City. Co-founder Lauren Melodia describes the goal as creating closer ties between upstate and downstate economies.[30] Many criminal justice policies affecting city dwellers lack support in rural areas, she observes, even as laws affecting farmers lack support in the cities. The goal of Milk Not Jail is to restore the upstate region to an economy that "depends on bringing city residents local, healthy food, not locking them up."[31]

Similarly, Noran Sanford and Growing Change in North Carolina are working with youth in the juvenile justice system to "flip" former rural prison sites. They are transforming "jail cells into aquaponics tanks, guard towers into climbing walls, the prison bus into a traveling museum, [and] the old 'hot box' into a recording studio."[32] The former administrative building will host returning veterans obtaining four-year college degrees in a residential internship program. With combined funding from universities, foundations, state agencies, and private business, they aim to flip six sites within a fifty-mile radius—even as they transform disaffected youth into experienced experts.

Communities, however, did not build the prisons on their own, and they cannot make this transition on their own. Mass incarceration reflects policy choices and public financial commitments far beyond any particular prison town.

The war on crime more than tripled state expenditures on corrections, rising from $15 billion in 1982 to $54 billion in 2001, and hovering in that range ever since.[33] In the late 1990s the federal government awarded roughly half a billion dollars every year for prison construction to states that agreed to enact tough new truth-in-sentencing laws.[34] Including required state matches, the federal law unleashed roughly $4 billion in prison construction, or roughly $5.8 billion in today's dollars.

Unwinding the carceral state will require similarly purposeful choices and similar levels of expenditure. Again we need to think not only in terms of money saved but also about money spent for other purposes—specifically, helping rural communities that are losing a mainstay of their economy. Last time it was for prison construction; this time it is for prison replacement.

Transitional assistance is a routine government function. Hillary Clinton, running for president, proposed a $30 billion plan to help communities dependent on coal adjust to a new clean energy economy.[35] This was only campaign talk, not a budgetary commitment or congressional appropriation—but it was an indication of real money being promised to fill a gap.

Post-prison America needs a similar economic program. State and federal agencies need to create grant programs to help prison towns make the necessary changes. Corrections professionals need help transitioning to new

careers. At the same time, academic researchers and philanthropic foundations need to study successful alternative uses of former prison sites. A literature needs to be developed, studies conducted and best practices imitated.[36]
The ultimate question is how communities can be reenvisioned to be less
dependent on government funding, or how the government can help a local-
ity transition to an economy that is healthy, adds value, and is sustainable
over time.

New York is leading the way. First, New York showed that it is possible to
reduce prison populations while also reducing crime.[37] Reforming the drug
laws alone reduced the number of people in New York state prisons for
drug crimes from 24,000 in 1996 to 6,700 in 2013.[38] To offset the impact,
the state created a fund specifically designed to help communities affected
by the closure of corrections or juvenile justice facilities.[39] The Economic
Transformation Program provides tax credits and $50 million in capital
funding for projects that create jobs and economic development in communities that lost their prisons. The fund is designed as a match to leverage investments from other sources, providing seed funding but far below the total
funds needed for any particular project.

The conversion of the Fulton Correctional Facility in the Bronx, described
above, used funds from the Economic Transformation Program.[40] Elizabeth
Gaynes, director of the Osborne Association, described the program like this:

> We advocated with the Governor's office and the local elected officials
> to get the state to turn over the facility at no cost to us, and we applied
> for funding from ESDC for the redevelopment of the site as a commu-
> nity reentry center. We received a letter of support for our proposed plan
> signed by every elected official in the Bronx, including City Council,
> State Senate, and the Assembly.
>
> We submitted tentative plans for the reuse, to include transitional
> residential capacity, and workforce development services. Since the
> Governor's goal was, to the extent possible, to replace jobs lost when a
> prison is closed, we are focused on programs that would create as many
> new jobs as possible. In order to access the ESDC funding of $6 million,

we needed to raise a 10 percent match; the Bronx Borough President agreed to capital funding of $657,000.

Although the New York Economic Transformation Program and the redevelopment of Fulton are very good news, they are also a very small story. The scale of transitional assistance is nowhere near the size of the problem. Funds for decarceration look nothing like the funds dedicated to incarceration in the 1980s and 1990s. Far more will be needed, in New York and everywhere else.[41]

Resources are not unavailable for rural economic development. The US-DA's Rural Business Cooperative Service offers programs to support business development and job training opportunities for rural residents.[42] The U.S. Department of Health and Human Services Rural Health Information Hub helps rural communities find and access available programs, funding, and research.[43] States offer similar resources, such as the Center for Rural Pennsylvania and the Illinois Institute for Rural Affairs.[44] The Citizens Institute on Rural Design helps communities develop local solutions for job growth and the local economy.[45]

But while it is all good, it is not nearly enough. Current rural development programs lack both specific knowledge about decarceration and funds on the same scale as those that were used to build the prisons and are needed to unbuild them. A crucial goal for reform is to increase this capacity.

There will be obstacles, of course—prison interests are well entrenched. Rebecca Thorpe, political science professor at the University of Washington, has documented the unsurprising conclusion that politicians in prison districts tend to support legislation that sends people to prison: "Political representatives in more rural areas with prison infrastructure support punitive criminal justice policies more than their partisan allies and their rural counterparts without any prison sites."[46] The Prison Policy Initiative has documented how the Census Bureau's practice of counting people in prison where they're incarcerated—not where they come from—pads the legislative districts of representatives with prisons, giving those politicians even more heft in the legislature.[47]

Here I list a few of the problems that lie in this direction, the better to understand and solve them.

Transitional problems are familiar to justice policy reformers. Drug treatment may cost less than prison; it may work better and save money. But changing the regime usually requires funding drug treatment up front and reducing prison populations later. In the meantime, the state is funding both the treatment and the prison, resulting in a short-term fiscal crunch.

In this case, the goal is to close prisons and redirect some of the savings back to the host community. Say a $30 million prison is closed, with $10 million redirected for treatment and investment in the neighborhoods the prisoners came from, $10 million returned to taxpayers as savings, and $10 million designated for reinvestment in the prison town. The money may sound like it breaks even, but the timing doesn't. The money can't go to both prison operations and investment at the same time. Something has to start first or end first, and additional money is needed during the transition. Bridge funding can be key to a successful transition.

A dirty secret of modern America is that there aren't enough jobs to go around. This hidden background problem haunts rural transition, just as it haunts prison reentry and "ban the box" proposals. There aren't enough jobs. There aren't enough jobs for people even without criminal records, there aren't enough jobs for rural areas without prisons, and there aren't enough jobs when the prison closes. There weren't jobs when the factory closed, and there still aren't.

Obviously the solution to that problem is beyond the scope of this chapter. America needs an industrial policy, needs to rebuild its economic infrastructure, and needs big thinking about how to grow the economy. We need manufacturing and trade policies to restore the productive part of our economy.[48] But the era of paying rural America to lock up urban America seems to be winding down. Perhaps when we get around to solving those larger problems, former or soon-to-be former prison towns can become laboratories for that democracy. In the meantime, let us not use our inability to solve that problem as an excuse to continue our failed experiment in mass incarceration.

Labor unions are often at the center of economic fights. Strongly on the positive side, unions bring working people together to advance their collective interests. Unions are associated with higher wages, better benefits, and upward mobility.[49] But on matters of mass incarceration, unions can be a retrograde force. Unions too often use their clout to fight for new prison space or keep old prisons open. Of course, they are doing the right thing by their members who pay their dues—but in this case that interest may not line up with the greater good. Indeed, it can even create conflict between members in corrections and members in other professions. One vivid example is the American Federation of State, County and Municipal Employees (AFSCME), a part of the AFL-CIO, with 1.4 million members. AFSCME has 80,000 members who are corrections officers, with the obvious personal interest in prison jobs and prison conditions.[50] But plenty of AFSCME's members are not correctional officers and have reason to be skeptical of mass incarceration, and they too pay their dues. And as a member union of the AFL-CIO, AFSCME is navigating the tensions of mass incarceration on a larger scale. At the AFL-CIO's national convention in 2013 it voted in favor of a resolution critical of mass incarceration.[51] The resolution focuses on private for-profit prisons, but it goes further. It resolves to support sentencing policies that are "fair" and "commensurate with the crime," and to manage "drug use as a public health issue," focusing on treatment rather than incarceration.

To help unions navigate the thicket of criminal justice reform, I offer these prospective recommendations when closures seem imminent. The goal is to protect union staff without creating needless roadblocks to reform. These ideas come from my time working at the Service Employees International Union, which represents corrections officers as well as many other professions in the public and private sectors.[52]

Close Private Prisons First

This is an obvious demand that unions can make as prison populations shrink. It is consistent with the AFL-CIO resolution, and it is fiscally and morally prudent. Private prisons don't save money, have a history of performance problems, and create conflicts of interest.[53] Indeed, the only advantage of private prisons is that they don't create the same long-term commitment to the workforce. Declining prison populations are the time to use that advantage.

Create a Soft Landing for Employees

If jobs will be lost as a result of prison downsizing, create exit options for affected employees. For more senior employees, offer buyouts or early retirement packages. For the staff at large, offer training options, transfers within the department of corrections, or favorable consideration for other public jobs within the jurisdiction. The goal is to soften the transition.

Allow Unions to Help Choose Which Prisons to Close

Unions should be at the table when decisions are made about which prisons to close and which to retain, offering their perspective and representing the interests of their members. The Pennsylvania Corrections Officers Association has made the case for commissions like the ones used when military bases are shut down to be used when closures are being considered.[54] Such a commission can consider prison population projections and security requirements while also considering "the human impact . . . [and] possible economic, environmental, and other effects on the surrounding communities."[55] Indeed, staff in Pennsylvania's Cresson prison learned of its impending closure from inmates who heard about it on television. That's no way to ease either personal or community transitions.

Fight for Those Grants

Unions should be at the forefront of asking to create redevelopment grants and transitional assistance for the affected community—not just in any particular closure but as a policy matter for all closures. That's a better use of effort than fighting closures.

This discussion raises as many questions as it answers, but still, it's a start. Some of those questions are presently missing from the reform agenda. We can't decarcerate by changing the justice system alone. As a policy matter, we need alternatives for the prison community in the same way we need alternatives for the sentencing judge and jobs for people coming home. As a political matter, reform will come easier if host communities are allies of change, not enemies. It will be hard to fix the push unless we also work on the pull.

Notes

1. Felicia Krieg, "Hundreds Rally Against Chateaugay Prison Closure," *Press Republican*, October 6, 2013.

2. Paul Egan, "Bill Would Allow Private Prison Near Baldwin to Reopen," *Detroit Free Press*, April 23, 2015.

3. "Petition Drive Held to Keep Tamms Correctional Center Open," KFVS-TV, Marion, IL, February 25, 2012.

4. Ryan S. King, Marc Mauer, and Tracy Huling, "Big Prisons, Small Towns: Prison Economics in Rural America," The Sentencing Project, February 2003, www.sentencing project.org/doc/inc_bigprisons.pdf.

5. Tracy Huling, "Building a Prison Economy in Rural America," in *Invisible Punishment: The Collateral Consequences of Mass Imprisonment*, ed. Marc Mauer and Meda Chesney-Lind (New York: The New Press, 2002).

6. Dan Strumph, "With Fewer to Lock Up, Prisons Shut Doors," *Wall Street Journal*, February 10, 2013.

7. States spend $48.7 billion and the federal government spends $9 billion. Counties spend another $26.3 billion on local jails, but they don't affect rural development in the same way. Tracey Kyckelhahn, "Justice Expenditure and Employment Extracts, 2012—Preliminary," Bureau of Justice Statistics, Department of Justice, NCJ 248628, February 26, 2015.

8. "Say No to Closures," *Adirondack Daily Enterprise*, August 7, 2003, www.adiron dackdailyenterprise.com/opinion/editorials/2013/08/say-no-to-closures.

9. Ben Jacklet, "Prisontown Myth: The Promise of Prosperity Hasn't Come True for Oregon's Rural Communities," *Oregon Business*, April 1, 2008; Gregory Hooks et al., "Revisiting the Impact of Prison Building on Job Growth: Education, Incarceration,

and County-Level Employment, 1976–2004," *Social Science Quarterly* 91, no. 1 (March 2010): 228–44; John Wiley, "Prisons May Not Be Economic Boon," *Spokesman Review*, July 18, 2004.

10. Tracy Huling, "Prisons as a Growth Industry in Rural America: An Exploratory Discussion of the Effects on Young African American Men in the Inner Cities," A Consultation of the United States Commission on Civil Rights, April 15–16, 1999, www.prisonpolicy.org/scans/prisons_as_rural_growth.shtml.

11. Tracy Huling, *Yes, in My Backyard*, 1999, http://itvs.org/films/yes-in-my-backyard.

12. Ernest Drucker, *A Plague of Prisons: The Epidemiology of Mass Incarceration in America* (New York: The New Press, 2011), 79.

13. Additional information can be found at the *Yes, in My Backyard* website, maintained by Tracy Huling, www.yesinmybackyard.org.

14. James J. Stephan, "Census of State and Federal Correctional Facilities, 2005," Bureau of Justice Statistics, Department of Justice, NCJ 222182, October 2008.

15. "Repurposing Prisons: One Architect's View," *Yes, in My Backyard*, May 10, 2013, www.yesinmybackyard.org/2013/05/10/repurposing-prisons one-architects-view.

16. Michael McMillen, "Adapting Jails and Prisons," *Correctional News*, September 12, 2012.

17. Denis Slattery, "Former Bronx Jail to Be Reborn as Reentry Center for Ex-Cons," New York *Daily News*, February 1, 2015; Empire State Development Corporation, Economic Transformation Program, http://esd.ny.gov/BusinessPrograms/EconomicTrans formation.html.

18. "Managing an Urban Prison Reuse Project," *Yes, in My Backyard*, May 22, 2015, www.yesinmybackyard.org/2015/05/22/urban-prison-reuse-project.

19. "Reusing Gainesville Correctional Institution," *Yes, in My Backyard*, October 2, 2014, www.yesinmybackyard.org/2014/10/02/reusing-gainesville-correctional-institution; Brianna Donet, "Former Prison to Turn into Homeless Shelter, Expand Nature Center," WUFT-FM Radio, November 20, 2013.

20. J. Adrian Stanley, "A Transformed Fort Lyon Promises Homeless a Second Chance," *Colorado Springs Independent*, September 4, 2013.

21. Ibid.

22. Tracey Porpora, "Construction on Broadway Stages Film Studio Could Start by Year's End," *SI Live*, January 30, 2015.

23. Brushy Mountain Development, http://brushymtngroup.com; "Reusing Brushy Mountain State Prison," *Yes, in my Backyard*, October 3, 2014, www.yesinmybackyard .org/2014/10/03/reusing-brushy-mountain-state-prison.

24. Teri Weaver, "New Camp Georgetown Owner Wants to Open Summer Science Camp There," Syracuse *Post-Standard*, May 13, 2013; Samantha Allen, "This Former NY Prison May Become a Yoga Retreat Center," Do You Yoga, n.d., www.doyouyoga.com /this-former-ny-prison-may-become-a-yoga-retreat-center-64937.

25. "Sports Facility Planned at Former Prison," *Warwick Advertiser*, September 11, 2014.

26. "File Drawers Replace Felons in Prisons," *Herald and Review*, August 10, 2014. The storage facility uses far fewer staff, however.

27. Tory Cooney, "Armory Arts Village in Michigan Used to Be a State Prison. Now It's an Artists' Community," *Humanities*, July/August 2014; "Case Study: Michigan Prison Transformed into Art Village," *Yes, in My Backyard*, March 20, 2013, www.yesin mybackyard.org/2013/03/20/case-study-michigan-prison-transformed-into-art-village.

28. Kirk Pinho, "Redico Plans $150 Million Redevelopment of Former Women's Prison Site in Northville," *Crain's Detroit Business*, June 2, 2015.

29. Fulton County Center for Regional Growth, Tryon Business Park, www.fccrg.org/parks/tryon-business-park; "Governor Cuomo Authorizes Transfer of Tryon Boys and Girls Center to Fulton County IDA," news release, Office of the Governor, New York State, September 20, 2012.

30. Von Diaz, "A Unique Alternative to a Prison Economy," *Colorlines*, September 23, 2013.

31. Milk Not Jails, https://milknotjails.wordpress.com.

32. Growing for Change, www.growingchange.org/reclaim-attain-sustain/site-usage.

33. Tracey Kyckelhahn, "State Corrections Expenditures, FY 1982–2010," Bureau of Justice Statistics, Department of Justice, NCJ 239672, December 2012; Kyckelhahn, "Justice Expenditure and Employment Extracts, 2012—Preliminary." Figures in real dollars.

34. The Violent Offender Incarceration and Truth-in-Sentencing (VOI/TIS) Incentive Formula Grant Program ran from FY 1996 through 2001; www.bja.gov/ProgramDetails .aspx?Program_ID=93. See also "Report to Congress: Violent Offender Incarceration and Truth-In-Sentencing Incentive Formula Grant Program," Bureau of Justice Assistance, February 2012.

35. Maggie Haberman, "Hillary Clinton Unveils $30 Billion Plan to Help Coal Towns," *New York Times*, November 12, 2015.

36. *Yes, in My Backyard* is starting this dialogue, www.yesinmybackyard.org.

37. James Austin and Michael Jacobson, "How New York City Reduced Mass Incarceration: A Model for Change?" Brennan Center, January 2013.

38. Budget testimony of Anthony Annucci, New York Department of Corrections, February 5, 2014, http://assembly.state.ny.us/write/upload/files/testimony/20140205 /20140205-PublicProtection-Annucci.pdf.

39. Empire State Development Corporation, Economic Transformation Program, http:// esd.ny.gov/BusinessPrograms/EconomicTransformation.html; fact sheet, http://esd.ny.gov /_private/BusinessPrograms/Data/Economic_Transformation/ETAProgramFactSheet Finalforwebupdated4714.pdf; Guidelines 2014, http://esd.ny.gov/BusinessPrograms/Data /Economic_Transformation/2014Guidelines_v8_FINAL.pdf.

40. Slattery, "Former Bronx Jail to Be Reborn."

41. "Managing an Urban Prison Reuse Project." The ESDC is the Empire State Development Corporation, the entity in charge of the Economic Transformation Program.

42. USDA, Rural Business Cooperative Service, www.rd.usda.gov/about-rd/agencies/rural-business-cooperative-service.

43. Rural Health Information Hub, www.ruralhealthinfo.org. Formerly the Rural Assistance Center.

44. Center for Rural Pennsylvania, www.rural.palegislature.us; Illinois Institute for Rural Affairs, www.iira.org.

45. Citizens Institute on Rural Design, www.rural-design.org.

46. Rebecca Thorpe, "Perverse Politics: The Persistence of Mass Imprisonment in the Twenty-first Century," *Perspectives on Politics* 13, no. 3 (September 2015): 618–37.

47. Prison Policy Initiative, www.prisonersofthecensus.org/impact.html. The author is president of the board.

48. Robert Scott, "The Manufacturing Footprint and the Importance of U.S. Manufacturing Jobs," Economic Policy Institute, Briefing Paper #388, January 22, 2015.

49. E.g., Richard Freeman et al, "Bargaining for the American Dream: What Unions do for Mobility," Center for American Progress, September 2015.

50. AFSCME Q & A, www.umass.edu/local1776/Flyers,%20Updates%20%26%20Documents_files/AFSCME%20Q%20%26%20A.htm.

51. AFL-CIO Resolution 17, 2013, "Prisons and Profits—The Big Business Behind Mass Incarceration," www.aflcio.org/About/Exec-Council/Conventions/2013/Resolutions-and-Amendments/Resolution-17-Prisons-and-Profits-The-Big-Business-Behind-Mass-Incarceration.

52. None of this is official SEIU policy.

53. E.g., Michigan Corrections Organization et al., "Pitfalls and Promises: The Real Risks to Residents and Taxpayers of Privatizing Prisons and Prison Services in Michigan," National Institute of Corrections, February 2012, http://nicic.gov/library/027650. One inherent conflict is between taxpayers and free society, with an interest in lower incarceration, and a for-profit corporation with an interest in more.

54. Jason Bloom, "Pennsylvania's Prison Workers Deserve Better," *Centre Daily Times*, August 22, 2013

55. Defense Base Closure and Realignment Commission, www.brac.gov.

Acknowledgments

Ernest Drucker: I would like to acknowledge my own gratitude to each of the authors for sharing their huge store of experience and knowledge about decarceration in this single volume as well as all the efforts of our New Press editors, Diane Wachtell and Jed Bickman. I'd also like to thank the many Soros Justice Fellows and OSF leadership who have made my own work possible for many years, and my academic colleagues at Montefiore/Einstein, John Jay College of Criminal Justice, and NYU's College of Global Public Health, who provided so much support and inspiration to me in this enterprise. To name just a few: Herb Sturz, Bryan Stevenson, Eric Manheimer, Howard Josepher, Jeremy Travis, Jeff Coots, Alice Cini, Ric Curtis, Baz Dreisinger, Glenn Martin, Vivian Nixon, Joanne Page, and Max Kenner. Finally, I want to dedicate this book to two dear friends who are no longer with us: Marianne Kennedy and Pyser Edelsack.

Judith A. Greene and Vincent Schiraldi: The authors would like to thank David Aziz, research director, NY Department of Corrections and Community Supervision; Reagan Daly, research director, CUNY Institute for State and Local Governance; Brian Leung, senior operations analyst, Fresh Direct; Freda Solomon, senior research fellow, NY Criminal Justice Agency; and Eric Sorenson, population research director, NYC Department of Correction.

Michael Romano: I'd like to thank my great friend, mentor, and partner in crime data analysis, Joan Petersilia.

Judge Robert Sweet: I would like to thank my mentor, the Honorable J. Edward Lumbard, for his deep understanding and dedication to criminal justice.

Danielle Sered: My thinking is indebted to many hardworking visionaries in the criminal justice reform movement. Particular thanks are owed to the formidable team at Common Justice and to the harmed and responsible parties who have taught us in our work. While any mistakes are my own, any insights are surely shared.

Elizabeth Gaynes and Tanya Krupat: The authors extend their deepest gratitude to Jomo Davis, Emani Davis, Kathy Boudin, Ann Adalist-Estrin, Daniel Beaty, Echoes of Incarceration, SFCIPP, Ebony Underwood, Tony Lewis Jr., and many more people who light the path forward. We also thank Diana Archer, Allison Hollihan, St. James Church, and the Sills Family Foundation.

Ross MacDonald and Homer Venters: Dr. MacDonald and Dr. Venters would like to acknowledge their supportive families for tolerating their work in jail over the years as well as the contributions of countless inspiring colleagues, including, among countless others, Zachary Rosner, Elizabeth Ford, Fatos Kaba, Amanda Parsons, and Patricia Yang.

Mujahid Farid and Laura Whitehorn: We thank the countless strugglers who laid the foundation we stand upon. This foundation is the uplifting of voices of currently and formerly incarcerated people and the disenfranchised. For far too long these vital views were ruthlessly diminished. All who paved the path to uplift must be credited with bringing to light the issues we present in the RAPP perspective.

Daliah Heller: The generosity and intelligence of so many people in my life over the past two decades—in the harm reduction community, in governmental public health, in advocacy and organizing, in research and academia—helped me to develop the ideas presented in this chapter. Thank you for sharing your wisdom.

Contributors

Ernest Drucker is a professor of public health at New York University's College of Global Public Health; professor emeritus in the department of family and social medicine at Montefiore Medical Center, Albert Einstein College of Medicine; visiting scholar at John Jay College of Criminal Justice, City University of New York; and a Fulbright Fellow and senior specialist in global public health. He is the author of *A Plague of Prisons: The Epidemiology of Mass Incarceration in America* (The New Press). Drucker is a founder of the International Harm Reduction Association, founding editor of *Harm Reduction Journal*, former chairman of Doctors of the World/USA, and a Soros Justice Fellow of the Open Society Foundations. He lives in New York City.

Natasha A. Frost serves as associate dean for graduate studies in the College of Social Sciences and Humanities at Northeastern University and teaches in the School of Criminology and Criminal Justice. She has served as a consultant for the Massachusetts State Parole Board, worked collaboratively with the Massachusetts Department of Correction, and done studies for the National Institute of Justice. Her book *The Punishment Imperative: The Rise and Failure of Mass Incarceration in America*, co-authored with Todd R. Clear, was published in 2014 (NYU Press). She lives in Massachusetts.

Todd R. Clear is provost of Rutgers University-Newark; previously, he was dean of the School of Criminal Justice. His most recent book is *The Punishment Imperative* with Natasha Frost (NYU Press). Clear has served as president of the American Society of Criminology, the Academy of Criminal Justice Sciences, and the Association of Doctoral Programs in Criminology and Criminal Justice. He was the founding editor of the journal *Criminology & Public Policy*, published by the American Society of Criminology. He lives in New Jersey

Carlos E. Monteiro is a senior research associate at the Institute on Race and Justice at Northeastern University's School of Criminology and Criminal Justice. He serves as co-project director for a National Institute of Justice-funded research project examining the sources and impacts of stress in the lives of correctional officers. He lives in Massachusetts.

Judith A. Greene's essays and articles on criminal sentencing issues, police practices, and correctional policy have been published in numerous books, as well as in national and international journals, and her work has been cited in outlets including the *Wall Street Journal*, the *New York Times*, and National Public Radio. She is a co-founder of Justice Strategies and has been a Soros Senior Justice Fellow, a research associate for the RAND Corporation, a senior research fellow at the University of Minnesota Law School, director of the State-Centered Program for the Edna McConnell Clark Foundation, and the Vera Institute of Justice. She lives in New York.

Vincent Schiraldi is a senior research fellow directing the Program in Criminal Justice Policy and Management at Harvard Kennedy School. Formerly, Schiraldi worked as the founder of the Justice Policy Institute think tank, director of the juvenile corrections in Washington, D.C., commissioner of the New York City Department of Probation, and most recently as senior advisor to the New York City Mayor's Office of Criminal Justice. He lives in Massachusetts.

Michael Romano is the director and founder of the Three Strikes Project at Stanford Law School. As counsel for the NAACP Legal Defense and Educational Fund, Michael co-authored two successful California statewide ballot measures, the Three Strikes Reform Act of 2012 ("Proposition 36") and the Safe Neighborhoods and Schools Act of 2014 ("Proposition 47"), which provided for the release of over 10,000 nonviolent prisoners. Romano was recognized by the Obama administration as a "Champion of Change" in 2016, and was named one of California's top lawyers in 2009. He has been profiled in numerous outlets, including the *New York Times Magazine, Rolling Stone, The Economist,* and in the PBS feature documentary *The Return.* He was a John Knight Fellow at Yale Law School and clerked on the U.S. Court of Appeals for the Ninth Circuit. He lives in California.

Judge Robert Sweet is currently a senior United States federal judge serving on the United States District Court for the Southern District of New York. With co-author Edward A. Harris he contributed a chapter to Jefferson Fish's book *How to Legalize Drugs.* Sweet is a member of Law Enforcement Against Prohibition and serves on its advisory board. He lives in New York

James Thompson is a litigation associate at Morrison Foerster, LLP, practicing out of the New York office. Prior to joining the firm, James served as a law clerk to the Honorable Robert W. Sweet of the U.S. District Court for the Southern District of New York.

Robin Steinberg is CEO of The Bail Project and director of Still She Rises. She was a founder of The Bronx Defenders, where she developed a client-centered model of public defense that uses interdisciplinary teams of advocates to address both the underlying causes and the collateral consequences of criminal justice involvement. Steinberg is a frequent commentator on local and national media outlets and has been honored by the National Legal Aid & Defender Association and the New York Bar Association. She was awarded Harvard Law School's Wasserstein Fellowship and is currently a lecturer in law at Columbia Law School in New York.

Skylar Albertson was previously Assistant to the Director at the Bronx Defenders, and is now studying for his JD at Yale Law School.

Rachel Maremont has been an intern at the Bell Policy Center, a progressive research and policy think tank in Denver, Colorado; the South Texas Pro Bono Asylum Representation Project, which provides legal representation to unaccompanied minors in immigration proceedings; and the Foundation for Sustainable Development in Cochabamba, Bolivia. She lives in New York.

gabriel sayegh is the co-founder and co-director of the Katal Center for Health, Equity, and Justice. He was a former managing director of policy at the Drug Policy Alliance. He has written for publications including the *New York Times*, the *Washington Post*, *Newsweek*, *Vice*, *New York Daily News*, *New York Post*, Associated Press, the *Huffington Post*, the *Village Voice*, *Gawker*, and has appeared in news outlets including CBS, NBC, Fox, and the BBC. He lives in Brooklyn.

Danielle Sered is the founder of Common Justice. She and her work have been featured in the Aspen Ideas Festival, the *Atlantic Magazine* Summit on Race and Justice, the *New Yorker*, the *Washington Post*, NPR, and more. Danielle sits on the advisory council to the New York State Office of Victims Services, the diversity advisory committee to the federal Office for Victims of Crime, the New York State Governor's Council on Reentry and Community Reintegration, and the advisory board to the National Initiative for Building Community Trust and Justice. Common Justice received the Award for Innovation in Victim Services from Attorney General Holder and the federal Office for Victims of Crime. She is a Rhodes Scholar and the author of *The Other Side of Harm: Addressing Disparities in our Responses to Violence, Expanding the Reach of Victim Services,* and *Accounting for*

Violence: How to Increase Safety and Reduce Our Failed Reliance on Mass Incarceration.

Elizabeth Gaynes is the executive director of the Osborne Association. She designed FamilyWorks, the first comprehensive parenting program in a men's state prison. She was co-chair of the reentry working group for the NYC Mayor's Task Force on Behavioral Health and Criminal Justice and serves on the New York State Council on Community Re-entry and Reintegration. She was on the steering committee of New York's Aging Reentry Task Force and was an advisor to Sesame Street Workshop in the development of their award-winning "Little Children Big Challenges: Incarceration" materials. In 2013, Gaines was recognized by the White House as a "Champion of Change" on behalf of Children of Incarcerated Parents, and she now serves as an advisor to the International Association of Chiefs of Police on the model protocol for safeguarding children at the time of a parent's arrest. She lives in New York.

Tanya Krupat is the program director of the New York Initiative for Children of Incarcerated Parents, Osborne Association. She lives in New York.

Ross MacDonald is the chief of medicine for Health+Hospitals Correctional Health Services in New York City, overseeing medical care for the city jail system, including Rikers Island.

Homer Venters is medical director and assistant commissioner of Correctional Health Services, and a faculty member at the NYU Center for Survivors of Torture, and a co-chair of a federal health advisory group on medical care for detainees. He has written widely and testified before Congress on these topics. He lives in New York.

Mujahid Farid is the lead organizer for the Release Aging People in Prison (RAPP) Campaign. When Farid was twenty-eight years old, he was sentenced to fifteen years to life for attempted murder. He was denied parole nine times, which ultimately added eighteen years to his incarceration. While confined, Farid earned four college degrees including two masters. Farid was part of a trio that created and proposed PEPA, the first HIV/AIDS peer education program in New York State prisons, and since his release, Farid has initiated the RAPP Campaign and the Rise and Shine Small Business Coalition. In 2013 Farid was an Open Society Soros Justice Fellow and was awarded a joint New York State legislative commendation for his community work and a Citizens Against Recidivism, Inc., award for social activism. He lives in New York.

Laura Whitehorn is a former political prisoner and is currently a Senior Editor at *POZ Magazine* in New York City. She is also a member of the New York State taskforce on political prisoners.

Daliah Heller is a professor in the Department of Health Policy and Management at the City University of New York. Previously, she served as assistant commissioner for the Bureau of Alcohol and Drug Use Prevention, Care, and Treatment, at the New York City Department of Health and Mental Hygiene and as the director of harm reduction in the Department's Bureau of HIV/AIDS Prevention and Control. Before joining government, she built and led one of the country's leading harm reduction service organizations, based in the South Bronx. She lives in New York

Kathy Boudin is the co-director and co-founder of the Center for Justice at Columbia University. She is an adjunct lecturer at Columbia School of Social Work where she has been the Director of the Criminal Justice Initiative, Supporting Children Families and Communities. Her work has appeared in such journals as *The Harvard Education Review* and *Journal of Corrections Education* among other outlets and she is editor and co-author of the book, *Breaking the Walls of Silence: AIDS and Women in a New York State Maximum Security Prison.*

Jeannie Little is the executive director of the Center for Harm Reduction Therapy. She developed the harm reduction therapy group model for the Department of Veterans Affairs and has trained therapists nationally and abroad. She teaches and consults with staff in outpatient clinics, drop-in centers, and supportive housing programs. She lives in California.

Jenifer Talley is an assistant professor and assistant director of clinical training at the New School for Social Research and assistant director of the Concentration in Mental Health and Substance Abuse Counseling. She lives in New York

Scott Kellogg is a clinical assistant professor of psychology at New York University.

Maurice Byrd is a harm reduction therapist who works in the Center for Harm Reduction's private practice and in community services with runaway youth. He is also a certified anger management facilitator. He lives in California.

Sheila Vakharia is a faculty member at Long Island University and a social worker at a grassroots HIV/AIDS and homelessness advocacy organization in Manhattan, where she provides harm reduction-based substance use counseling.

Eric Lotke is an author, activist and scholar whose legal advocacy includes groundbreaking lawsuits against private prison companies and over the exploitative cost of phone calls from prison.. His books include *Making Manna*, *The Real War on Crime*, and *2044: The Problem Isn't Big Brother, It's Big Brother, Inc.*

Celebrating 25 Years of Independent Publishing